The Investor's Guide to
Nanotechnology
&
Micromachines

The Investor's Guide to
Nanotechnology
&
Micromachines

GLENN FISHBINE

John Wiley & Sons, Inc.

Published by John Wiley & Sons, Inc., New York
Published simultaneously in Canada.

This publication is designed to provide accurate and authoritative information in
regard to the subject matter covered. It is sold with the understanding that the publisher is not engaged in rendering professional services. If professional advice or
other expert assistance is required, the services of a competent professional person
should be sought.

Designations used by companies to distinguish their products are often claimed as
trademarks. In all instances where John Wiley & Sons, Inc. is aware of a claim, the
product names appear in initial capital or all capital letters. Readers, however,
should contact the appropriate companies for more complete information regarding
trademarks and registration.

Library of Congress Cataloging-in-Publication Data:

Fishbine, Glenn.
    The investor's guide to nanotechnology and micromachines / Glenn Fishbine.
        p. cm. — (Wiley finance series)
    Includes index.
    ISBN 0-471-44355-7 (cloth : alk. paper)
    1. Microelectronics industry—Finance.   2. Semiconductor industry—Finance.
    3. Nanotechnology—Economic aspects.   4. Investments.   I. Title.   II. Series.

    HD9696.A2 F55 2002
    338.4'76213815—dc21   2001046539

Printed in the United States of America.

10 9 8 7 6 5 4 3 2 1

Contents

Preface

Throughout history, governments have actively supported piracy. Sir Francis Drake was one of the top 10 pirates of all time. He was financed by Queen Elizabeth, who provided ships, crews, and money in support of his piracy. The queen ultimately knighted Drake for his maritime success against the Spanish, which included the taking of slaves, destruction of ships, and theft of cargo. Pirates who had the sanction of their government were given the name *privateer* to distinguish them from common thieves. These days governments are reticent about the taking of slaves or plundering foreign ships, yet the economics of piracy remain intact—domination of a market by financing expeditions of discovery and conquest. Today, nanotechnology has the attention of worldwide governments as the new economic high ground to be explored and conquered.

History reveals that most pirates failed to find treasure, and many of those who did either were hanged or lost their treasure to mutiny, other pirates, or their government sponsors. Their failure was usually due to the fact that pirates happened to be in the wrong place at the wrong time with very little direction. The basic plan consisted of looking for sails on the horizon, chasing them, and—once in a while—looting them. Economic success was a chancy thing, and elusive to most.

Each investor needs to know two things before setting sail in the economic maelstrom of today's world:

- Where do you look for opportunities?
- What exactly are you looking for?

This book is the map you need to explore the opportunities in nanotechnology. Part I of this book answers the first question—where to look. These chapters investigate an investment landscape not yet established, identifying where opportunity exists and where it will emerge. Knowing where to find opportunity in nanotechnology is perhaps the most arduous task for any individual, requiring skill and homework.

Part II of this book answers the second question—what to look for. There are countless investment opportunities in nanotechnology. Some are worth billions of dollars. Some are exciting but fundamentally worthless. These chapters explore the core technology issues that the investor must understand to evaluate emerging investment opportunities. Knowing which technology issues have value and which do not is the key to making sound investment decisions.

Acknowledgments

Writing a book is a lonely task. You spend hours struggling over single words, single sentences, and then when you think you are done, you give it to someone to read and they have the unmitigated gall to want it to be better. Then back you go, behind the keyboard, seeking the approval of loved ones and strangers alike. It is amazing how many people deserve the credit for keeping me on my course and providing encouragement when my thoughts focused on dropping my computer into the lake. First, my parents and brother deserve thanks for tolerating both early drafts and me. Nancy, Jenna, and Karis get a special thank-you for the inspiration that comes from trying to make loved ones proud, and for reminding me of what a phoneme is. I want to thank Lynn for her encouragement and support. Kathy holds a place of honor, for only she had the courage to say, "This is crap," rather than preserve my fragile ego; and thanks to her son Matt, whose insight kept my tone even. My agent, Anne Hawkins, deserves special mention for believing in me; she kept waiting for me to whine, but never once permitted me to act discouraged. Diane, the eternal skeptic, gets a supporting role for keeping the scotch flowing freely and reminding me that investing is supposed to be fun. And, of course, I offer my deepest respect to my editors at Wiley, Chris Heiser and Jeanne Glasser, who questioned everything and made me honest.

There are many others who deserve thanks for the hours they invested in interviews, which too often resulted in nothing more than a dry sentence or two. Special thanks go to the Connecticut Venture Group, which hosted my search for angels and institutions that would answer simple-minded questions about what they do and why. This is a group that makes the world anew every day. I also thank the thousands of researchers throughout the world whose citations I shamelessly omitted.

There are those who, while they had no participation in this book, were teachers whose lessons gave me the courage and knowledge needed to undertake this task. Gordon, who earned my eternal respect by spending $3 million giving me the finest education money can buy. Steve, who taught me the true meaning of the phrase, "It's just business." Jack and Jack, who each, in their own way, had faith in my abilities before I had ever proven myself. Yoshimasa, who gave me the *how* of Japanese business, and Bill, who gave me the *why*. Katsuya, whose labors gave me insight into the practice of aspects of Japanese industry. Messieurs Dong and Zhang, who taught me the true meaning of cultural revolution. And lastly Brownie, who napped on my monitor giving me companionship during my search for my muse.

To all who contributed to my task, I thank you. Of course, none of you can share the responsibility for all errors, omissions, or misstatements that cropped up in this book. Those I had to do on my own.

The Investment
Landscape

CHAPTER 1

The Nanotech Landscape

An Emerging Market

There are those among us who believe one can outperform the Standard & Poor's 500 Stock Index by choosing stocks wisely. There are some who actually succeed. Among the success stories is that of a fabled six-year-old chimpanzee named Raven, who has been taught to pick stocks by throwing darts at the *New York Times* stock pages. This sharp-shooting monkey, whose portfolio selection is based entirely on the symbols penetrated by the darts, has allegedly outperformed 95 percent of all fund managers for each of the past five years. Whether Raven is a fable or a solid blue-chimp investor, he exemplifies the fact that there is a degree of uncertainty in predicting the performance of individual stocks.

Predicting a stock's performance is partly a matter of luck, partly a matter of the prevailing political and economic conditions of the day, and partly a matter of careful due diligence. While an individual stock's performance may be a difficult prediction best managed by a dart-wielding chimp, sector stock performance is usually somewhat more predictable. Sector stocks, which are collections of all stocks in selected industries, have the advantage of relying less on any single company's performance and more on the general long-term trends of an entire industry. It takes only modest simian insight to predict that in the long run, some industries will expand while other industries will contract. It should come as no surprise that even Raven could have predicted that the compact-disc industry will continue to expand, while vinyl is headed for the museum.

Established industrial sectors are relatively easy to predict. They have the advantage of precedent, with histories, trends, multiple market players, and a well-defined set of consumers who have predictable behaviors. But the industrial sectors that do not *yet* exist and therefore have no track record—like nanotechnology—these are the more interesting sectors.

At the end of the nineteenth century, there was an emerging industrial sector called the automobile industry. This industry was widely predicted to grow over time, and there was no question that early investors in automobiles had the potential to make tremendous returns on their investments. However, if you can picture yourself as an investor in New York City in 1899, the fundamental question you would have had to resolve was which automotive technology to invest in. Turn-of-the-century technology gave you a choice of electric, steam, and gasoline power sources propelling various forms of modified buggies. The industrial forecasters of this time had a clear bias against gasoline-propelled automobiles because of the difficulty in finding the rare refined oil that was required to fuel these vehicles. Had you been sufficiently prescient to have placed your bets on gasoline-powered vehicles, virtually none of the companies that you could have backed would have survived the impact of the upstart Henry Ford, who, in 1903, created the company that dominated the automotive industry for decades. In the short span of 20 years, technologies that competed with the gasoline engine were abandoned, and most of the early automobile companies simply ceased to exist. The sector as a whole, however, did extremely well.

Recent scientific progress has left virtually no question that nanotechnology will become a tremendous and significant part of worldwide culture. Likewise, there is no question that those who back the right technologies and the right companies at the right times will end up with pocket change sufficient to rival the gross domestic product of some third-world countries. So, as with the early automotive industry, the questions remain the same: Which technologies? Which companies? And when?

This book defines the core issues of investing in nanotechnology. Like every early-stage industry, nanotechnology is ill conceived, full of potential technology pitfalls, and crowded with revivalist-style, bible-thumping evangelists. In spite of the many shortcomings that would drive a traditional investor to mutual funds, nanotechnology has already become a global industry consuming nearly $1 billion each year in investment from the governments of technologically advanced nations. Relying on some of the most sophisticated technologies the world has ever seen, nanotechnology has received the global sanction of virtually every government capable of funding research and development (R&D). It has caught the attention of Hollywood and has been subjected to scathing attacks from pundits of social conscience. The level of investment shared by many different governments, coupled with the high social visibility it has attracted, lends some credence to the thought that nanotechnology, whatever it is, is going to be big.

AN INVESTOR'S DEFINITION OF NANOTECHNOLOGY

There are few people today who would agree as to what is and is not the scope of nanotechnology. The word *nano* is derived from the Greek word *nannos,* which, roughly translated, means "little old man." In today's English usage, *nano* is a technical term used in measurement, meaning 1 billionth of something. It is usually compounded with the word *meter.* A *nanometer* is a measure of distance of 1 billionth of a meter—approximately the distance occupied by 5 to 10 atoms stacked in a straight line. The word *technology* has a common meaning, also derived from Greek, which can be generally defined as *the application of the scientific method to commercial objectives.* So *nanotechnology* very generally means the manipulation of exceptionally small things, approximately at the atomic scale, toward some commercial objective. In a nutshell, nanotechnology involves the manipulation of individual atoms to make a profit.

However, of the hundreds of millions of dollars being spent on nanotechnology, virtually no money is being invested in the manipulation of individual atoms to some commercial end. *Most* of the money is going toward the development of things that are thousands of times larger than individual atoms. This results in some confusion as to what nanotechnology really is. In the pure sense, it should be technologies that work at the scale of atoms. However, actually manipulating atoms one at a time is an extremely difficult and expensive task and has no near-term product potential. Thus, the term *nanotechnology* today, having caught the media spotlight as *the* catchall marketing term for something really cool, has evolved in its meaning to broadly encompass those technologies that are so small that they cannot be seen without a microscope. If something cannot be seen because it is the size of an atom, or if it is the size of a dust mite, it really does not matter, because both are equally invisible. Purists, of course, will disagree, but the simple fact is that most of the money earmarked for nanotechnology R&D ends up in a technology called *microelectromechanical systems* (MEMS)—a technology concerned with devices thousands of times larger than a nanometer.

The term *MEMS* refers to microscopic devices that perform mechanical operations—say, for example, a steam engine the size of a dust mite. They are made by the same technologies that are used to make the electronics of integrated circuits. The major difference between integrated circuits and MEMS devices is that a MEMS device will usually incorporate something that moves. A typical MEMS device will incorporate components with features about 1 millionth of a meter in size. Thus, the smallest MEMS components are approximately 1,000 times larger than the size of potential nanotechnology components and, unlike nanotechnology devices, are already in common use in a variety of commercial products. The most visible MEMS device in commercial use is the accelerometer, which triggers the inflation of the air bags when a car collides with something.

Again, purists may disagree, but the best guideline for an investor considering what is or is not nanotechnology is simply this: *If you need a microscope to see the details, it must be nanotechnology.* This definition seems to be sufficient for the U.S. government's nanotechnology initiative, which is quietly pumping just under $500 million into nanotechnology research—mostly into technologies that actually fall in the MEMS category.

The most important question for an investor is not the size of the devices, but rather, why is it that these kinds of devices should be valuable? Furthermore, if large-scale investment in these technologies is good enough for the feds, where are the opportunities for private investment?

There is a rather complex answer to these core questions. It starts with the basic fact that nanotechnology is not *quite* ready for prime time. The number of public companies claiming to be focused on nanotechnologies is less than the number of fingers on your hands. The number of these companies that are profitable—well, just say it is less than that. Nanotechnology is an *emerging* technology breaking into an emerging market. It doesn't quite exist yet, but it will. When it does, it is going to have some rather incredible impacts on the way in which the world works.

Imagine a machine the size of a bacterium. This machine will have a complete set of robotic tools including arms, legs, eyes, brains, and senses, and it will be programmed to do a variety of biological repair tasks. Since this robot is the size of a bacterium, doctors will inject swarms of these robots into a vein, and they will then seek out and destroy every cancerous cell or invading pathogen in the body. Industry will manufacture these robots by the billions for a few dollars per billion. When these robots work as a team, they will destroy bad cells, repair old cells, and essentially reconstruct human bodies one cell at a time, giving people eternal youth and vigor. Ponce de Leon spent 10 years of his life conquering Florida in search of this miracle fountain of youth. From an investor's point of view, this sounds like rather good stuff. Exactly how much would the average consumer pay for a single injection of a few million microrobots that promises eternal disease-free youth? From the evangelist's point of view, the concept alone is worth a few trillion dollars, and is one of the core objectives of nanotechnology.

Stepping back a bit and focusing on something that *will* happen in the next few years: Imagine a disposable machine the size of a postage stamp, costing less than $10. This machine has a complete chemistry lab replete with protein, DNA, and chemical sensors. When you place a single drop of blood in this machine, it will give you a complete genetic analysis, blood-chemistry analysis, microbial and viral analysis, and a cross section of every medical test that can or will be derived from a blood sample. More amazingly, you can have the results in 10 minutes. The core MEMS technologies for this machine already exist and are commercially viable today, representing a multi-billion-dollar opportunity in the next few years.

Between the lab-on-a-chip realities and the distant fountain of youth, there are other potential uses for nanotechnology. One of the more popular ideas is the carbon nanotube, which is nothing more than a pipe made of carbon atoms linked together in such a way as to create a thread of pure carbon with a tensile strength perhaps 60 times that of steel. When a way is found to make carbon nanotubes of arbitrary length, it will be possible to braid a rope that would have the ability to stretch from the earth's equator to a geosynchronous orbit 22,000 miles above without breaking. If a way could be found to lower the rope from orbit and bolt it to the earth, an electric elevator could literally climb this rope and place people and machines into orbit for a few dollars per pound. Access to space would become cheaper than flying from New York to Boston. The fact that the longest nanotube on record is a fraction of a millimeter is no deterrent to the dozens of university and private research programs working on finding a means to create this unusual material.

INVESTING IN EMERGING INDUSTRIES

Managing investment in an emerging industry is not a task for the faint-hearted. In a mature industry, you know what people are buying, what they are willing to pay, and which features they want. You know who your competitors are, and what the technical triumphs and hurdles are likely to be. In an emerging industry, none of these things are known. There is only certainty that there will be a viable market, products, and revenues. Beyond that, take a lesson from history and count on your competition springing out of nowhere. Few guessed in 1903 that Henry Ford would own 50 percent of the automotive market in less than 15 years.

The major investment problem of emerging industries is not the technology. Rather, it is the ability to capture intellectual property that has real commercial value. For example, if you are running a company in a mature industry, such as producing digital versatile disc (DVD) players, then the technology problems have long since been resolved. As a DVD player manufacturer, you can either purchase components on an original equipment manufacturer (OEM) basis, or manufacture them according to industry standards. The issues you have to focus on are keeping the costs out of the products, incorporating features that make the products attractive to consumers, and setting up marketing and distribution systems that ensure that consumers want what you have and can get it when they want it. Even if a better, cheaper, faster DVD replacement technology becomes available that can produce higher quality at lower cost, the inertia of the installed base means that current consumers and producers of DVD program material will take years to evaluate the new technology and consider whether to embrace it. As a mature player in a mature market, you must be responsive, but you have plenty of time and staying power to weather the occasional storms.

An emerging industry has much nastier problems. What you have today may look good to the consumer, as long as you have their attention, but two booths down, a competitor may be selling what you are selling at half the price with more features. The problem is really quite simple. While an industry is emergent, there is no safety blanket of standards. *Every* technology is a breakthrough technology, and each player has a wrinkle that no other player has yet. Investors who get involved with emerging technologies have a simple requirement: Whatever the technology is, either it must be proprietary or it must be irrelevant to the success of the product. If the technology *is* proprietary, then it is a one-of-a-kind technology that is owned by one company and available to no one else. If it is also *valuable,* then the company has an asset of some value, perhaps great value. If it happens to be the *best* technology, then the company *may* have a winner. If the company can get market share, then it probably *does* have a winner. However, even in the case where all these answers are yes, things may not happen in a fiscally happy way.

Consider the experience of Sony during the early days of consumer videotape recording. In 1975, Sony introduced the consumer-grade Betamax videocassette recorder. A year later, rival JVC introduced the VHS videocassette recorder. Sony took the path that the Betamax system was proprietary and exclusive to Sony. JVC became part of an open-standards effort that permitted other companies to enter the fray on the side of VHS. From Sony's point of view, Betamax met the four basic requirements of a successful product:

- It was proprietary technology, owned by Sony.
- It was valuable, in that it permitted anyone to record video.
- It produced a better-quality picture than the competing technology, VHS.
- Sony's worldwide marketing capabilities were unrivaled when it came to product introduction, management, and consumer sales.

But consumers had to choose either Betamax or VHS, and throughout the mid- to late 1980s, a marketing battle of epic proportions was waged. In the end, Sony's Betamax lost, and VHS won. Sometimes, it's not what *is* real that counts, it's what people *think* is real that counts. Marketing will sometimes prevail over quality.

From the starting gate, there are problems for product development in nanotechnology because of the federal government's large investment. What exactly constitutes proprietary technology becomes a rather difficult issue when federal dollars are providing most of the development money. When the federal government funds an R&D program that results in valuable intellectual property, the government technically owns the rights to the property, but access may become public domain. Having your core intellectual property owned by the government promotes extreme insecurity and substantial competitive risk, and it can increase the paperwork challenges by an order of magnitude. This is a major turn-off for many investors. As shown later in this book, there are some ways to extricate valuable intellectual property from federal coffers without inciting a revolution or committing theft.

SOURCES OF FUNDING

As mentioned earlier, most nanotechnology funding comes from a variety of federal sources. The private investment arena provides a pittance, with estimates topping out at $30 million, invested by traditional venture-capital or seed-capital sources. That is roughly 6 percent of the government's $500 million infusion. Corporate research programs operated by the *Fortune* 1000 may be investing 10 times the amount provided by private investors, depending on how one draws the line between nanotechnology and other small technologies.

From an investor's point of view, the opportunities to invest in nanotechnology are extremely limited because of the nature of the current funding process. The government is doing the bulk of all financing at this time. What private-sector investment has occurred to date has been in the form of private placements and a few initial public offerings (IPOs). There is little opportunity to invest in publicly traded stocks, simply because the number of public nanotechnology companies is less than 10. *Private placement* is the most common means of investing in nanotechnology companies. In a private placement, the fledgling company attempts to raise between $1 million and $5 million to start the company's operations. Under the Securities and Exchange Commission (SEC) regulations that control investment, the reporting requirements for a company at the lower end of the scale are relatively minimal compared to the reporting requirements of a public company. This permits the company to focus on the business of being a business without being bogged down by the quarterly and annual filing requirements of a public company. Most nanotechnology start-ups are in this early phase of capital formation.

Because most nanotechnology investment is in private placement, most investors are not qualified by the SEC to participate in these kinds of investments. Rule 215 of the Securities Act of 1933 defines a *qualified* (or *accredited*) *investor* as someone with a net worth of $1 million or an annual income of at least $200,000. The typical investment agreements also include legal language that states that the investor is willing and able to lose the entire value of the investment.[1] The actual act of investment is usually handled by individual accredited investors, or seed venture-capital funds that solicit funds from accredited investors. Of the 40 million Americans who invest in some manner, there are approximately 250,000 who are active accredited investors—with a maximum potential pool of about 2 million more who are not currently active. Most accredited investors focus on bricks-and-mortar investments, where physical property represents the bulk of the company's assets if they should need to be liquidated. It is a very rare accredited investor who is willing to plunk down a few hundred thousand dollars into an intellectual-property idea or esoteric custom technologies that may or may not find a niche in an ill-defined marketplace.

The ultimate hope of the accredited investor is that at some point the company will do well enough to go for an IPO. If the company gets to this step, the stock that the investor previously owned loses its "restricted" legend and can be bought or sold at the prevailing market price. Unless the company gets to the IPO stage, the stock is generally worthless.

In an emerging industry such as nanotechnology, the key to creating assets that can lead to investment that can lead to an IPO is the acquisition of proprietary intellectual property. Intellectual property, like Sony's Betamax technology, is the coin of the realm in defining future value. In the case of nanotechnology, however, the federal government owns most of the intellectual property. There are, however, two key mechanisms by which a fledgling company can acquire the intellectual property to give it a suitable monopoly to potentially persuade an investor to believe that if a product results, it will be unique and exclusive. These two mechanisms, which are dealt with in depth in later chapters, are the Small Business Incentive Research (SBIR) program and the Bayh-Dole act.

The SBIR program was initiated in 1982 and is administered by the U.S. Small Business Administration through 11 participating federal agencies. The intent of this program is to help small businesses explore their technological potential and to provide the incentive to profit from the technology's commercialization. Most active nanotechnology companies are involved with one or more SBIR programs.

The Bayh-Dole act was originally passed in 1980. It encourages the dissemination and commercialization of federally sponsored research (typically in university and national laboratory settings). This act promotes the control and licensing of technology developed under federal funds. One of the offshoots of this act is that more than 200 universities and all national laboratories now maintain technology transfer offices, which have the task of selling and licensing technologies to prospective buyers. One of the more interesting results of this activity is that a number of university technology transfer offices actually operate in a venture-capital mode by supporting the creation of new companies that are developed around a particular piece of intellectual property developed and paid for by federal funding.

Both of these mechanisms represent significant investment opportunities for investors wanting a piece of the nanotechnology pie. However, since these mechanisms are highly regulated and controlled by federal law, they are not opportunities to be explored casually. Separate chapters are devoted to each of these mechanisms.

THE PLAYERS

As you work through the hurdles of how to invest, you will also have to understand where the investment opportunities can be found. For nanotechnology, there are five kinds of R&D programs that need to be considered:

- The first kind is the traditional university setting, dominated by individuals who work in an academic environment and strive to solve the thorny and difficult problems that plague any emergent technology.
- The second kind is the national laboratory system, which often competes with academics for federal dollars to develop new and esoteric capabilities of value.
- The third is the traditional industrial research setting. Large companies in the Fortune 1000 class devote significant money to developing technologies that they hope will ultimately find their way into future products.
- Fourth are the nonprofit institutional philanthropists, who attempt to create the political and investment climate that encourages the funding of new initiatives and programs.
- Fifth are the actual for-profit companies—the entrepreneurs who invest their lives and careers on behalf of shareholders in hopes that they can create products of value before the cash runs out.

Subsequent chapters explore some of the dynamics of these five groups.

GOING FORWARD

The intent of this book is to provide the investor with a blueprint for developing an investment strategy focused on nanotechnology. The chapters that follow explore what is happening today. This book explores the scope and impact of the federal nanotechnology initiative and who is benefiting and why. It looks at the major commercial players and the kinds of activities they are undertaking and have planned for the future.

This is followed by a detailed view of the intent of the nanotechnology initiative and how the federal dollars are earmarked and distributed. This book pays special attention to Sandia National Laboratory's MEMS program, which has some of the most remarkable short-term product potential among comparable programs. This is followed by a detailed look at the SBIR program to see how companies use this program to bootstrap their technology, and how and when an investor should take a close look at the opportunities that are created from this type of federal funding.

The Bayh-Dole act is explored in some depth. The most important outcome of this act is the new practice among public institutions of spawning private, for-profit corporations. This has resulted in a steady trickle of small start-up companies with a better-than-average history of survival. This book explores how technology transfer offices spin off these companies and how an investor can participate.

Industrial giants such as IBM and Intel have long-standing ongoing research programs in nanotechnology. These programs represent significant investments in the future of these companies. While it is unlikely that these companies will spin off small companies with great investment potential, they do represent current investment opportunities for now and in the foreseeable future.

One interesting exploration is the analysis of a typical nanotechnology start-up, focusing on how several emerging nanotechnology companies have leveraged private and federal dollars to create technologies that they are trying to bring into the market. These companies, which are the closest to making IPOs, represent some of the more exciting near-term investment opportunities, provided they don't run out of cash first.

Finally, this book looks at international activities. The United States is not the only country that has a strong interest in nanotechnology. Offshore investment is nearly double in value to that being made in the United States. More than half of the investment opportunities in nanotechnology are not covered by SEC regulations, although offshore investing has its own set of risks and problems.

There is a lot of ground to cover in setting the stage for investing in nanotechnology. There is much to learn about how to extract private money from federal programs without going into the fascinating details of what is on the threshold of discovery. The subsequent chapters will guide you through a complex but manageable quagmire of potential value. If you are lucky, this book will help you avoid the mistakes of the investors of Henry Ford's time, without invoking the predictive capabilities of Raven the chimp.

NOTES

1. Typical legal language covering participation in a private placement includes the following: "Investor has experience in investing in compa-

nies in the developmental stage, such as the Company, and acknowledges that it is able to fend for itself and to assess the economic risk of this purchase, recognizes that this investment involves a high degree of risk and may result in a loss of the entire investment, and has such knowledge and experience in financial and business matters that it can be assumed to be capable of evaluating the merits and risks of this investment and/or protecting its interests in such an investment."

CHAPTER 2

Current Activity in Nanotechnology

During the height of the *Washington Post*'s investigation of the Watergate break-in, reporters Bob Woodward and Carl Bernstein relied on a Nixon insider, the infamous "Deep Throat," for the guidance they needed to unearth the facts that ultimately toppled the Nixon administration. This insider gave the two reporters one simple rule for their investigative process: *Follow the money*. In any investigation with uncertain outcomes, this may be the cardinal rule for investors. In terms of this book, it will be the guiding light on the rather murky path that leads from technology evangelism to the world of real and potential investment. Tracing the Watergate money led Woodward and Bernstein to a myriad of surprises regarding who was involved and what secrets had been hidden away in the closets of intrigue. In exploring the potential of nanotechnology, there is quite a bit of intrigue before one finds unassailable investment potential. By following the money, you can shake loose those things that are of real value and discard those that are simply spin.

There is an ongoing worldwide investment of approximately $1 billion finding its way into the microscopic visions of researchers and developers. In the absence of clearly defined products and markets, there must be reasons why so much money is being spent on something that has such limited short-term payoff.

If one were simply to itemize where the money goes, it would be like summarizing the task descriptions of every division of a *Fortune* 500 company. It could certainly be done, but the knowledge gained would be about as helpful as reading the yellow pages in an effort to determine the basis of a region's local economy. When investors choose to follow the money, nanotechnology gives them a more difficult time than most other technologies, because there is virtually zero private investment going into nanotechnology. Thus, there is no profit motive that investors can trace. There are, however, sources of money that investors can identify, and their motives and intentions are relatively easy to find.

WHO IS SPENDING?

To qualify as an investment target, here is a simple rule for following the money: The collective investment of the target group must be in excess of $100 million. The first group, the U.S. government, has created the National Nanotechnology Initiative (NNI). This office serves as a central clearinghouse for the conceptualization and prioritization of government-sponsored funding in nanotechnology. Second are those companies involved in microelectronics. They face highly competitive markets that require ever smaller and more efficient components. The third group is represented by consortia of universities that operate in their traditional role of developing novel research that expands the scope of human knowledge. More than 50 percent of the funding for university nanotechnology research comes from both government and corporate sponsors. So, your task is to follow the money and see where these groups are focusing their dollars and why.

WHAT TO CHOOSE

To understand how money is directed to a particular kind of research, you need to understand how value is assessed for something that does not yet exist. For those who fund research for a living, this is an everyday problem. The standard question asked by grants program administrators is "How do you select a program for funding, when no one really knows if the program will ever amount to anything?" The selection process will typically focus on research that may solve problems based on one of four kinds of needs:

- *Solving problems that are here and now and require solution for an economic purpose.*   If people are dying of a disease, the need is to find a solution that ends the disease.
- *Solving problems that are identified as a result of a consensus process that defines a need.*   If all the experts think that the problem is important, then solving the problem is important.
- *Solving problems because of the protracted and effective efforts of evangelism.*   If someone preaches long enough, eventually the sermon acquires the ring of truth and is awarded a commensurate budget.
- *Solving problems that are promoted by those who've successfully and publicly solved problems before.*   If a researcher has a history of solving problems, the odds are that he or she will do it again.

Each of these needs plays a role in defining what kinds of research are carried out by different kinds of institutions.

Companies such as IBM and Intel are drawn to research in nanotechnology because they face a clear and present danger from competitors who may gain market share by developing exclusive technologies that create faster, smaller, and cheaper devices. This is defensive research, focused on maintaining and expanding the market share of an established company. If Intel were to cease all research and development (R&D), the next generation of microprocessors would certainly be manufactured by one of Intel's competitors. Because of the vast profits that can be made by being in the top position in electronics fabrication, maintaining that position requires a never-ending research program to develop smaller, cheaper, faster devices that are used by more and more system integrators.

Although no immediate commercial advantage is visible, government funding agencies will often support popular R&D programs. Their rationale is based on what the experts within a research community believe will have significant long-term benefits that will ultimately produce something of value. From a political point of view, this type of funding is usually proposed as maintaining or developing *national means*. This is a concept that says that a nation's defense and economy will rely on the country's ability to independently produce and control new technology. If other countries beat a nation to the punch, it may become a supplicant to the policies and programs of another nation. The hydrogen-fusion reactor is an example of a program that was funded for decades, through billions of dollars, because the expert consensus suggested tremendous returns if an economical fusion reactor could be built. Of course, even a government-sponsored R&D program will be abandoned if there is little or no progress in a generation or two.

Evangelism is an extremely effective means of acquiring R&D funding. In these cases, highly vocal and visible individuals promote an idea with such conviction that they develop a community of like-minded followers who, through their protracted and unceasing efforts, convince someone with money that R&D funding is well spent on that endeavor. The Search for Extraterrestrial Intelligence (SETI) program is perhaps the best current example of this R&D funding model. Those who fund evangelic R&D proposals can be any mix of government, business, or private financial sources. There need not be a promise of short-term economic benefit. This type of research borders on philanthropy, and a certain vagueness of appeal is required to generate the funding that pours in. The hope is that there will be significant economic payoffs for future generations.[1]

Prominent researchers with established credibility within their academic and funding communities will often receive R&D money simply because of who they are. The motivation is that if credible people are funded based on their track record, they will be successful again. The credentials of the researcher alone are often sufficient to justify support. IBM's fellows program is one example of a case in which researchers are funded simply because, whatever they do, it will probably be of great value when they are finished.

Most of the money funneled into nanotechnology is distributed as a result of the grant proposal process. The ultimate goal when writing a grant proposal is to merge all four funding rationales into a single proposal that generates significant funding interest. Researchers collaborate in the development of a proposal, and the proposal is in turn submitted to a funding source. As discussed earlier, there are three major investors in nanotechnology—government, the microelectronics industry, and universities. Each of these investors serves a different constituency and uniquely balances the needs that must be emphasized in funding proposals. Each of these investors is covered in a full chapter, to fully explore how they create investment opportunities and assess the needs for providing R&D funding.

GOVERNMENT FUNDING

The focal point for government funding of nanotechnology is the NNI. The National Science and Technology Council operates the NNI. This cabinet-level council was created in 1993 by the executive order of President Clinton to coordinate federal investment in science and technology. The president chairs the council, which includes the vice-president, members of the cabinet, and the heads of various agencies with long histories of funding federal R&D programs. In July 2000, the NNI produced an operations plan for R&D development of nanotechnologies through federal sponsorship. Approximately $500 million was included in the fiscal 2001 federal budget to support the initiative's plan, which included R&D spending allocated among:

- The Department of Commerce
- The Department of Defense
- The Department of Energy
- The Department of Transportation
- The National Aeronautics and Space Administration (NASA)
- The National Institutes of Health
- The National Science Foundation

As part of the initiative, agencies selected strategic research areas, which are agency-specific focuses for the possible outcomes of nanotechnology research. Approximately 70 percent of the funding goes directly into university research programs. The balance is distributed among the national laboratories and the various grants programs administered by the agencies. The distribution of funds is about one-third for fundamental research, one-third for grand challenges,[2] and one-third distributed among infrastructure, facilities, and social issues development. Grand challenges are policy concepts thought to be potentially valuable to the future economy of the country and the well-being of all citizens.[3]

THE MICROELECTRONICS INDUSTRY

The microelectronics industry's investments in nanotechnology are narrowly focused on the development of technologies that permit the semiconductor manufacturers to maintain their competitive position. In 1965, one of Intel's founders, Gordon Moore, was preparing a presentation for a conference, and he graphed the performance of integrated circuits over time. It appeared that the number of transistors on an integrated circuit doubled approximately every 18 months. His observation became known as *Moore's law*. Through the present day, his law has in fact been the way of the microelectronics world. However, many people have noted that this "law" has some pending problems. Over the next 10 years, microelectronic devices will become so small that individual atoms will have to be the fundamental components, and when this becomes the case, there will be nothing smaller that is known that can be used to make electronic devices. In addition, the technologies for producing integrated circuits have become so advanced and complex—not to mention expensive—that it is no longer obvious how microelectronics will be fabricated in the future. Today, the smallest lines in an integrated circuit are a mere 300 nanometers in width, with future requirements pushing toward the molecular and atomic scales. While it is not a natural law that integrated circuits should double in complexity every 18 months, there is tremendous competitive pressure within the industry to maintain technological leadership in the production of ever smaller and more efficient components. As a result, almost every major semiconductor company maintains a family of active and expensive research programs, each of which is focused on developing the technologies for future generations of integrated circuits, directed to both the short-term and the long-term potentials of microelectronics. The short-term programs are dedicated to the *next* generation of devices, the ones that must become commercially viable within a few years. The long-term programs are dedicated to future generations of devices. Much of the work in the long-term programs is focused on managing the manufacturing costs, which will otherwise skyrocket.

One thing that Moore's law didn't dwell on is the fact that the factories that manufacture each new generation of electronics double in cost with each doubling in performance. A current state-of-the-art microelectronics fabrication facility costs in excess of $1 billion. Unless this trend is broken, one can forecast facilities costing in excess of $10 billion within a few years. Clearly, there are strong incentives for finding means to keep the costs of these facilities well below the gross domestic product of a small country. Much of the research dedicated toward nanotechnology is focused on a concept called *self-assembly,* a hypothetical means whereby devices would have the innate ability to assemble themselves without requiring massive and incredibly expensive manufacturing facilities.

UNIVERSITY RESEARCH PROGRAMS

Universities represent the third tier of funded research into nanotechnology. Universities have a politically and ethically delicate mixture of responsibilities. On one hand, universities operate under the dictum of academic freedom. This means that once professors have been admitted into the community of scholars, their scholarship is subject only to peer review. Academic freedom gives members of the faculty freedom to research anything they want, provided that their peers agree that what they are doing is meaningful and significant.

On the other hand, universities also require funding to support this scholarship. In an era in which an atomic force microscope (a basic tool for nanotechnology research) can cost well over $100,000, someone has to pick up the tab for all manner of expensive equipment. So faculty members in research programs often find themselves in the difficult position of balancing true scholarly research with the influences of funding available from federal agencies and large companies. When researchers come up with some invention of value, they are often torn between the desire to be scholars and the desire to acquire the funding necessary for continued scholarship. As a result of these conflicts, many universities have developed programs that encourage the commercialization of the inventions derived from research. Some universities actually try to spin off companies to commercialize their inventions.

One of the most well-known philosophers of science, Thomas Kuhn, articulated significant elements of the interaction between research and the development of knowledge.[4] Kuhn described the scientific process as being as much a social phenomenon as a logical phenomenon. Each generation of scientists comes into their professional maturity with a set of ideas about what is valid research. These generational ideas are deeply ingrained into the social and economic foundations of research. Each generation of scientists believes in common research fundamentals, the practices that constitute the scientific method, as well as the plausible research outcomes that should be funded. Scientists who strike out on their own are deviations from the community process of science and usually become outcasts. If they are extremely talented and extremely well thought of, they become the leaders of the next generation of scientific thought. The dominant paradigm of any given generation of research will endure through a generation of scientists, only to be replaced at some later time by a new paradigm that had as its midwife some radical whose detractors failed to destroy his or her ideas.

Nowhere but in a university setting can radical thinking be sustained to the point where actual dollars are spent on proving or disproving the radical ideas. In the case of nanotechnology, Eric Drexler is credited with collating most of the defining paradigm.[5] In his book *Engines of Creation* (New York: Anchor Books, 1986), he proposed many of the possibilities and future directions of nanotechnology, and thereby created the paradigm that drives much of the current university-sponsored nanotechnology research.

Each of the three sources of research funding has a slightly different spin on what constitutes value for research dollars. All three sources, however, spotlight the development of investment opportunities that are available to a much wider audience. In the case of the government, the NNI has the clearly stated objective of funding research that has the potential for commercialization within a three- to five-year period. As this book explores the SBIR programs through which much of this money is made available, you will see how the government intends to commercialize its success. In the case of the microelectronics industry, the maintenance of stock prices through continuing commercial success represents an investment value today for those who would speculate about the future of nanotechnology. For universities, the prevalence of technology transfer programs and the growth of spin-off operations within those programs present an obvious and valuable opportunity for private investment.

NONPROFITS

While a nonprofit organization is, by definition, an inherently bad choice for investment, nonprofit institutions play a significant role in defining and directing the opportunities for investment. In nanotechnology, nonprofit organizations such as the Foresight Institute and a half dozen others operate in much the same way as a combination clearinghouse and lobbying institution. By sponsoring conferences, publishing research, and participating in hearings before agencies of the government, nonprofits and the paths they promote represent a significant force in determining what kinds of investment will be made and who will receive the money. Because of their influence, nonprofit organizations focused on nanotechnology must be carefully watched and monitored by potential investors. The effects of their lobbying are profound and striking, especially when there is $500 million to play with.

HOW TO SHOOT A DUCK

Every year, several million migratory birds are shot dead in flight or on the water as a result of the nation's desire to kill waterfowl and eat gamy and stringy meat. Virtually none of these birds are deprived of their lives by means of a single bullet. The approach that blasts a bird from the sky is given the term *shotgun* because the shotgun is the most effective means of killing a bird in flight, which is otherwise too hard to target and shoot. When the shotgun sprays hundreds of pellets in the general direction of the bird, a few of them may actually hit the bird and send it to its maker. Research funding programs are in many respects similar to the shotgun approach in hunting. When dissecting the structure of the funding that comes from the NNI, you will see that the funding is earmarked to virtually anyone who has a credible idea worth funding. Roughly half a dozen federal agencies have solicited proposals for 300 to 400 funding opportunities in the range of $50,000 to $1 million per year. Each funding agency puts a slightly different spin on the proposal requirements. The National Institutes of Health have scant interest in proposals that focus on micropropulsion systems, whereas NASA has scant interest in proposals that focus on gene activation. Of the thousands of proposals that are submitted, of the few hundred that are actually funded, some small percentage of the results are going to hit the bird dead on. Most, however, will go wide of the mark and be buried and lost in the files of the funding agency. Shotgun research, however, is the unique prerogative of federal R&D sponsorship. The next chapter dissects how this funding works and discusses how to find opportunities.

NOTES

1. The signal-processing complexities of the current SETI program are so vast that a means was found to distribute the processing by means of software that anyone can download from the SETI web site. The software permits literally millions of home personal computers to share the gargantuan amount of signal processing required to differentiate an artificially produced radio signal from the natural background noise. One spin-off of this has been the commercialization of massive parallel-processing tools that permit for-profit companies to execute computationally complex tasks by enrolling large numbers of home PCs.

Companies pay a fee to home-computer owners to gain approved access to their PCs.

2. A *grand challenge* is a fundamental technology issue that has broad implications for the development of future technology if resolved.

3. The NNI program overview is included in Appendix A. Much of the motivation and strategy for the program is found in this overview.

4. Thomas Kuhn, *The Structure of Scientific Revolutions* (Chicago: University of Chicago Press, 1996).

5. Eric Drexler is currently with the Foresight Institute, the major non-profit nanotechnology advocacy group.

CHAPTER 3

The Feds

There is an old adage in the oral history of political science that states that our system of government consists of four branches—the executive, the legislative, the judicial, and the bureaucracy. About the bureaucracy, Hyman Rickover is quoted as remarking, "If you're going to sin, sin against God, not the bureaucracy. God will forgive you but the bureaucracy won't." In spite of significant and perhaps well-deserved negative press, the federal bureaucracy is capable not only of conducting research, but, more important, of turning this research over to the private sector for economic exploitation.

THE COHERENCE OF FEDERAL RESEARCH AND DEVELOPMENT

With a $1-trillion-plus annual budget, the U.S. government actually has a piteously small amount of discretionary money for pure research. For the last half century, the government has accepted and institutionalized the idea that federally funded research is best if administered by federal agencies but performed by others. The origin of the current system of federal research and development (R&D) administration was the Manhattan project, which developed the atomic bomb during World War II. Originally, the major research facilities at Los Alamos and Oak Ridge were administered and controlled by the U.S. Army. It became apparent very early in the program that a measure of civilian control was required. Most of the brainpower that was needed for the project could neither be drafted nor ordered to execute research under the uniform code of military justice. Over time, the administration of the nuclear weapons program was shifted from direct military control to contractual arrangements with civilian institutions. Over time, this created a cross-connected set of national laboratories managed by a diverse set of civilian contractors. For example, the Los Alamos National Laboratory is currently operated under a contract with the University of California. About 50 miles away, the Lockheed Martin Company manages the Sandia National Laboratory. Both national laboratories are operated on behalf of the Department of Energy. By comparison, the Department of Health directly controls the National Institutes of Health, which are also members of the national laboratory system. In turn, the National Institutes of Health manage 25 separate institutes and centers under a mixture of direct, corporate, and university programs. The specific logic of how these agencies are operated has more of a historical justification than any pragmatic justification. The key concept however, is that although the R&D funding may come from a single operational budget (i.e., the Department of Energy), the control of programs and projects at any one particular laboratory is likely to be quite different from that at any other particular laboratory. For this reason, tapping into investment opportunities within the national laboratory system is an activity that requires significant homework to find out where technology investment opportunities are. Nonetheless, the national laboratory system consumes about one-third of all federal dollars that are pumped into nanotechnology research.

THE NATIONAL NANOTECHNOLOGY INITIATIVE

The National Nanotechnology Initiative (NNI) has the role of coordinating the nanotechnology efforts of four cabinet-level departments (Commerce, Defense, Energy, and Transportation) as well as the National Institutes of Health, the National Aeronautics and Space Administration (NASA), and the National Science Foundation. By federal standards, the NNI has an almost insignificant $500 million in its budget. Therefore, NNI is not in a position to dictate policy to any of these agencies, let alone disburse funds through the extended and complex matrix of operating agencies, universities, and companies. The management task alone would consume most of the money. Thus, the approach taken by the NNI has been to funnel funds to each of its constituents so that they, in turn, can directly fund or solicit proposals for funding within their respective research programs. Although NNI estimates that 70 percent of the distributed funds will end up in programs operated by universities, a significant amount will end up in the hands of nanotechnologists working within the national laboratory system.

THE LAW

Before getting into some examples of how private investors can participate in federally funded research, it will be helpful to try to untangle the rather complex web of law that defines the commercialization of federal R&D. The national laboratory system consumes approximately $25 billion each year. A major portion of this money goes into research programs for both civilian and military programs. The military technology is generally classified and for sale only to foreign agents. However, not all research ends up in classified weapon systems. Congress has enacted a number of laws to ensure that the public will reap the benefits of this research.

In 1974, the Federal Laboratory Consortium was established to organize the transfer of technology between members of the national laboratory system. At the time, although there was a certain legitimate trickle of technology from the national labs into the commercial sector, it was relatively unregulated and uncoordinated. In many cases, technology was simply given away, with no sense of the value that had been captured in the research. In 1980, the U.S. Congress adopted two laws, the Stevenson-Wydler act and the Bayh-Dole act. The Stevenson-Wydler Technology Innovation Act set out the requirement that each member of the federal laboratory system had to establish an office of research and technology applications, which would have the responsibility of transferring technology to other federal, state, or local governments, or into the private sector. The Bayh-Dole act set the standard that universities that conducted research under federal funding were to be encouraged to commercialize inventions resulting from that funding. It provided that universities were entitled to own patents generated by their research, but that the patents could and should be licensed to private businesses whenever possible. Together, these laws provided means by which the researchers who produced technology could be rewarded for their efforts, as well as means for returning some money back to the laboratory systems that had developed the technology.

Subsequent amendments to these acts culminated in the Technology Transfer Commercialization Act of 1999, which pulled together and amended prior legislation to provide a coherent federal policy for all technology emanating from federal research dollars. The outcome of this was the establishment and support of a wide variety of federally funded technology transfer offices for both the national laboratory system and any other recipients of federal money. The purpose of these offices, established through decades of legislation, is to transfer the results of federal research into the commercial sector, primarily through technology and patent licensing. This is your in as an investor.

THE PRACTICE

To understand how this network of law translates into investment opportunities, here is an examination of one particular program out of the 700 national laboratories operated within the federal R&D system, which demonstrates how the money flows and how opportunities wind their way from the federal sector into the private. The chosen exemplar of nanotechnology R&D within the national laboratory system is the Sandia National Laboratory's Intelligent Micromachine Initiative (IMI).[1] The IMI focuses on the development of the technology and capabilities that are required to produce mechanical devices composed of parts as small as one-millionth of an inch. The IMI is focused on an effort to develop the technology infrastructure for what it estimates to be a future industry with an annual value of $100 billion. The initiative is housed in the Microelectronics Development Laboratory on Kirtland Air Force Base, and is managed by the Albuquerque office of Sandia National Laboratory under contract to Lockheed Martin by the Department of Energy. The IMI has access to a modest 30,000-square-foot Class 1 clean-room fabrication facility for its technology development programs.[2]

The focus of the IMI is on the development of micromachines fabricated by essentially the same technologies that are used to make microelectronics. The difference is that rather than complex circuits interconnecting discrete electronic devices, micromachines consist of discrete mechanical components that perform the same mechanical functions performed by larger machines. Some examples of the types of machines that have been fabricated by the IMI include:

- *Microengines.*   Devices that perform linear or rotary motion.
- *Microtransmissions.*   Devices that convert between different rotational speeds.
- *Microlocks.*   Devices that operate in much the same way as a combination lock.
- *Micromirrors.*   Devices that reflect light at selectable angles.
- *Steam microengines.*   Literally, microscopic steam engines.
- *Gas microsensors.*   Devices that detect the presence of explosive vapors.

Applications developed by other facilities include fuel injectors, relays, nozzle pumps, strain gauges, optical switches, mechanical switches, biohazard detectors, cooling systems, and many other devices. In all, the Sandia IMI probably represents less than one-fourth of the total global R&D activity dedicated to microelectromechanical systems (MEMS). However, with a market potential estimated by the IMI to be in excess of $100 billion per year, you need to know how investors can get their hands on the opportunities that emerge from work performed by the IMI. To understand how this works, you have to focus your attention on the machinations of several different programs devoted to the commercialization of federally developed technology.

In 1989, the National Technology Transfer Act (NTTA) established the National Technology Transfer Center (NTTC), its stated purpose "to strengthen US industrial competitiveness by identifying industry's needs and matching those needs with technologies and commercialization services required to bring new products/services to market."[3] The operational mandate of the NTTC is to establish and build strategic partnerships among industries, government agencies, and universities by providing:

- Business and product-development services that identify industry's needs; technology mining and assessment; market analysis; and business planning, licensing, modeling, and incubator mentoring assistance.
- Support for the development of regional entrepreneurial businesses.
- Information products and services that facilitate and improve the transfer of federally funded research and development. These products and services develop out of the collection, enhancement, maintenance, analysis, and dissemination of federally sponsored research and technology information.
- Professional development programs that develop high-quality training workshops and alternative delivery training products focused on improving the technology commercialization capability of professionals in the public and private sectors.

In a nutshell, what the NTTC is supposed to do is take technology that has been developed with federal dollars and make it available to private companies through licensing. Ideally, the licenses apply to intellectual property covered by patent, but the technology may also include know-how and methods that cannot be covered by patent. The NTTC operates through local branch affiliates. Each of the federal agencies that performs or administers research receives a small amount of funding intended to support a local or regional technology transfer office. For example, the regional office housed at Sandia National Laboratory is called the Corporate Business Development and Partnerships Center. This office serves three functions:

1. Developing strategic partnerships with private industry
2. Creating relationships with universities
3. Collaborating with other government laboratories

Each federal agency or laboratory has a similar center, although often with a different name. The primary purpose of a technology transfer center is to find some means of commercializing whatever technology has been developed. Each office is local, administered by the particular laboratory's operations management. While day-to-day operations may differ from one office to another, they all share the same common broad objective. Each laboratory also has a personnel policy that describes how employees can interact with the local technology transfer office. Sometimes, the policy is comprised of guidelines explaining federal laws regarding technology transfer. But sometimes the policy can also include tangible incentives for employees to actively participate in technology transfer, as is the case at Sandia where employees can receive benefits such as:

- *Entrepreneurial leave.* Employees can take time off without pay for an extended period to participate in the operations of new companies that attempt to exploit their technology.
- *Receipt of a percentage of royalties.* Employees get a share of royalties that are paid to the laboratory as part of any licensing agreement.

With these types of incentives in place, and with virtually every federal R&D activity supported by some kind of technology transfer office, there is a clear opportunity for private participation in federally developed research in many technology fields, including nanotechnology. However, it is extremely common for a regional office to develop a close relationship with a local economic development office or a private venture-capital firm that will have, if not first pick, at least a first look at what may be emerging out of that technology transfer office. These local affiliations with private commercialization funds (which are encouraged by statute) are both a boon to the federal process of technology transfer and a barrier to others seeking access to federally developed technology. The simple fact is that the entire process is managed locally, and with 700 laboratories participating in technology transfer, there is no single operational practice that an investor can follow to gain access to all of them. Each one must be dealt with on a case-by-case basis.[4] The NTTC also maintains an active list of available technologies and affiliated organizations that it supports.[5] When you get through to the local office, you can spend an hour or so learning who the office routinely interacts with in its region and what its normal business interactions are like.

HOW TO FIND INVESTMENT OPPORTUNITIES

In spite of the wide diversity in the operation of technology transfer, the investor has only one means for tapping into this technology—licensing. However, there are two ways in which licensing provides investment opportunity. Using Sandia's Intelligent Micromachine Initiative history, here are two examples of how commercial opportunities for investment develop under the general practice of technology licensing. The first is an example of licensing technology to an existing company. In this case, a portion of the MEMS technology developed at Sandia was licensed to a private company called Microcosm Technologies, Inc. (now Coventor), of Cary, North Carolina, in December 2000. The R&D investment represented in this agreement was valued at approximately $60 million. Essentially, this licensing agreement gave Microcosm, and subsequently Coventor, access to the manufacturing know-how developed at Sandia, and it permits Coventor to apply this know-how in any profitable manner that Coventor chooses. Should Coventor actually sell products developed under this license, royalty payments will be made to Sandia. From an investor's point of view, then, the emphasis shifts from the work done at Sandia to the actual performance of the licensee. In this case, Coventor (as of this writing) is a privately held company with a venture-capital backing of just under $30 million. The company intends to use this licensed technology for the development of MEMS-based products, which it intends to sell to a broad prospect base. Obviously, if the company's performance matches the current investor's interests, Coventor will be looking at an initial public offering (IPO) within a few years, at which time private investors can invest in the technology developed at taxpayer expense by Lockheed Martin employees under contract to the Department of Energy. The value of the license both to Sandia and to Coventor will not be known until Coventor's financial statements enter the public arena.

A second way in which investment opportunities arise is through the direct creation of a private company. Again, using Sandia as an example, new companies can be created to exploit the technology developed with federal R&D monies. In this case, a company called MEMX was created in October 2000, with the purpose of commercializing optical switch technology developed by Sandia's Intelligent Micromachine Initiative.[6] The NTTC affiliate, Sandia's Corporate Business Development and Partnerships Center, generated the necessary venture-capital contact that provided the seed-stage financing to start the new company. Again, the actual technology provided by Sandia to MEMX is under license. Funds from private venture-capital sources initiated the operations of MEMX once the licensing agreement was consummated. Assistance in developing the business plan, legal support, and infrastructure development under federal guidelines came from the laboratory's technology transfer office. In this case, several employees of the laboratory left to start the new company.

These two examples demonstrate two diverse means of taking R&D from federal laboratories and agencies and converting it into private investment opportunities. In both cases, investors have several entry points to participate in the technology. At the level of a certified investor, the opportunity exists in finding an appropriate venture-capital fund that focuses on the exploitation of technologies developed under the NTTA. At the level of a noncertified investor, the opportunity exists in following a privately held company closely and participating in the company's IPO, or post-IPO free-trading stock. The lesson for the investor is that it is important to follow the companies that license or spin off technologies supported by the NTTA. Learn the technologies, the nature of the licenses, and, most important, the viability of the management and the business plans. Once the license is granted, the emerging company has all the advantages and potential problems of any other classic start-up company.

SMALL BUSINESS INCENTIVE RESEARCH PROGRAMS

Technology transfer programs are not the only means the investor has for gaining access to programs operated at federal laboratories. One of the other means of commercializing federal research is through the Small Business Incentive Research (SBIR) programs. Much of the money distributed by the National Nanotechnology Initiative is earmarked specifically to the SBIR, the Small Business Technology Transfer (STTR), and the Fast Track programs, which are discussed in the following paragraphs. Each of these three programs represents a direct or indirect opportunity for private investors.

The SBIR program is ostensibly operated under the auspices of the Small Business Administration, but it is managed rather independently by a wide assortment of federal agencies and programs. The purpose of the SBIR program is to provide up to $850,000 in early-stage R&D funding directly to small technology companies (or individual entrepreneurs who form a company) that are willing to undertake research and development activities directed by a particular federal agency's annual broad policy goals. The long-term intent of these programs is to commercialize the outcomes of the research.

The STTR program is managed primarily by Department of Defense (DoD)–related agencies and NASA. The purpose of the STTR program is to provide up to $600,000 in early-stage R&D funding directly to small companies working cooperatively with researchers at universities and other research institutions; again, the caveat is that these activities must be within the scope of a broad agency goal. The long-term intent of these programs is also to commercialize the outcomes of the technology transfer.

The Fast Track program is almost exclusively managed by DoD agencies. This program rewards companies that have in place some degree of private investment. As a reward for finding private investors, the Fast Track program offers a higher chance of an SBIR or STTR award, and continuous funding, to small companies that can attract outside investors. For the investors, Fast Track offers an opportunity to obtain a match of $1 to $4 in DoD SBIR or STTR funds for every $1 invested—a funding system initiated by National Public Radio. The intent of these programs is to motivate private investment at the earliest possible stage of the program's life.

Approximately two-thirds of the federal money disbursed for nano-technology is directed into one of these three funding approaches, although SBIR programs tend to dominate. This is rather important because the structure of each of these programs requires concerted efforts by the grant recipients to commercialize the outcomes of their research.

The SBIR program is managed by 11 agencies of the U.S. government:

- Department of Agriculture
- Department of Commerce
- Department of Defense
- Department of Education
- Department of Energy
- Department of Health and Human Services
- Department of Transportation
- Environmental Protection Agency
- National Aeronautics and Space Administration
- National Science Foundation
- Nuclear Regulatory Commission

The U.S. Small Business Administration (SBA) is the originator of the SBIR program, but does not itself perform any of the grant solicitations or fund disbursements. Under the SBA guidelines, each of the 11 agencies has the discretion to issue solicitations for research relevant to the agency's specific annual goals and objectives. The SBIR program is a competitive grant program that encompasses three phases of funding. The program is operated in one of three modes, called *phases*.

Phase I is the seed phase. During this phase, grant awards are given to applicants to evaluate the scientific and technical merit of a particular idea for a period of up to six months, and awards may be funded for an amount of up to $100,000.

Phase II is available only to prior Phase I participants. If the Phase I results are considered promising, an award for a period of two years with an amount of up to $750,000 is possible.

Phase III is the commercialization of the Phase II results. No additional money is available at this time; however, the intent is that the prior phases will have demonstrated significant commercial value so as to interest private investors in the technology.

The SBIR program represents a unique opportunity for investing in nanotechnology, directed at the outset toward the commercialization of whatever technology results. To participate as an investor in programs resulting from an SBIR grant, you have to find the Phase II grants. Again, in keeping with the bureaucratic processes of government, there is no single source of information for SBIR grant recipients. At some future time, the

NTTC *will* have a complete summary of this information, but not yet. In order to get information on nanotechnology-related SBIR programs, each of the participants in the NNI must be contacted. Information for SBIR awards for each of these agencies can be found at the agency web sites.[7]

Unfortunately, none of these sites, except that of the National Science Foundation, are searchable directly for nanotechnology. Thus, the savvy investor needs to print out a list of the many award recipients and determine which of the Phase II awards are related to nanotechnology, and whether the funded organization is appropriate for possible investment. This task is probably more suited to venture-capital firms that specialize in technology transfer and technology start-up operations. In support of small businesses, the SBA maintains a list of investment companies that either directly invest in or loan money to small businesses of the same class as the recipients of SBIR and STTR grants.[8] You should contact local investment firms for a given region to see if they manage funds dedicated to SBIR or STTR recipients, especially those dedicated to nanotechnology.

CONCLUSION

Federal technology transfer programs provide a means to find developing private companies focused on the commercialization of nanotechnology. The entire federal technology transfer system is specifically and legally required to support the commercialization of technology developed through federal funding. The purpose of the NTTC is specifically to assist private industry in finding and exploiting technological capabilities developed by the national laboratory system. The savvy investor looking for opportunities will find an extremely supportive, albeit cumbersome, federal bureaucracy ready, willing, and able to support investment.

NOTES

1. This program encompasses only the MEMS activities at Sandia and does not include other nanotechnology activities undertaken by the laboratory.
2. A typical modest production facility for semiconductors would include a production facility with 75,000 to 150,000 square feet of Class 1 clean room. A clean-room class represents a level of air filtration that admits no dust particles beyond a specified level.
3. See www.nttc.edu.
4. For information about how to contact a regional office affiliated with the NTTC, call (800) 678-6882.

5. See the NTTC web site at www.nttc.edu.
6. Information on MEMX can be found at www.memx.org.
7. As of this writing, the appropriate web sites are:
   Department of Commerce
   National Institute of Standards and Technology
   http://patapsco.nist.gov/ts_sbir/awards.htm
   Department of Defense
   www.dodsbir.net/awardlist/awardlist.htm
   Department of Energy
   http://sbir.er.doe.gov/sbir/Awards_Abstracts/award_Abstract_main.htm
   http://sbir.er.doe.gov/sbir/Awards_Abstracts/sttr/sttr_a&a_main.htm
   Department of Transportation
   www.volpe.dot.gov/sbir/previous.html
   National Aeronautics and Space Administration
   http://sbir.gsfc.nasa.gov/SBIR/awdarch.htm
   National Institutes of Health
   http://grants.nih.gov/grants/funding/sbir.htm#data
   National Science Foundation
   www.fastlane.nsf.gov/a6/A6AwardSearch.htm
8. See www.sba.gov/INV/.

CHAPTER 4

The Universities

As the previous chapter shows, there is a complex path that ultimately leads the investor to investment opportunities in nanotechnology that are funded within the national laboratory system. This chapter looks for the same kinds of opportunities within the nation's university system. Although the federal government does not control the nation's university system, a significant amount of the research performed by universities is funded by federal money. The two-thirds of the National Nanotechnology Inititiative (NNI)'s funds earmarked for universities represents a major proportion of the dollars spent by universities on nanotechnology research. By accepting this money, universities become subject to federal law in much the same way that the national laboratory system is subject to federal law. Thus, much of the commercialization that could occur from university research in nano-technology has many of the same restraints as seen in the previous chapter. In order to understand how to gain access to these potential investments, this chapter goes through another web of interlocking federal requirements. First, it looks at an overview of the university system as a whole. Then it explores the relevant federal law regarding commercialization of technolo-gies developed in universities. Finally, it looks at two examples of how to break investments out of the universities. This concludes with a guide to finding the nanonuggets that are buried in institutions of higher learning.

UNIVERSITY RESEARCH

Over 14 million Americans enter or return to the postsecondary education system each year. Most of them are engaged in efforts to improve their knowledge or their career options—choosing to ignore Robert Goheen, who said, "If you have both feet planted on level ground, then the university has failed you." Some 1 to 2 million of these students are engaged in graduate-level studies. Often earning less than minimum wage under the austere title of *research assistant,* hundreds of thousands of these students are engaged in that most hallowed of academic processes, university research.

Representing well over $200 billion of investment in education each year, the U.S. university systems manage a budget fully one-fifth the size of the U.S. government's. With a significantly higher proportion of their budgets earmarked for research and development (R&D) than the U.S. government's,[1] university research programs represent the cutting edge of much of the technological innovation developed in this country. Almost two-thirds of all nanotechnology R&D funding is directed toward university researchers, while additional funding for nanotechnology research comes from university budgets, endowments, and private industry. There is no clear picture as to how much money university researchers spend on nanotechnology research, but most of the money that is spent ends up in university research programs.

Universities tend to operate in a relatively independent mode and are therefore not required to report their funding and allocation statistics, except when such monies come directly from federal programs. In the absence of major public relations programs and legal reporting requirements, most of the information available on university nanotechnology research comes from professional publications in the variety of fields touched by nanotechnology. With several hundred thousand journals published in the academic arena, significant research programs are often buried in clouds of paper and manage to become known to relatively few outside the closed circles of academia. However, some universities have dedicated public nanotechnology R&D activities. Some of these programs are within departments, and some are spread across many departments within one or more academic institutions. Globally, at least 78 universities have active public programs involved in some aspect of nanotechnology (see Appendix B for a partial list). Many hundreds of other universities participate in nanotechnology research through less publicized programs, individual research projects, or faculty members engaged in nanotechnology topics.

The preceding chapters dealt briefly with the Bayh-Dole act. This act encourages universities to commercialize R&D that is funded by federal sources. To help you understand how to extract value from university research, the next section looks deeper into the Bayh-Dole act, and how universities throughout the country have implemented the various provisions of the act. As with the federal laboratory system, there is no single means of waltzing into the treasures of university R&D.

BAYH-DOLE GOES TO COLLEGE

Perhaps the most influential person in creating federal technology transfer law was Vannevar Bush. Prior to World War II, Bush was one of the world's earliest computer scientists, and he developed advanced analog computers used by the military during the war. As a scientific adviser to President Roosevelt, Bush proposed in 1944 that the process of cooperation between science and government that had been developed to create the atomic bomb should be institutionalized because of the rich rewards that would emerge from the convergence of government research, science, and society. The immediate postwar legacy was the creation of the first of many government institutions—the National Institutes of Health, the National Science Foundation, and the Office of Naval Research. For the next 30 years, federal technology was placed into the public domain largely without restriction or control. When licenses were granted for federal patents, they were granted to whoever requested them. This process produced an environment that preempted any competitive advantage for companies interested in the technology, which in turn led to virtually no exploitation of federally funded research.

In 1980, the Bayh-Dole act was passed with the intent of providing commercial incentives to develop federally funded technology. The key provisions of the act included:

- A uniform federal patent policy was adopted.
- Universities were encouraged to collaborate with business to promote the utilization of inventions arising from federally funded research.
- Universities could elect to retain title to inventions developed under governmental funding.
- Universities were required to file patents on inventions they chose to own.
- The government retained a nonexclusive license to practice the invention throughout the world.
- The government retained march-in rights.[2]
- Preference in licensing had to be given to small business.
- Uniform guidelines for granting licenses were provided.

Over the next decade, the outcomes of this legislation were exactly as intended, with the university systems reaping large benefits:

- The number of universities engaged in technology transfer increased by a factor of 10.
- The number of university-originated patent applications increased by a factor of 4.
- The number of patent licenses increased by a factor of 5.
- The amount of money returned to the universities through patent licensing increased by at least a factor of 4.

Estimates for the year 1998 were that as a direct result of the Bayh-Dole act, university research generated $33.5 billion in revenue, created 280,000 new jobs, and launched 384 new companies.[3] Estimates for the fiscal year 1999 were that licensing had generated approximately $640 million in direct revenue for universities. Sometimes you can measure the impact of a law. For the universities, this was a windfall of unprecedented proportions.

HOW UNIVERSITIES IMPLEMENT TECHNOLOGY TRANSFER

Unlike federal laboratories, universities are not required to license technology. Nor are they required to patent technology or transfer it. The Bayh-Dole act merely tells universities what rules they must follow if they choose to patent, license, and transfer technology that was developed with federal money. Otherwise, they can focus on teaching if they wish.[4] However, universities have one need that is never satisfied—money. The Bayh-Dole act provides a means for a university to create a revenue stream—and, in some cases, a lot of revenue.

Universities come in two flavors, public and private. The difference is the source of the funds that permit the university to operate. In the case of a public university, the money comes from a mixture of sources, including state government—a funding source not available to private universities. The obvious implication for the public university is that work performed by the university is work performed by the government, subject to state law regarding the ownership and spin-off of any technologies. In contrast to this, work performed at a private university is subject to the policies and guidelines developed over the life of the university by its board of regents. A private university can do anything it wants with technologies it has developed, provided their development was not financed by government funding sources. As a result, the technology transfer office operations of a private university are somewhat different from those of a public university.

Public Universities

By definition, public universities are funded primarily by their state legislatures and are subject to many of the same restraints as other state agencies. University employees are subject to the same employment standards as other state government employees. However, with the passage of the Bayh-Dole act, much legislation ensued that permitted universities and their employees to engage in activities that would otherwise be considered a conflict of interest for a state employee. There are as many different laws as there are states, but there is some uniformity in the practices implemented by most states. Under the Bayh-Dole act, a university—and therefore the state government—is permitted and encouraged to commercially exploit federally funded inventions developed by university employees. The Bayh-

Dole act defines the university as the "owning entity" and strongly encourages the transfer of inventions into the private sector. In order to exploit this, most public universities have developed a three-tiered approach to generate revenues from their inventions.

The first step is to establish a technology transfer office directly within the administrative structure of the university system. This office develops the guidelines and policies for the university. More important, the office maintains a staff of specialists who are familiar with patent law, the Bayh-Dole act, the R&D activities of the university's faculty, and various companies that may be interested in licensing patents. At a minimum, the function of this office is to review patent recommendations from the faculty, apply for patents, and seek out potential licensees for the patents. As the previous chapter shows, investors can focus on the companies receiving these licenses as potential investment opportunities. Any licensing agreement that is made available by a technology transfer is available to the public, as is the disposition of any patent, which is also public information. An investor interested in contacting the proposed or actual recipient of a technology patent has full legal access to that information through the public university. Of course, since the staffing level of technology transfer offices is usually low, it could take some concerted effort to actually get this information.

The second way universities generate revenue is by establishing a royalty payment system for patent licenses. The payment system typically allots percentages of the royalty payments to the university system, the department housing the inventors, and the inventors named on the patent. This structure tends to be relatively generous to the inventors when compared to patent assignments found in the private sector. It is not uncommon for a faculty inventor to get as much as 25 percent of the royalties generated by a patent.

More revenues can come from the development of a commercial technology transfer operation. Although not as common as technology transfer offices, many states have enacted legislation that creates private nonprofit companies, owned by the university or the state, which have the specific function of commercializing patents developed under the rules of Bayh-Dole, including the launching of for-profit companies. University-sponsored nonprofits usually do not provide direct funding to their for-profit start-ups,[5] but rather serve as a kind of intellectual property incubator, providing technology licenses, know-how, and access to private funding sources. In return, they often get a large chunk of stock in the start-up and some royalty payment arrangements for the licenses. From an investor's point of view, these nonprofits are the focal point of interest, because they are usually funded under state budgets. This means that their activities are in the public domain. Likewise, information on the for-profit companies that they create, or are in the process of creating, is also public. The resulting for-profit companies are usually considered seed-stage start-ups, with all the risks and rewards inherent in such companies. Only qualified investors can participate in these start-ups until the companies get to the initial public offering (IPO) stage of growth.

One of the major problems with public-university technology transfer offices is the high rate of turnover, severely restricting how effective these offices can be. The people who perform the patent and license work are routinely paid at levels far below their private-sector market value, which makes it not uncommon for good people to remain only a very short time before moving on to higher-paying positions in the private sector. Because the nature of their job is to generate money for everyone except themselves, it is also very common for senior managers in technology transfer offices to join or start venture-capital firms, or leave to manage one of their own start-ups. With this in mind, it is normal to see the operation of a given technology transfer office schizophrenically flip-flop its emphasis between pure patent licensing and startup incubating, depending on the current focus of the management. This often restricts the office's ability to respond to information requests from individual investors. The key for investors, when contacting technology transfer offices, is to ask about their most recent history of activities. All offices will know if their emphasis is on licensing, start-ups, or both. Those engaged in licensing are probably the best bets to follow. However, be sure to check back at the other offices every six months or so, because the emphasis can often change without much warning.

Private Universities

Private universities operate without any state-imposed restrictions. Essentially, a private university is capable of operating in exactly the same manner as a venture-capital firm, which some do. The only restraints on a private university are those imposed by the use of federal funds for research. A private-university technology transfer office is essentially based on the same model as a public university office, except that a private university can and may directly fund the start-up of a new company. A private university has more opportunities for commercialization, due to the absence of state law governing the process. Otherwise, the outcomes and pitfalls are the same. From an investor's point of view, however, the office's information is not in the public domain. As a result, gaining access to current opportunities and plans is a function of whether the office supports the appropriate infrastructure required to answer questions from prospective investors. In most cases, however, the office will welcome you into the fold. The investment access points for private universities are essentially the same as for public universities. Companies that license the technology are one potential investment target. Companies that are incubated by the university are the other targets.

NANONUGGETS

One of the nice things about universities is that they work together much better than government agencies do. They have centralized databases that provide valuable information regarding what is available and how to get to it. The Association of University Technology Managers (AUTM), for example, represents approximately 2,300 technology managers working at universities, government agencies, research hospitals, and other research institutions (see Appendix L). At the time of this writing, AUTM membership includes 546 organizations, of which 224 are university technology transfer programs. The AUTM does not maintain a directory of available technologies; directories are usually maintained by the member technology transfer offices. AUTM research indicates that the major impetus in generating licensable technologies from the university setting is not the activity of a technology transfer office, but rather direct relationships between the licensing company and the researchers at the university.[6] Three out of four licensing activities originate from personal contacts between researchers, whereas only one out of four licensing activities originates from the marketing efforts of the technology transfer office. The implication of this for the investor is somewhat discouraging. When contacting a technology transfer office, only one time in four will the office have any idea what licensing activity is likely to occur. Usually, a researcher comes to the office with a licensing candidate in hand, and the office then proceeds to implement licensing activities. An investor tapping into this resource needs to be in regular contact with those offices to know both which patents the office is actively marketing and which licensing candidates have recently emerged from within the university.

That said, tracking nanotechnology originating from universities is actually a task that can be done relatively easily. The key is to understand the life of the academic researcher, which can be summed up in a simple phrase: *Publish or perish*. Survival within an academic institution depends on one's ability to publish research—frequently. This accounts for the existence of approximately 40,000 paper journals dedicated to the pursuit of knowledge. The exact number of online journals is probably unknowable, and it is growing at an outrageous pace. In looking for investment opportunities you need to focus on the technology that can be found without myopically plowing through megatons of bound paper journals. Various estimates suggest that for all scientific research, 150 journals account for half of all citations to research and about a quarter of all that is published.[7] For the average investor, narrowing the field from 40,000 journals to 150 is not much help. However, there are two journals that cover significant research results derived from nanotechnology research—*Science* and *Nature* (see Appendix L). This does not mean that significant publications do not occur elsewhere—they certainly do. However, these two journals have a strong editorial interest in nanotechnology and have published reports of some of the more striking advances in nanotechnology. Perhaps the most important aspect of these two journals is that they both maintain searchable online article libraries. Depending on the subscription level purchased (and it would be wise to purchase a full level), current research on nanotechnology—including information on the authors, their affiliations, and how to contact them—is readily available to anyone. It is not always the case that the investor is going to understand each and every article, but when performing due diligence on an opportunity, or looking for a new one, these two journals represent the single most significant source of university-based information available.

Given that you know where to look, the question of what to look for still remains. This, of course, is the $100 billion question. There is no obvious answer in an emerging technology. However, there are some general topical areas that show promise for short-term commercialization. The following sections itemize some of the more interesting things to look for in university-published research, as suggested by the NNI's implementation plan.

Materials and Manufacturing

When objects are built at the atomic or molecular scale, they can become lighter and stronger than other materials. Such materials would have lower failure rates and unprecedented strength, and they could be used in a variety of existing industrial processes in rather revolutionary ways. The investor should be on the lookout for nanotubes, fibers, and other structures or coatings that have unique and novel characteristics that can replace or improve existing materials and manufacturing techniques. Some of the successful start-up companies discussed later have focused solely on the production of materials fabricated at the nanometer scale. There are a significant number of university-based research programs focused on nanomaterials.

Nanoelectronics and Computer Technology

Electronic devices fabricated at the nanometer scale have the promise to outperform existing computational electronics by several orders of magnitude. In addition, some of the computational schemes proposed for nanodevices (such as quantum computers) suggest capabilities that make a modern Pentium seem slow as a glacier. Furthermore, sensor and display systems for electronic devices and signal transmission may be radically transformed with these technologies. Given the prevalence of electronics in modern society, devices derived from nanotechnology have the potential to completely replace all the systems currently in place today, as well as add new capabilities hitherto undreamed of. Advances in device technology, especially quantum computing and fabrication technologies for devices smaller than 30 nanometers, are of special interest to investors.

Medicine and Health

Nanotechnology has the potential to interface with living systems at the molecular scale. There are a wide variety of diagnostic and treatment capabilities that are possible with fabricated devices designed to interact with living organisms. Devices and materials have the potential to totally reshape the arena of medical diagnosis and the treatment of disease. Of particular interest are the half dozen or so companies working on biochip technologies for DNA sequencing, diagnostics, and other kinds of research. Future developments that work within the cell or attack specific pathogens can be expected in the near term. Drug-delivery systems that can directly attack sites of disease are of extremely high interest to investors. In addition, new diagnostic tools, devices, and instruments that operate directly within the human body are also of strong interest.

Aeronautics and Space Exploration

Aircraft and spacecraft are incredibly expensive technologies. The sheer weight of materials used in their fabrication contributes greatly to their cost. Nanotechnology has the potential to dramatically reduce the weight and efficiency of materials and devices that are required, thereby dramatically reducing the costs. Some materials have the potential to revolutionize the practice of earth-to-orbit operations. Materials and devices that can impact the costs of space exploration are of considerable interest to the National Aeronautics and Space Administration and the aerospace industry. Various devices that can operate as swarms or which are smaller than insects are under development and have high potential as investment targets. These devices would permit fleets of vehicles to be built at low cost, permitting wide geographic coverage and minor losses if any single device is destroyed. Of especial interest are any developments in the manufacturing of nanotubes that may be capable of supporting structures that extend from the surface of the earth into geosynchronous orbit. These would include any fiber materials with tensile strengths 60 times greater than steel.

Environment and Energy

Nanomaterials and nanocomposites have the potential to revolutionize the efficiency of the fossil fuel industries. It is possible that higher-efficiency engines and transportation systems will result from nanocomposites. Nano-materials may dramatically improve the efficiency of the systems used to convert oil into the familiar variety of useful fuels and lubricants. Some materials may reduce dramatically the release of toxic materials into the environment. As the costs of oil and transportation increase, the research into reducing and managing these costs has a strong nanotechnology flavor. Nanomaterials are on the horizon that can enhance the performance of cat-alytic converters and oil-refining processes. Any of these materials represent strong investment opportunities if they can be fabricated cheaply and com-mercialized.

Biotechnology and Agriculture

The same generic technologies that will be applied to medicine and health can be similarly applied to the creation of chemicals, pharmaceuticals, and agricultural products. The production of new kinds of drugs, fertilizers, and other chemicals is the focus of active R&D programs. Similarly, the devel-opment of more nutritious and disease-resistant plants and animals is of strong interest to many university programs. The modification of plant and animal genetics has already begun in several commercial applications. Any materials, methods, or treatment systems that improve crop production and the nutritional content of food plants and animals have a strong commercial potential. Many of these opportunities will be derived from genome re-search currently underway at many universities.

National Security

Military applications cover a wide variety of potential applications. Battle-field dominance being the generic objective of any military organization, improved electronic warfare capabilities, better weapons systems, and im-proved camouflage and intelligence systems are on the Defense Depart-ment's active R&D list. Any new technology, including nanotechnology, receives significant support from a variety of military sources. University publications in these areas, however, are likely to be much less common than publications in the other arenas. Most of these opportunities will ulti-mately be developed within the R&D departments of established defense industries. However, nanomaterials that can improve the performance of batteries, microsensors, and pathogen detectors are likely to emerge from university settings, and these represent excellent investment opportunities.

WHAT TO DO?

Maintaining awareness of the current opportunities arising from universities is not a trivial undertaking. Because nanotechnology is a highly technical topic, finding the nuggets in the mix is an activity that requires steady and applied effort. University programs are producing an increasing rate of research publications, some small fraction of which describe developments that have tremendous commercial potential. A determined investor can gain access to these nuggets very early in the process, or wait several years for the initial public offering. Discovering which opportunities will turn into grand slams is not an easy undertaking, but as this chapter shows, there are ample opportunities arising from the university system.

NOTES

1. *AUTM Licensing Survey: FY 1999* (Northbrook, IL: Association of University Technology Managers, 1999). 1999 estimates put federal R&D at 2 to 2.5 percent of the federal budget. University R&D represented approximately 10 percent of university budgets in the same year, or approximately $23.5 billion.
2. This is the right of the government to require, under certain conditions, that an exclusive license be revoked. In such cases, a variety of provisions are possible, but the idea is that under certain conditions, the government can force an exclusive license to become nonexclusive.
3. Wendy H. Schacht, *R&D Partnerships and Intellectual Property: Implications for U.S. Policy,* Report for Congress 98-862 (Congressional Research Service, 1998).
4. John Ciardi said, "A university is what a college becomes when the faculty loses interest in students."
5. It is not uncommon for the nonprofit to provide significant capital for a start-up. A direct investment of several hundred thousand dollars from the nonprofit is not uncommon.
6. Jerry G. Thursby and Marie C. Thursby, "Industry Perspectives on Licensing University Technologies: Sources and Problems," *Journal of the Association of University Technology Managers* 12 (2000).
7. *The Scientist* 10(17):13 (2 September 1996).

CHAPTER 5

Private Industry

Nanotechnology is not the exclusive province of government and university research and development (R&D). There are a number of companies that have active R&D programs or that are genuine nanotechnology companies. As of this writing, there are less than half a dozen publicly traded companies that have nanotechnology as their primary focus. Globally, several hundred companies are engaged in some aspect of nanotechnology. The issue for this chapter is to identify opportunities originating from private industry that will result in a significant return on investment.

Not all companies involved in nanotechnology are good investments simply because they invest heavily in nanotechnology. For example, even though IBM has significant activities in nanotechnology, and some of the highest corporate spending on nanotechnology R&D, IBM's nanotechnology products will not dramatically boost IBM's stock price. IBM has too many business units for any single program to compel investment. Some companies, however, concentrate on nanotechnology as their primary focus for product and revenue.

Opportunities within the private sector are thankfully free of federal laws, except for those enforced by the Securities and Exchange Commission (SEC). To set the stage for finding these kinds of investments, this chapter has a slightly less torturous path to follow. First, this chapter reviews the major private sector investors in nanotechnology and identifies the types of interests that they have. Since large companies do not do everything internally, it also examines their supply chains to determine who is providing products for their R&D programs. Finally, it briefly touches on some of the more interesting public and private companies that have the potential to actually make a profit on nanotechnology products.

CHIP MAKERS

Almost all of the private-sector nanotechnology activity is in the semiconductor industry—the leader in the development of commercial products based on ever-smaller electronic device structures. The industry has been reducing component sizes to such a degree that the current crop of products contain electronic structures smaller than one-millionth of an inch. With current technologies scaled to about 350 nanometers, semiconductor products are at the forefront of profitable nanotechnologies. However, the industry has found that improvements in technology come at an extreme cost that can no longer be supported by single companies. As a result, since the 1980s companies have looked for assistance from the U.S. government and have also looked for means by which they can share costs with other companies. The major competitive factors in the industry do not rest on the technologies required to produce ever-smaller devices. The industry competes on the basis of product function and product price. Thus, there is little competitive disadvantage in sharing technical know-how with other companies.

Representing an industry with annual revenues on the order of $100 billion, the Semiconductor Industry Association (SIA) husbands the issues associated with emerging semiconductor technologies. Its membership, the SIA claims, represents 90 percent of all U.S. semiconductor production. In order to support the technological needs of its affiliated membership, the association works in conjunction with three other organizations dedicated to the semiconductor industry:

- The Semiconductor Research Corporation (SRC)
- Sematech
- The Focus Center Research Program

SIA's objectives were traditionally aimed at maintaining both U.S. leadership in technology and market share for U.S.-based industries. In recent years, the focus has acquired a distinctly international flavor. The major research arm of the SIA, the SRC,[1] sets research objectives for the collaborative development of technologies that are of significant interest to the future of the industry and funnels R&D money to both private and university research activities (see Appendixes C and D).

With a 2001 operating budget of approximately $75 million, SRC operates two distinct kinds of research. The first is collaborative research with industry; the SRC directly invests in companies working in a variety of fields, including nanotechnology, to the tune of approximately $40 million per year. The second type is directed through a subsidiary organization called the Microelectronics Advanced Research Corporation (MARCO). MARCO provides task-oriented funding to professors and graduate students at approximately 70 universities, distributed among approximately 350 grants (see Appendix D). The results of the research are made available to the SRC's paying members. The SRC has set four broad objectives with corresponding programs as the focus for its R&D sponsorship. Of greatest interest to investors is the Nanostructure and Integration Sciences program. The SRC provides multiyear funding for research into nanotechnology topics in this core research area, with grants of $50,000 to several million dollars per program. The results of this university-sponsored research are available to the members of the SRC consortium on a royalty-free basis. The disposition of funded intellectual property is at the discretion of the researchers and their corresponding university programs.

The SRC also provides multi-million-dollar funding to magnet universities that support general SRC program objectives. At the time of this writing, the SRC is supporting major research centers at the Georgia Institute of Technology, the University of California at Berkeley, the Massachusetts Institute of Technology (MIT), and Carnegie Mellon University. At least two other university centers are expected to be added in the near term. The SRC, at this time, does not engage in direct commercialization of technology, nor does it engage in the development of spin-off companies to exploit developed technology. However, companies have been spun off as a direct result of SRC-sponsored projects.[2] Most of the SRC's involvement with universities is independent of university-based technology transfer offices. The technology transfer offices may become involved if the researchers at the institution think it is appropriate, but there is no overarching legislation such as Bayh-Dole that regulates their activities.

Although the SRC is a significant provider of funds for research in nanotechnology topics, finding the investment opportunities requires additional homework. The first source of information is the SRC's annual report, which summarizes the general thrust of SRC's R&D activities.[3] The process of finding investment opportunities under SRC's programs is essentially the same as that of finding Small Business Incentive Research (SBIR) participants in university programs—working the phone and calling the universities. In many cases, however, the technology transfer office is unaware of much of the funding that comes from SRC programs. Therefore, the four SRC-sponsored research centers—Georgia Tech, the University of California at Berkeley, MIT, and Carnegie Mellon—should receive the most attention from prospective investors.

OTHER RESEARCH AND DEVELOPMENT SUPPORT

Large companies that are heavily invested in electronics tend to invest in nanotechnology as well. How they invest is often as much a function of the tax code as of their interest in the future. There are several ways in which a profitable company can gain a tax benefit from conducting R&D under the federal tax code. A company can perform the R&D itself and take the credit that the Internal Revenue Service grants, or it can contribute to a cooperative service organization of operating educational institutions. A company can also contribute to a 501(c)(3) nonprofit foundation. With these options, a profitable company will distribute its tax credits depending largely on the nature of the credit and the nature of the R&D that it needs to undertake. If the R&D is directly related to short-term product development, then a direct R&D tax credit is the preferred means. This keeps the outcomes of the R&D under the complete control of the company. If the R&D is more strategic, the tendency is to contribute to educational institutions or foundations, depending on the degree to which the R&D is viewed as proprietary. There is a wide variety of mechanisms by which a company can get credits for R&D; in larger companies, these provide not only clear tax advantages, but also degrees of ownership for the results of the research.

From the investor's point of view, while there is a tremendous amount of internal corporate R&D from companies such as IBM, Intel, and others, the results of this R&D are not generally accessible as direct investment opportunities, unless the interest is simply in purchasing stock. As mentioned earlier, the university programs are one access point for corporate-funded research. What remains to be considered are the 501(c)(3) companies.

NONPROFITS

Section 501(c)(3) refers to that portion of the federal tax code that regulates the creation of nonprofit companies whose primary function is to provide religious, charitable, scientific, literary, or educational services. In the case of investing in nanotechnology, there are several 501(c)(3) companies that have been created to assist other companies in exploiting this portion of the tax code. The companies described earlier, including SRC, are 501(c)(3) companies, which accounts for their heavy support from private industry. There are several other 501(c)(3) companies that exist to exploit nanotechnology:

- *The Beckman Institute for Advanced Science and Technology.* This is a small 25-person research institute housed at the University of Illinois at Urbana-Champaign. One of its programs focuses on the development of molecular and electronic nanostructures.
- *The Nanotechnology Competence Center.* This center, based in Kaiserlauten, Germany, focuses on the use of nanotechnology in the fields of medicine, sensors, electronics, energy, coatings, and nanoparticles. It coordinates the efforts of about 150 research programs in Germany.
- *The Center for NanoSpace Technologies.* This is a Texas-based foundation focused on developing nanotechnologies for aerospace, education, energy, life sciences, shipping, and transportation.

- *The Foresight Institute.* This is probably the premier nonprofit nanotechnology organization devoted to the development of the general enabling technologies that will support the coming age of nanotechnology.
- *The Michigan Molecular Institute.* This nonprofit is primarily focused on plastics but has an ongoing interest in composite materials fabricated from nanomaterials.

OTHER INDUSTRIES

Commercial activity in nanotechnology is not limited to the semiconductor industry. While companies that focus only on nanotechnology have modest performance at best, there is a large number of companies that would not think of themselves as being in the nanotechnology business, but the industries in which they work have some clearly defined element that involves nanotechnologies. These industries include:[4]

- Micromachines and microelectromechanical systems (MEMS) involve those industries that produce extremely small machines and components. Often directly fabricated with supporting electronics, these are found in sensors, small mechanical structures, accelerometers, gas sensors, flow sensors, velocity sensors, and some kinds of biological sensors, as well as micromotors, microvalves, micronozzles, microprobes, micropumps, optical switches, and microswitches.
- Autofabrication is used to produce solid objects of any shape or structure from raw materials under the guidance of a computer-generated model of the object. Most of these techniques are associated with rapid prototyping techniques used in modeling components before they are fabricated. Many of the newer techniques involve composition of the objects at extremely high resolution and precision. Some of the newer technologies involve a process called *self-assembly* in which the objects assemble themselves through a variety of clever and novel techniques.
- Nanolithography is used primarily by the semiconductor and MEMS industries. The fabrication of integrated circuits and many micromachines fall in this category. Most of the R&D money from the semiconductor industry is focused on pushing the resolution of these techniques towards the molecular and atomic scales.
- Microscopy creates images of objects as small as individual atoms. A variety of different technologies exist, including scanning probe microscopes, atomic force microscopes, magnetic resonance force microscopes, scanning electron microscopes, and scanning tunneling microscopes. These systems also include families of control and imaging

software that manage the image scanning process and assist researchers in viewing pictures of what they have scanned.

- Software that permits the evaluation of atomic or molecular interactions falls in this category. Simulation software assesses hypothetical molecular and atomic structures. Other software permits the analysis of mechanical properties of structures fabricated at the atomic level. Yet other software evaluates the quantum interactions of individual atoms and permits the simulation of their utility in computational, mechanical, and chemical interactions. Applications for this software include the simulation of materials, new drugs, genetics, chemical processes, and biotechnology.

- Nanoscale and nanophase materials are fabricated in such a way that their atomic and molecular structure is well defined and understood. These materials can be used to create new materials with improved hardness, strength, wear resistance, adhesion, and lubricity. They can also be used to create bondings, coatings, capsules, catalysts, plastics, and even cosmetics. Some of these materials are used as catalysts, pigments, and ceramics. Certain materials are fabricated to evaluate future electronic systems; these include nanodots, quantum logic gates, quantum wires, and optical coatings. Most activities are focused on the fullerene family of materials, which includes nanotubes, nanowires, and, in some cases, specially fabricated strands of DNA and RNA.

- Novel nanoscale materials have unique properties simply because they are fabricated at such a small size that the quantum effects of atomic structure dominate their behavior at the macro level. These materials include fullerene powders, some piezoelectric materials, and dendrimers.

- Other analytical processes that determine the atomic and molecular structure of compounds, materials, or organic structures include X-ray crystallography, mass spectrometry, nuclear magnetic resonance (NMR) imaging, DNA sequencing, RNA sequencing, protein sequencing, chromatography separation, chromatography assay techniques, and some molecular biology reagents.

PUBLIC COMPANIES

There are several companies that exist solely on the basis of nanotechnology and their efforts to bring this technology to market. The world has not been kind to these companies thus far. As shown in Table 5.1, their performance has been something that would not bring joy to the heart of most investors.

While Table 5.1 is incomplete, and there are certainly new companies making initial public offerings (IPOs), the historical performance of public nanotechnology companies has not been stellar. The star in the table, Nanometrics, is in the measurement technology business, providing instrumenta-

TABLE 5.1 Stock Performance of Nanotechnology Companies

Company	Symbol	High Trade	Current Trade*	Profit in 2000
Nano World Projects Corporation	OTC:BB:NAPH	16.5	0.01	−$ 3 million
Molecular Robotics	OTC:BB:NTEH	—	—	Delisted
Nanogen	NASDAQ:NGEN	101.93	7.60	−$18 million
Nanometrics, Inc.	NASDAQ:NANO	63.87	23.84	$11 million
Nanophase Technologies, Inc.	NASDAQ:NANX	22.06	10.41	−$ 4 million
Nanopierce Technologies	OTC:BB:NPCT	6.62	0.64	−$ 3 million

*Price as of market close, May 12, 2001.

tion that improves the yield of semiconductor manufacturing processes. However, revenues for Nanometrics decreased in 2001 from their 2000 levels.

PRIVATE COMPANIES

A pre-IPO company has one curse and one blessing. The curse is that finding money for operations is one of the constant preoccupations of management. The blessing is that there are virtually none of the SEC reporting requirements that impose onerous burdens on early-stage companies. A pre-IPO company is relatively free to perform, subject to the convictions and whims of its sources of funding. This provides a great degree of freedom of operation and permits companies at this stage to shift direction literally overnight if the technology or market conditions are favorable. However, at some point the investors will inevitably want to see a return on their investment, which ultimately leads private companies either to the IPO stage, to acquisition, or to death.

In the absence of SEC reporting requirements, detailed information about private nanotechnology companies is difficult to obtain. Investors who wish to participate in these companies have to wait for the IPO, invest directly as qualified investors, or invest with venture-capital firms that have provided or will provide capital to these companies.

Even learning that these companies exist is sometimes difficult. When these companies are in an emerging market with a limited and rather dismal performance history, there is a wide variety of ways in which the companies manifest themselves. Two companies in particular demonstrate the extremes that can be found:

■ Zyvex
■ NanoSciences

Zyvex is probably the most publicized private nanotechnology company on the planet. Zyvex's mission is "to be the industry leader in adaptable, affordable molecular manufacturing." As an investment opportunity, Zyvex represents an interesting challenge. This is how Zyvex describes itself as an investment opportunity on its web site (see Appendix L):

> Nanotechnology is exciting, and a company devoted to making it happen seems like a great investment. It's probably not; pioneering companies often fail to capitalize on their inventions. So here are some reasons why you might want to hold on to your money for a while:
>
> ■ Zyvex is a private company, which intends to remain private for some time (no liquidity).
> ■ There is no formal financial reporting currently required, and very little planned (no SEC reporting).
> ■ The period to investment payback is unknown, and possibly infinite (no guarantees).
> ■ We're far out on the risk frontier—some scientists claim molecular nanotechnology isn't even possible (no fear).
>
> If you are a small investor wishing to buy stock in a nanotechnology company, we commend you for your foresight, but cannot accept your investment.
>
> If you would like to make a contribution to the field, we suggest a tax-deductible contribution to the Foresight Institute, a non-profit educational and informational organization, or to the Institute for Molecular Manufacturing, which sponsors nanotechnology research.[5]

With this encouragement to the prospective investor, Zyvex answers some questions about its products:

What will your first product be?

Who knows?!? Our time horizon of five to ten years is a very long time, and people's needs for products will change over that time. We currently expect our first product will be some type of assembler, which others can buy and set to work to make useful things for the market they are already familiar with. We don't expect to go conquer all known markets and make all possible products by ourselves. The assembler will be enough for starters.[6]

Most investors, even qualified investors, would start pricing land in the Gobi desert as a more pragmatic investment alternative. However, the fact is that Zyvex has achieved significant private funding, has hired some of the best people in the industry, and is focused on some of the most fundamental core issues facing nanotechnology development. At this time, only a qualified investor with a return-on-investment horizon of decades would be interested in investing in this company.

At the other extreme is a struggling private company called Nanosciences Corporation. Nanosciences was founded in 1995 around a single unique nanotechnology—micromachining ultrasmall channels in silicon. The company leveraged this technology into two types of investment:

- Several SBIR grants, including both Phase I and Phase II grants
- Private investment from a privately held manufacturing company

The technology developed by Nanosciences has the potential for wide use in the fabrication of low-light imaging devices, which, if successful, will create a comfortable and lucrative niche product family for the company. How the company proceeds with soliciting future investments is yet to be determined. A company such as Nanosciences is an excellent, albeit difficult, find for a potential investor. Naturally, all the due-diligence issues of any investment apply to a company at this stage of development.

DUE DILIGENCE

Private industry is a reasonable bellwether for investment opportunities. Many public and private companies have a significant interest in nanotechnology. What is clear, however, is that nanotechnology itself is a dicey investment at this time. Investment in the solution of problems that require the utilization of nanotechnology techniques is definitely valuable. As in all investment opportunities, investing in solutions to real problems carries relatively low risk. Investing in broad visions of the future carries high risk.

Because of the early stage of nanotechnological development, it is very important for prospective investors to be wary of companies claiming to be at the forefront of some broad vision of nanotechnology. Even with SEC oversight, many companies that have no clue how to make a profit will make inroads into the investment community without necessarily ever having a product to sell. There are two interesting companies that merit discussion as examples of the importance of due diligence (see Appendix L):

■ Atomasoft
■ Nanotechnology Holding Corporation

A casual investor looking for nanotechnology investments will come across both of these companies in very short order. Preliminary investigation will indicate that both companies are on the forefront of nanotechnology and have the potential to become major industrial giants capitalizing on nanotechnology. However, due diligence would raise some red flags that a casual investigation might not reveal. In the case of Atomasoft, the investor would soon discover that the company's chief executive officer is a brilliant but academically struggling undergraduate at a Canadian university who operates the company from his dorm room. In the case of the Nanotechnology Holding Company, the investor would soon discover that Atomasoft will be developing its first commercial product (as of May 2000). For an investor being asked to participate in a multi-million-dollar private placement or IPO involving either of these companies, the management of these companies would be of concern. While both companies may create remarkable returns on investment, it would be prudent to focus on companies such as Nanosciences, which have remarkably boring but *credible* prospects.

There is truth to the ancient Latin slogan, *caveat emptor:* Buyer beware!

NOTES

1. The Semiconductor Research Corporation (SRC) is a private nonprofit company that operates on the basis of charging fees for participation in its programs. It has experienced a historical growth rate of approximately 20 percent per year since its inception in 1982. Organizations and companies in some way affiliated with SRC as of 1999 can be found in Appendix C.
2. See especially www.neolinear.com. This private company was spun off in 1996 as a direct result of SRC-funded R&D.
3. This report can be obtained from the SEC's North Carolina office. See Appendix L for contact information.
4. Adapted from information from Paul Green, Nanothinc.com. An incomplete list of companies that are involved in some way with nanotechnology as of this writing can be found in Appendix E.
5. See www.zyvex.com/Corporate/investment.html.
6. See www.zyvex.com/Corporate/faqs.html.

CHAPTER 6

International Activity

Many other countries have initiated significant national research and development (R&D) nanotechnology programs with much the same focus as that of the U.S. National Nanotechnology Initiative (NNI). About two-thirds of all investment occurs outside of the United States. While none of these other programs have the breadth of the NNI, the initiatives are designed to ultimately support the development of market presence or dominance in economic sectors already important to the local economies. There is often government funding available for nanotechnology through preexisting national R&D programs, which have been expanded to support nanotechnology programs. University and industry programs will often support some level of activity even when there is no government involvement. With this vast array of R&D sources, it is understandable that the net global investment in nanotechnology is valued at well over $1 billion each year.

From an investor's point of view, government support makes opportunities in most countries public domain. The countries that support nanotechnology as a specific national objective include:

Australia	Korea
Belgium	The Netherlands
Bulgaria	Russia
China	Singapore
Finland	Spain
France	Sweden
Germany	Switzerland
India	Taiwan
Israel	United Kingdom
Japan	

A 1999 National Science and Technology Council (NSTC) report estimated that worldwide expenditures in nanotechnology research and development in fiscal 1998 were at least double those of the United States, totaling just under $1 billion.[1] In 1998, government spending in Europe and

Japan each exceeded the support provided by the U.S. government. The NSTC report also concluded that different countries had leads in various broad nanotechnology disciplines.[2] The United States had the lead in the areas of synthesis, assembly, and high-surface-area materials, while it tied with Europe on biological approaches, applications and dispersions, and coatings. Japan, however, was on top in nanodevices and consolidated nanomaterials. Overall, the report found that the growing knowledge about nanotechnology was a global phenomenon, with only marginal leads held by any one country. The report stressed that nanotechnology was likely to be one of the driving economic forces of the twenty-first century and therefore was of extreme strategic interest to the U.S. government. The report was subsequently used as part of the justification in increasing the federal funding level of the NNI for fiscal year 2001.

This chapter examines the scope of global nanotechnology programs. Most of the focus is on investment opportunities in Europe, Japan, and Asia. While these regions do not include the totality of global opportunity for R&D and investment, they constitute the bulk of the investment currently in process. With almost two-thirds of R&D happening outside of the United States, serious nanotechnology investors must consider their opportunities on a global basis. However, investors looking for offshore opportunities have some unique problems in assessing potential investments beyond the inevitable language and regulatory issues that are built into the equation. As in the United States, opportunities to invest in emerging companies are accessed primarily through local stock exchanges, and enterprising investors should be able to find pre-IPO companies through much the same means as are used for their U.S. counterparts.[3] It is important to keep in mind when seeking offshore opportunities that Security and Exchange Commission (SEC) regulations do not necessarily apply. Furthermore, there are different legal systems associated with foreign investment, with the accordant higher risks.

EUROPE

Europe has an R&D and commercialization infrastructure similar to the infrastructure found in the United States. Although European activities encompass many different nations (not all of which are contained geographically within the European continent), there are some elements of a common government that manage much of the European commerce and R&D. The history of the modern European Community goes back to the end of World War II, when, as an outgrowth of the Marshall plan, numerous treaties, agreements, and programs began to transcend national boundaries in hopes of developing conflict-free economic cooperation among the countries of Europe. Over the next five decades, these efforts included the development of the Common Market, a European parliament, and extensive agreements on legal, economic, and codevelopment activities. One of the consequences of this multinationalism is that R&D activities often include cooperative ventures between national and multinational governmental agencies. Where cooperation exists, there is tremendous opportunity for developing support for favored R&D programs. It is not uncommon to find a particular program or project that has a mix of financial support from university, corporate, and national sources and one or more European agencies. There are several trans-European R&D programs spanning the continent that sponsor and support nanotechnology research.

One of the intentional outcomes of the European response to global competitiveness has been the development of a network of Innovation Relay Centers (IRCs). Created in 1995 by the European Commission, IRCs serve essentially the same function as the National Technology Transfer Center (NTTC) in the United States. There are nearly 70 regional IRCs that support technology transfer centers in at least 30 countries that are affiliated with the program (see Appendix F). Each IRC is set up as an independent business and technology consulting organization with a specific geographic territory. Their primary intent is simple: Bring two companies together, one with a problem and the other with the solution. An IRC will often work in close concert with one of the European Commission's 30-odd Regional Innovation and Technology Transfer Strategy (RITTS) programs. These programs are topical business-support programs that attempt to develop technology within a region by providing networking and technical support for businesses. Funding for RITTS programs tends to be split equally between the European Commission and the local governments. In general, these programs provide no funding for development-stage companies or technologies, but they do provide significant consulting and networking support for emerging technologies, companies, and companies in search of technology solutions. Most emerging European nanotechnology companies will pass through either an IRC or a RITTS at some point.

Nanotechnology programs are funded in much the same way that U.S. programs are funded. There are some national programs, especially in Germany. There are several European research institutions (the European Laboratory for Particle Physics [CERN], the European Synchrotron Radiation Facility [ESRF], the European Molecular Biology Laboratory [EMBL], and the European Southern Observatory [ESO]) and several ongoing technology development programs (the European Cooperation in Scientific and Technical Research [COST] program, the European Space Agency [ESA], and the Europe-wide Network for Industrial Research and Development [EUREKA]) that transcend national boundaries for developing new technologies. The EUREKA program, for example, provides outright grants for

R&D with the intent of developing businesses from the products that result from the R&D. Countries that provide grant funding under EUREKA include Austria, Norway and the United Kingdom. Otherwise, support in the form of loans or nonrepayable subsidies is available in Belgium, Germany, Slovenia, Iceland, and Israel. In most cases financial support is no greater than 70 percent of what is required to complete the program. Local governments or other resources are expected to participate in the programs and pay the balance of the bills. In essence, the EUREKA program operates in much the same way as the Small Business Incentive Research (SBIR) program, without the confounding phases or caps on the financial investment (see Appendix L).

Germany

Germany has a unique program that is of strong interest to potential investors in European nanotechnology. The Ministry of Education and Research (*Bundesministerium für Bildung und Forschung*) manages a budget of approximately $7 billion,[4] one quarter of which goes into technological innovation research funding. EXIST is a subsidiary funding program of the ministry with a specific goal, the creation of new companies from university and other research settings. One of the most innovative government-sponsored start-up opportunities on the planet, the EXIST program is extremely valuable to researchers. One feature of EXIST funding is that it will pay salaries for researchers and university students for a period of up to five years, during which time they are expected to create a functioning business (see Appendix L).

Germany also supports a national initiative for nanotechnology R&D. This initiative attempts to coordinate the large number of German companies that are either directly or indirectly involved in developing or applying nanotechnology to their products (see Appendix G). The Ministry of Education and Research oversees R&D activity in Germany and coordinates much of the funding and focus of German nanotechnology research. Unlike the U.S. program, which includes the kitchen sink, German R&D focuses on relatively narrow topical areas that show the largest near-term commercial value. The ministry has defined market opportunities with revenue values of such significance that it believes that sponsored research will give Germany a lead in capturing these markets. The focal areas and their corresponding revenue potential are:

Ultrathin layers[5]	$20 billion
Lateral nanostructures[6]	$2 billion
Ultraprecise handling of surfaces[7]	$12 billion

| Measurement and analysis of nanostructures[8] | $13 billion |
| Nanomaterials and molecular architectures[9] | $4 billion |

European Nonprofits

Other European nanotechnology activities may lack the focus of German activities, but they cover the full spectrum of possibility in nanotechnology. Many of the universities and companies listed in Appendixes C and E have significant research or commercial interest in nanotechnology. Of particular interest are the corresponding nonprofit nanotechnology support organizations that function in much the same way as their U.S. counterparts. The United Kingdom hosts the Institute of Nanotechnology, which serves as an education and lobbying arm for much of the European community. Established as a charity in 1997, the institute is an information and support organization for the public, educators, researchers, and private industry. The institute maintains membership offices in a number of European countries (see Appendix H). It also maintains current information on the state of global nanotechnology initiatives as well as funding opportunities for startups in the European arena (see Appendix L). It is a reliable source of current information on the state of funding and research of various programs in the European community. The institute is relatively new to the world of nanotechnology and is still finding its way. It can, however, be anticipated that it will soon rival the Foresight Institute in the United States, and it is definitely an organization that should be constantly monitored by investors interested in potential European investment opportunities.

JAPAN

Japan's investment in nanotechnology has a growth rate of 15 to 20 percent per year. While there is clearly definite government support for nanotechnology, the distinction between what is government, corporate, and university support is more difficult to separate because the economy is run in a manner somewhat different from that of the U.S. or European economies. The Ministry of Economy, Trade, and Industry (METI) is the predominant organization charged with directing research and distributing money for R&D.[10] One of the METI's operating arms, the National Institute of Advanced Industrial Science and Technology (AIST) has the responsibility of directing research programs and funding to specific areas of national interest, including nanotechnology. The AIST operates 15 research institutions, 23 research centers, 2 divisions, and 7 research initiatives. One of the research centers is the Nanoarchitectonics Research Center. One of the institutes is the Nanotechnology Research Institute. The Japanese concept of nanotechnology is much broader than the U.S. concept. It incorporates all the concepts of nanotechnology along with biotechnology. For example, technologies that deal with DNA at the molecular level fit cleanly within the Japanese definition of nanotechnology. A majority of Japanese activity focuses on either the semiconductor industry or the biotechnology industry.

The perception of long-term global market opportunities for nanotechnology fits well within the Japanese structure of joint government and corporate R&D. It is not uncommon for a Japanese company to undertake a research program on behalf of the government with a contract value that is insignificant compared to the R&D expense incurred by the company. R&D programs lasting a decade are not uncommon under this type of government-corporate partnership. Ultimately, the company and the government will culminate the project after many years when the government purchases products from the company at a price that recoups the company's R&D investment to that point. The company has the security during the R&D phase of knowing that when the government's role is finished, the company will be in a competitive position to provide products in a global marketplace. The government gets sponsored research for its own needs, knowing that the cost will be recouped later by future tariffs or an improved position in the global economy. Companies that have ongoing research or research collaborations in nanotechnology tend to be affiliated with some of the larger Japanese industrial giants (see Appendix I).

Not all of the Japanese research support is directed to large companies. The METI also coordinates support for the development of new businesses through its Small and Medium Enterprise Agency. This agency has a division called the Business Start-up and Alliance Promotion Division that has the responsibility of providing virtually interest-free loans to companies that might be considered bad credit risks by traditional lending sources. Through this division, small companies composed of at least one individual can receive support for the development of a technology and a business. The METI hopes that many of these companies will ultimately develop into larger companies that, in turn, will compete in the global marketplace. These companies in particular represent potential investment opportunities under the Japanese model of R&D. While public information for these companies is available from the METI, access to this information requires an excellent source of Japanese language skills and familiarity with the METI model of corporate financial aid. Organizations such as the Tokyo IPO Corporation provide English-language investment support and would be one path to access the emerging nanotechnology companies found in the Japanese economic system.

ASIA

Lumping 50 percent of the world's population into a few paragraphs may be the height of conceit. However, the balance of nanotechnology fits into the broad scope of the Asian experience. Two dominant players are China, and Korea. Although there are notable nanotechnology activities in other parts of Asia, the major thrust of Asian nanotechnology development is in the semiconductor product arenas. These two countries have national programs that sponsor R&D activity in nanotechnology. The future economy of both these countries is believed to depend on the development of their domestic nanotechnology industries.

China

Through the Chinese Academy of Science, China manages many of the country's nanotechnology R&D programs. Most of the emphasis is directed toward semiconductor fabrication technologies. Much of the focus is on the development of nanotechnology-based electronic devices. There is also a surprising interest in using nanomaterials for the preservation of archeological artifacts. One of the more successful applications was the recent product release of an air conditioner that featured antibacterial materials fabricated from novel nanomaterials.[11] China maintains a number of research centers that include departments or divisions dedicated to nanotechnology R&D (see Appendix J). In addition, there are an estimated 200 enterprises actively engaged in the commercialization of nanotechnology-derived components and products (see Appendix K). At this time, while foreign investment in China is clearly growing at a rapid pace, it is unlikely that worthwhile investment opportunities will exist for individual investors for a number of years. For now, corporate and institutional investment seems to be the high road to China.

Korea

Korea is focused almost exclusively on microelectronics applications of nanotechnology. Through the Tera-Level Nanodevices Initiative, sponsored by the Korea Ministry of Science and Technology, Korean universities and industries are concentrated on the development of next-generation microelectronic devices that will create memory devices with terabit capacities and processing components operating at terahertz speeds.[12] Generic nanotechnology R&D is also ongoing at the Seoul National University. Two programs within this university are the Center for Science in the Nanometer Scale (CSNS) and the Center for Near Field Atom-Photon Technology (CNAT). The CSNS program is developing the technologies that will manufacture the next generations of memory and storage devices. The CNAT program is focused on the development of measurement and lithographic technologies that will operate at the molecular and atomic scales.

Samsung, one of Korea's largest corporate conglomerates, maintains an Advanced Institute of Technology that performs research and commercialization development of microelectronic technologies and supports an extensive variety of microelectromechanical system applications.

Korea's KISC program (see Appendix L) provides reasonably good tracking for start-up opportunities in Korea and is a first line source for exploring investment opportunities derived from Korean nanotechnology activities. Another source is the Korea Trade-Investment Promotion Agency, which provides information to offshore investors and will help track specific economic sectors for investors who are willing to invest at least 50 million won (approximately $38,000 as of May 2001; see Appendix L).

GLOBAL SYNOPSIS

With these few examples, it is clear that nanotechnology R&D and investment opportunities exist on a global scale. The global economy almost universally supports start-up opportunities in nearly every country on the planet. Many countries directly support the development of nanotechnology, intending to make this technology the core of future industries. Investors who are willing to dive into the international arena will find nearly double the opportunities overseas as in the United States.

NOTES

1. NSTC, *Nanostructure Science and Technology—A Worldwide Study* (National Science and Technology Council, September 1999).
2. The absence of standard definitions of nanotechnology preempts the ability to place this study's categories in the classification schemes used elsewhere as well as in this book. The categories used in this study are retained from the original study to demonstrate national capabilities as of 1998.
3. Japanese IPOs can be tracked by Tokyo IPO Corporation. European IPOs can be tracked by EO P.L.C. Korean IPOs can be tracked by KITC Co., Ltd., or through the nonprofit Korea Trade-Investment Promotion Agency's KISC program. See Appendix L for contact information.
4. All currencies converted to U.S. dollar equivalents at the exchange rate of May 15, 2001.

5. These are technologies that produce films of perhaps a few atoms in thickness that improve the quality of mirrors, chemical reactions, adhesion, and other properties of commercial value.
6. These are linear structures, often associated with matrixes of wires that can provide interconnections between devices. They can also be used to guide the production of small holes in surfaces to produce novel devices such as extremely high quality displays for computers.
7. These are technologies and techniques that permit the precise positioning of materials for processing. For example, when producing integrated circuits, as many as 50 layers of material must be placed on the substrate, aligned with extreme precision and accuracy.
8. These are techniques that are used to measure and test fabricated devices that are sized in the nanometer range. A typical example might be a 300-nanometer wire that is used to interconnect two electronic components on an integrated circuit.
9. These are unique materials that are fabricated at the atomic or molecular scale. A wide assortment of possible devices including molecular computer components, water-filtration devices, or advanced automotive catalytic converters is possible.
10. In January 2001, METI replaced the old Ministry of International Trade and Industry (MITI). Substantial reorganization was in process at the time of this writing.
11. 100,000 air conditioners were ordered from the Shadong Small Duck Group.
12. A terabit device would contain 1 trillion (1,000 billion) bits. A terahertz device would operate at 1 trillion transactions per second.

CHAPTER 7

Future Prospects for Investment

The previous chapters have shown a number of ways an investor can find investment opportunities in nanotechnology. What has been missing from this discussion is how to evaluate the companies and the technologies that are found at the end of the search. Assume that an investor has spent the requisite time to grind a way into a university's technology transfer office and is now looking at the prospectus for a new company. The question remains, how does an investor distinguish between technologies that are merely fascinating, and those that have true commercial value? Further, given that most of these companies are in the start-up phase of life, how can an investor determine that the technology will go anywhere, given that the management of the company may be rich in PhDs but lacking in business experience?

There is something compelling about investing in a technology that promises to place a million Pentium-class processors in a space the size of a pinhead. If, however, there is no way to connect these processors to anything, the value swiftly vanishes. Because of the imprecise nature of emerging technologies, there are many opportunities to invest in something that is fantastic, but which in the final analysis ends up on the dustheap of scientific endeavor.

INVESTMENT MODELS FOR TECHNOLOGY

Emerging technology companies tend to be started by the techies who approach the world with integrity, the best intentions, an acute vision of the future, and the business sense of a ticket scalper in a blizzard (sales training is usually missing from most graduate education programs). Having an incredible technology is of little value if no one knows it exists, and telling the world about the virtue of a product is pointless if you can only make a single copy. Further, if you can sell a million copies but lose $1 on each sale, there is no way that you can make up for it in volume.

The first quality any investor should be looking at in a company is the *management team*. No matter how good or exciting the technology and no matter how close to production it is, if the management team does not have its act together, the technology might as well be on the moon. For any prospective investment, prudence suggests that there are four functions that must be fulfilled by the members of the management team:

- *Leadership.*   The chief executive officer (CEO) or president should provide this core function of not only executing the goals of the company, but also communicating these goals to employees, customers, stockholders, and the public. A good CEO need not know very much about the technology, but must sure as hell know how to sell the vision and explain what to do with it. As things stand with nanotechnology, the ideal CEO has prior experience with high-technology start-up companies and an excellent reputation with the investment community.
- *Finance.*   Financial management is usually provided by a chief financial officer (CFO). This must be an individual who has the ability to count every penny and manage the cash flow and the investors with an eye to making payroll and product, while simultaneously managing times of explosive growth and famine. Prior experience working with government contracts and grants programs is of special value to nanotechnology companies. Because the exit strategy of most investors will be through the initial public offering (IPO), the CFO should have prior experience in taking a company public.
- *Sales.*   Sales is usually directed by a vice-president of sales, but in early-stage companies may be directed by the CEO. This must be an individual who can explain the most complex ideas to a six-year-old child, and simultaneously leave that child begging to invest every penny he or she has in some venture. If this person also has sufficient integrity to never *do* that to a six-year-old child, then this person is worth his or her weight in nanotubes. An individual with prior technology sales experience, especially in marketing and market development, and familiarity with government agencies and original equipment manufacturers would be of special value to a nanotechnology company.
- *Technology.*   There must be the person who knows how everything works. Typically, this is a chief technology officer (CTO) who has the ability to complete whole sentences without coaching yet can mentally solve nonlinear differential equations and can cheaply transform a pile of graphite into products valued at thousands of dollars per ounce. If this individual has prior start-up experience in bringing high-technology products into production, he or she would be of great value to a nanotechnology company.

If the management team is in place, then it is time to actually listen to the story. Remember, whatever the story is, it will be a good one. A stockbroker once claimed that in 30 years of investment banking he had never heard a *bad* story. People who are looking for money rarely stand before an investor with their hat in their hands and say, "I really don't know if it will *ever* work." Instead, they hide their doubts behind credible optimism about how good it will be *after* they get the funds needed to solve a few minor problems on the path to mass production of products for the eagerly awaiting market.

Investors should listen to the story, not so much to find out how rich everyone is going to be, but to investigate whether the management team has its act together, especially to determine whether the team has sufficient sales presence to sell to customers. If, during the story, you are presented with stale Oreos and instant coffee, the sales side of the company is definitely in trouble. However, if you are presented with beluga caviar and fine champagne, then the financial management side is in trouble. If only a savvy investor could gauge the management team simply by the snacks offered during the presentation.

Levity aside, sales ability and the quality of the story are the ultimate drivers of corporate success. The key problem with nanotechnology is that the general markets will be worth billions, but the immediate markets are often worth very little. In reviewing the stories, an investor should focus not on the long-term potential, but on the immediate markets for the products. For example, a good story might suggest that the technology will be applied within a year to provide a better, lower-cost solution to an existing technology problem, and this might be accompanied by a list of customers, some of whom have provided serious letters of intent. A bad story might suggest that the company will someday have a lock on everyone who will need a particular nanotechnology capability. Extravagant claims tend to be unrealistic.

After the story and snacks, it is important to review the company's financial statements. This is the make-or-break point for classes of investors and stages of companies. Simply put, the company would not be looking for investors if everything were working fine. Perhaps the research and development (R&D) program burned through all the cash. Perhaps the most senior investor wants to cash out and spend his retirement years fishing in Iceland. Whatever the reasons, something is not going quite right, and that something has to be sitting on the table, right where they want you to sign the check. This is where investor taste comes into play. No guide can tell you what kinds of problems you should invest in. The best advice is to invest in problems that you understand. If you do not get it, get out.

The following chapters discuss both technologies and companies in terms of where they fall in various phases of opportunity. Every company will fit into one of three phases defined here.

Figure 7.1 displays a curve that shows the net assets of a company as a function of time since the company was founded. The assets of a company, excluding any cash received as investments,[1] go negative immediately because the company is spending money to create something that it has not yet sold. Phase 1 of this process is the R&D phase. This is when the company has the worst possible story. There are no customers, the technology does not quite work, and the staff resembles a mixture of evangelists and kids who look like they will never be old enough to vote. Usually, the company is emerging from a Small Business Incentive Research (SBIR) grant or a university research program. This is the realm of the professional investor and the venture capitalists, private placements, angels, and rich uncles. The upside potential of these investments is fantastic. The downside is the total loss of the investment.

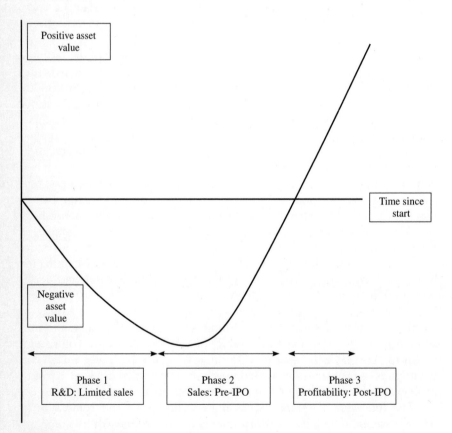

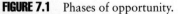

FIGURE 7.1   Phases of opportunity.

Phase 2 begins with sales. As sales happen, the rate at which a company is losing money starts slowing, and at some point, the company breaks even. Most investments and many IPOs will happen at this stage in a company's life. However, the company is not out of the woods yet. Many bad things can still happen. Most investors can participate in a company at this stage through either an IPO or a secondary offering. The upside potential of these investments is good. The downside is the total loss of the investment.

Phase 3 begins when the company is actually worth something. At this stage, it is making money, it has cleared its early debt, and there is a stable product that seems to sell no matter what mistakes are made by the management team. Most investors at this stage will buy and sell the company's stock on one of the major exchanges. Anyone who can drive a computer or call a broker can participate in a company at this stage. The upside potential of these investments is modest. The downside, obviously, is the total loss of the investment.

ASSESSMENT METHOD

Given the various factors that go into evaluating investment risk and potential, this section presents a guide to help assess the companies and technologies that an investor is likely to encounter. This guide can help focus the prospective investor on the risk/reward opportunity of the investment under consideration. The assessment method is not an assurance of either success or failure; rather, it will help determine the risk threshold—the lower the score, the riskier the company.

1. Determine the quality of the management team. Possible scores are:
   - *10 points if it is good.* Management has a prior history of successfully bringing high-technology products to market.
   - *5 points if it is okay.* Management has a prior history of bringing products to market.
   - *0 points if it is bad.* Management has no prior history.
2. Determine which phase the company is in (see Figure 7.1):
   - *10 points if it is Phase 3.* The company is a going concern and is successful in this or other markets.
   - *5 points if it is Phase 2.* The company is making sales, but is not yet profitable.
   - *0 points if it is Phase 1.* The company is still losing money and has not yet sold anything.

3. Determine how long it will be before the company has a working tech-nology:

   - *10 points if it is less than one year.* The company will be making sales soon, and probably needs investment to expand operations or sales.
   - *5 points if it is less than three years.* The company has a handle on a market, but either the technology or market is not quite mature enough for sales.
   - *0 points if it is more than three years.* The technology or market has yet to be proven.

4. Determine how much money it will take to get a working technology:

   - *10 points if it is under $1 million.* The technology needs a slight nudge to get it into the marketplace.
   - *5 points if it is under $10 million.* The technical hurdles are serious, but not insurmountable.
   - *0 points if it is under $100 million.* The technology is the stuff of dreams; reality has yet to be found.

5. Determine how long it will take the market to actually buy a working technology:

   - *10 points if it is less than one year.* The market exists; replacement of existing technologies is ready to happen.
   - *5 points if it is one to three years.* The market exists, but entrenched suppliers of alternative products exist, or proof of viability of the product is pending.
   - *0 points if it is more than three years.* The market may exist, but it must be farmed to prove its existence.

6. Determine the actual market size, assuming no competition. A Frost and Sullivan report would be a typical source for this information:

   - *10 points if it is over $1 billion.* There is a significant demand for a product that solves an established need.
   - *5 points if it is over $100 million.* There are niche consumers who understand the value of the product.
   - *0 points if it is over $10 million.* The few buyers tend to be aca-demics, researchers, or other start-up companies.

7. Sum up the scores in each of the preceding steps, yielding a number from 0 to 60. The closer the number is to 0, the more risky the invest-ment. The closer the number is to 60, the less risky the investment.

No two investors would likely get the same number in looking at the same company. However, this assessment gives an individual investor a means to compare opportunities and focus on the most common strong and weak points of the emerging companies in this arena. In high technology things often change very fast. Thus, the watchword for the investor is a simple mantra—*due diligence.*[2]

POSSIBILITIES

In principle, anything that is manufactured today will be impacted in some way by nanotechnology. There are five broad avenues of current development that warrant consideration:

- Biological applications
- Chemical applications
- Nanomaterials and composites
- Aerospace applications
- Military applications

Biological applications of nanotechnology have proven to be the most fruitful to date. Numerous bioengineered crops currently exist that have increased disease resistance and improved yields. While public acceptance of this technology continues to be argued in the political and ethical arenas, the manipulation of DNA to enhance or produce new traits in organisms is a well-established technology. Similarly, the design of specialized organisms, and ultimately machines that work within the human body, will provide unprecedented changes in health care and the treatment of disease.

Traditionally, a chemist's work has consisted of developing new substances by manipulating existing substances and forcing often-complex chemical reactions until the target substance is finally produced. Nanotechnology promises to build new chemicals with new properties by assembling these chemicals one atom at a time. In addition, chemical-sensing systems may provide new tools for diagnostics and process control systems.

New materials are one of the realities of nanotechnology. When control of a material is at the atomic level, novel and unique properties can emerge. Some substances, such as carbon, when arranged correctly, acquire tensile strength 60 times that of steel. Such strength makes possible a world of space elevators and virtually indestructible fabrics. The development of devices fabricated at microscopic or even quantum scales has created materials with a number of unique and valuable optical and electromagnetic properties. Similar developments in creating surfaces with special properties may result in highly efficient water-purification systems, or reduce oil refineries to the size of a desk.

In the arena of aerospace, high-density fuel storage under pressures not unlike those at the core of Jupiter, spy planes that resemble a gnat, and interstellar probes the size of a beer can are also on the agenda for nanotechnology. Given that such micromachines can be fabricated, their obvious potential in aerospace is huge. Research has already created insect-sized vehicles that cheerfully flutter about research labs at several campuses, and spin-off technologies from the Strategic Defense Initiative are producing designs for spacefaring probes that (because of their tiny size) could be propelled to other stars with transit times measured in years rather than centuries

The battlefield of the future will be the scene of a war of information in which soldiers have the ability to know anything about enemy disposition and capabilities. Systems are under development to provide troops with complete pictures of their own and the enemy's positions using roving scouts not much larger than insects. Fire-and-forget munitions that guide themselves to enemy soldiers and material have had nearly a decade of successful deployment. Body armor, medical monitoring, and power systems for individual soldiers are also being developed. The Defense Department's objective for these systems is to totally dominate the battlefield using systems derived from nanotechnology.

PERSPECTIVES

In any emerging industry, there are always competing viewpoints as to how to classify and organize the emerging technologies. At least three models should be considered for nanotechnology:

- The first is the *incremental model,* which considers nanotechnology as a natural evolution of technology, based on the projection of today's technology into tomorrow's marketplace. This approach is appropriate when considering the evolution of the semiconductor industry and its never-ending balance between component size and component fabrication costs.
- The second is the *strategic model.* This is the one chosen by the National Nanotechnology Initiative (NNI) for its selection of funding directions for basic research. In this model, various near-term possibilities that enhance national priorities get the emphasis for funding, while those which are longer term, or of little national interest, are passed over for consideration.
- The third, the *quantum leap model,* looks toward broad capabilities that will create revolutionary changes to society, the economy, and the quality of life for future generations.

Each model has its proponents and its advantages. None is capable of covering all the possibilities for investment or potential outcome, and surprises will happen for reasons that make sense only in hindsight. The Internet boom is an obvious example of a dramatic global phenomenon that no one—absolutely no one—could have predicted with any certainty.

Part II of this book presents a model with a technology framework intended to help investors know what they are looking at. The criteria for selection were rather straightforward:

- *Technologies that are hot in the summer of 2002 might well be lost opportunities by the summer of 2003.* The investor's assessment of new opportunity must have a context that works today and for years to come.
- *The model has to be realistic.* The evangelist may make claims about what is possible, but the horizon of possibility must be within the investment lifetime of mature investors, rather than their children. Discussing breakthroughs that will happen within the next 50 years makes for fascinating material, but investors never lack for opportunities that will pay out or fail within three to five years.
- *The model has to be coherent.* The NNI, by comparison, is the kitchen-sink approach to nanotechnology. From the NNI's point of view, size matters more than focus. Had the NNI's perspective been chosen, investors would be trying to grasp how nanotubes will affect space travel, cell phones, body armor, transistors, and new generations of televisions. Ultimately, serious investors will have to discover how nanotubes may do all these things, but a coherent foundation in the scope of nanotechnology is required to bring perspective.
- *The model has to be understandable.* Nanotechnology is chock full of scientific concepts and jargon that are difficult to follow even by those with advanced degrees in physics. To dive into the quantum structure of nanotubes would leave most investors shaking their heads and searching the Sunday paper for fast-food franchises. Thus, although the core physics of nanotechnology may be the debating ground of the American Physical Society, the core investment opportunities must be explainable to virtually any literate human being.

The selected approach meets the preceding criteria (although it may not satisfy the authors of the NNI) by exploring the key technologies that will be used to create productive nanomachines and micromachines. This book traces the technological requirements, status, and futures of what it takes to make fully functioning micro- and nanorobots. This process keeps a common thread through the discussion, yet introduces the investor to a wide range of technological challenges currently under development.

The dream of creating billions of tiny machines tailored to reshape the world is not a trivial undertaking. If these machines are going to be practical, there are four things they must do:

- They must be capable of independent action over extended periods of time in the execution of the tasks they have been programmed for.
- They must be capable of manipulating and changing the real and unpredictable world outside of laboratory environments.
- They must be cost effective.
- They must never ever turn an angry eye on their creators.

Essentially, what is required is an inexpensive robot, smaller than dust, which does what it is programmed to do under incredibly harsh conditions without much guidance. For those working in the field of robotics, there are quite enough difficulties in figuring out how to get a robot to do something under *any* conditions. Solving the issues of useful work and harsh conditions can come at a price—but smaller than dust? Most contemporary robotics labs would likely lose funding if they followed the path that nanotechnologists prefer and openly started developing invisible machines. The development of micromachines is much like the old-time flea circus, where spectators stood around a small plate and watched invisible trained fleas perform amazing acts of acrobatics and heroism. The state of the art required to produce invisible robots that do real work is not quite past the flea-circus stage. There is truly a lot of science fiction in the current proposals. There is also a remarkable amount of core technology with valuable consequences being developed. Yet translating core technologies into real-world solutions has never been an easy task. Determining what a micromachine *could* do is far easier than determining how it is going to do it.

There are some serendipitous events occurring in the universities and research labs, which, either by accident or by brilliant design, will result in some incredible microrobots in just a few years. In the robotics labs, significant progress has been made in designing the key pieces that will make a robot largely autonomous while it walks or rolls or swims around a room, or around the world. In the nanotechnology labs and micromachine labs, fabrication techniques now exist that permit rudimentary machine parts to be constructed from a few atoms. There is no question that as robotics and nanotechnology evolve, there will be a convergence of ideas and capabilities that will result in a remarkable redefinition of the industrial society.

One recurring theme is that the boundary between mechanical devices and biological devices is becoming blurred. In many cases, there are biological solutions that work as well or better than manufactured solutions. Although this book focuses on the mechanistic side of engineered solutions, there is no doubt that solutions to engineering problems will often be a hybrid of biological and mechanical engineering. There are many obvious lessons from nature's bounty that show how to make machines, that point to explicit and effective solutions that are too obvious to ignore. The creation of tiny robots that perform momentous tasks will work best when a combination of approaches is integrated into a working system.

Part II of this book (dealing with the key elements of a microrobot) details the investment opportunities that exist for the core technologies that will be used to fabricate these tiny robots. It examines the essential components of a robot, or a paramecium, and shows which aspects are current technology, worthy of investment, and which are not yet ready to open the kimono. The technologies that follow provide a perspective with an investment horizon that covers a time span from today to at least a decade into the future.

NOTES

1. In this analysis, it is important to exclude cash received from private placements, IPOs or other nonrevenue sources. You need to see the company's position as a pure debt/credit structure.
2. Due diligence is the investigation of the details of a potential investment, including an examination of operations, management, and market and verification of facts.

Searching for Gold

CHAPTER 8

The Technology Landscape

The invisible world has been a prominent focus for investment since that dim time in prehistory when Paleolithic tribes herded mastodons over cliffs to the Texas-style barbecues of the early Stone Age. Whether carving a totem to a god of the hunt, fermenting mead in a lambskin tank, or fleeing the horror of the Black Death, humans have invested heavily in the invisible forces of nature that somehow control the course of their lives. Over time, humanity has shifted its perspective from being controlled by the unseen forces of nature to controlling them. The invisible has become knowable, and humans have taken the first steps toward creating the tiniest of objects to perform the most profound tasks in their history.

Close to $1 billion is spent each year to develop the technologies of the invisible world of nanotechnology, mostly through government sponsorship. Although there are those who may doubt it, not *all* government spending is fruitless. In fact, investment in nanotechnology may be one of the most significant investments of the twenty-first century—but its roots have been centuries in the making.

When Robert Hooke published his book *Micrographia* in 1665,[1] the world was introduced for the first time to accurate pictures of the invisible world, with precise drawings of what Hooke saw under his microscope. With drawings of ants, molds, and razor-blade edges, the book showed what it meant to be small—how nature was composed of a tiny latticework of structures. In 1674, Antonie van Leeuwenhoek published the first-ever drawings of microorganisms.[2] By showing that microscopic life exists in this unseen world, van Leeuwenhoek's drawings utterly transformed medical practice. Thus began the process of changing the foundations of the medical world from the study of invisible mystical foul vapors to informed diagnosis and treatment. Almost immediately, the 7,000-year-old arts of winemaking and brewing transformed themselves into a science as wineries and breweries invested heavily in the classification and breeding of new strains of yeast. Shortly after 1680, the first nanotechnology—the scientific use of yeast in brewing and winemaking—became a commercial practice.

Hooke and van Leeuwenhoek were not the first to consider the smallest of things. They were merely the first to have the technology to see them. In 440 B.C., the Greek philosopher Leucippus proposed that matter consisted of small indivisible units (which his student Democritus called *atoms*). Since that time, physicists have speculated that large things can be chopped into smaller things until some ultimate limit is reached beyond which no further chopping can occur.

For three centuries, the world of the small was investigated descriptively as biologists and mineralogists studied, drew, and photographed ever-smaller objects and creatures. The idea of actually controlling the microscopic world had to wait until December 29, 1959, when Richard Feynman (one of the twentieth century's most renowned physicists) gave his speech "There's Plenty of Room at the Bottom" to the American Physical Society. This speech is generally credited as being the seminal act that made nanotechnology credible. Feynman, who pointed out that there is absolutely no physical reason why artifacts cannot be built one atom at a time, proposed that it was not just possible but inevitable that the manipulation of single atoms would ultimately lead to the fabrication of useful devices.

In the 40 years since Feynman's lecture, nanotechnology has found a place in the world of science and technology, inspiring research in a broad range of areas from theoretical physics to common household devices. The physics of this often-whimsical world dominates many of the issues that determine the success of investments in nanotechnology.

WHY NANOTECHNOLOGY IS IMPORTANT

Just because something is small doesn't mean it is valuable. In fact, this culture tends to think that bigger is better. People supersize their lunches for only 39 cents and gaze in awe at ever-taller skyscrapers, longer bridges, or more massive supertankers. The idea that smallness might be a virtue is relatively new in this culture, circa the birth of the microprocessor in the early 1970s. Intel's first commercial microprocessor—the 4004, released in 1971—contained about 2,300 transistors. Thirty years later, the microprocessor had shrunk into something containing over 7.5 million transistors and operating almost 10,000 times faster than devices built in the 1970s. For Intel's stockholders, smaller proved better.

There are many proponents of nanotechnology who claim that Intel-like financial performance can be expected as technologies evolve and shrink in size. In 1986, Eric Drexler published *Engines of Creation* (New York: Anchor Books), which summarized the speculative possibilities of nanotechnology. Moving far beyond Feynman's proposals, Drexler proposed a world of technological capabilities with profound social and economic possibilities. The list of possibilities grows with each year, but the basic starting point for Drexler's speculation included devices with the capability to end disease, create wealth for everyone, end pollution, provide unlimited energy, and manufacture goods at virtually no cost. These speculations are based on the idea that inexpensive autonomous machines will be fabricated by the billions, each of which will manufacture things of value one atom at a time using only the crudest of raw materials. If they operate inside the human body, they will identify disease and destroy it or transmute it into harmless chemical ash.

Clearly, there is some value in nanotechnology if only a fraction of this speculation is achievable. Amazingly, some of it has already been achieved *and* commercialized. The semiconductor technology of the Information Age is nothing more than an offshoot of *one* direction of nanotechnology research. The electronics that make the Information Age possible are made of devices whose smallest parts are less than one-millionth of an inch across. The increasingly difficult process of stuffing more transistors on a chip is just one of the research paths directed by nanotechnology. This process alone accounts for nearly 70 percent of the growth in the gross domestic product of the United States.

HOW SMALL IS SMALL?

One of the wonders of nature is the gecko lizard. Aside from being cute, the gecko is well known for being able to walk straight up walls, even windows, and geckos can often be found hanging upside down from a ceiling. It has been reported that some enterprising researchers, in trying to unravel the mystery of the upside-down gecko, placed the lizards inside glass bell jars and evacuated all the air to determine whether the gecko employs some kind of microscopic suction cup to hang upside down. Reportedly, the geckos in these studies did not fall, although survival time in a vacuum is limited. In June 2000, researchers at the University of California announced that the gecko's ability to walk upside down is based on something called *van der Waals forces*. These forces are created by microscopic hairs on the sole of the gecko's feet and could, in theory, have a holding force of about 45 pounds. The attractive forces between the wall and the hairs, which are 10 microns in diameter, account for this unusual ability of the gecko.

The hairs on the foot of the gecko prove that the behavior of small things can have profound consequences for big things. When discussing smallness, there is a special vocabulary that describes invisible proportions and aids in one's understanding of just how small is small. To begin with, consider exactly what the *nano* part of the word *nanotechnology* means.

The *nano* in *nanotechnology* comes from the term *nanometer,* which is a distance of *one-billionth* of a meter. That *is* pretty small. (More generally, *nano-* is a prefix that means one-billionth of any unit of measure.) Table 8.1 gives some perspective.

Being small creates a new set of problems that are quite different from the problems of being big. These problems involve basic natural forces, which change in importance as things get very small. In the normal human world, you think in terms of gravity and friction—two dominant forces. You can add to these natural forces those tamed by humans, such as the contained explosions of the internal combustion engine or the electromotive forces of the motors that drive washing machines. At the normal human scale down to about a millimeter, these are the dominant forces that enable industrial technology.

Gravity is one of the fundamental forces of nature. When an object, such as the earth, has mass, it creates gravity, which draws things to the center of the mass. On a large scale, this is what binds a planet to itself, or lets the planets circle the sun. At the normal human scale, gravity is a significant force that that you engineer around or with, depending on the issue at hand. If you build a bridge, you engineer around gravity. If you build an automobile, you engineer with gravity. As shall be seen, gravity is a factor that becomes relatively unimportant as things get smaller.

Working with gravity in the normal world is friction. Friction is the resistive force of two things sliding against each other. Without friction, steering a car would be dependent on the ability to bounce off of objects

TABLE 8.1   Notions of Size

Unit	English Measure	As Big As
Meter:		
1.0 meter	3.28 feet	Small child
Centimeter:	0.39 inches	Tip of little finger
0.01 meter		
Millimeter:	0.04 inch	Grain of sugar
0.001 meter		
Micrometer:	0.00004 inch	0.025 diameter of a
0.000001 meter		human hair; size of
		a bacterium
Nanometer:	0.00000004 inch	5 to 10 atoms end
0.000000001 meter		to end
Angstrom:	0.000000004 inch	1 atom; 10 times the
0.0000000001 meter		wavelength of an
		electron

alongside the road. Usually, you think of gravity and friction working together when you make machines that do work. The automobile relies on gravity to keep it on the road, and friction to steer the way. At the normal human scale, friction is *also* something that determines how you engineer machines. However, like gravity, friction becomes relatively unimportant as things get smaller.

Combustion is another vital natural phenomenon. Combustion accounts for 39 percent of the world's energy consumption and 97 percent of the world's transportation. The burning of fossil fuels is one of the principal means of turning machines from static objects of art into functioning, productive tools. Combustion, along with gravity and friction, is one of the many things of the normal human world that changes as things get small.

To understand how they change, consider which forces are important as things shrink in size from the scale of meters down to the scale of nanometers. At the size of a millimeter, gravity, friction, and combustion are still factors, but they do not have quite the same relevance as they do at a larger scale. Things still fall down, and they still rub against each other, but combustion becomes difficult, if not impossible. Minor forces of nature, such as the formerly weak electrostatic forces, start influencing how things work, as air starts taking on the consistency of thick honey. The electrostatic forces are the *interesting* change.

Somewhere between a millimeter and a micrometer, the world becomes gooey and sticky as electrostatic forces become more important. The electrostatic force is the primary interaction between and among protons and electrons. The electrostatic force between two protons is a trillion trillion trillion times stronger than the gravitational force between two protons. Gravity normally dominates in the universe when enough matter is present, so an object the size of the earth creates a significant amount of gravity—which, at a large scale, is the dominant force. But as objects get smaller, the *relative* effect of gravity becomes less important *locally* than the electrostatic force. At the size of a millimeter, electrostatic forces become significant. By the time things get to the size of a micrometer, electrostatic forces become more important than gravity. There are two aspects of these forces that are important in nanotechnology. The first is van der Waals forces, and the second is brownian motion.

Van der Waals forces are named after Johannes van der Waals, who was a Dutch physicist of the late nineteenth and early twentieth centuries. He pointed out that even electrically *neutral* particles interact with each other in significant ways. Electric fields around molecules are not uniform, because the geometry of a molecule is rarely round. Rather, the geometry of a molecule can be virtually any shape. As a result, the electric field around a molecule is not uniform either. This lack of uniformity creates an asymmetrical electric field, which permits molecules to alternately attract or repel each other depending solely on their relative orientation to each other at any point in time. In one orientation, a molecule might attract. In a different orientation, it might repel. This permits the gecko lizard to walk up walls.

Another unusual effect encountered at this scale is brownian motion. In 1827, a British botanist named Robert Brown noticed that under a microscope, pollen grains (about 250 micrometers in diameter) that were suspended in water seemed to be in constant motion. Brown was honored by having this constant motion named after him. In 1905, Albert Einstein, who had a penchant for solving all kinds of problems, came up with an explanation. He found that molecules in a liquid or gas are in constant motion due to the heat energy in the system. As the molecules move, they randomly bounce off of the pollen grains and impart visible motion. Brownian motion makes it difficult for things to stay where you put them. On the other hand, it is also one of the important means by which nanotechnological devices may be powered.

As sizes further shrink between the scale of the micrometer and the nanometer, there is a further decline in the importance of gravity and friction and an increase in the importance of electrostatic forces and brownian motion. Further changes start occurring as sizes approach the nanometer scale. At this scale, a new collection of effects is caused by the most esoteric of physics—quantum mechanics. Quantum mechanics is neither easily described nor easily understood. Even those who developed the theory were disturbed by its implications. Erwin Schrödinger was one of the founders of the theories that make up quantum mechanics. He described his feelings about quantum mechanics in this way: "I don't like it, and I'm sorry I ever had anything to do with it." Richard Feynman, who was also a significant contributor to the theory, said, "I think that I can safely say that nobody understands quantum mechanics."

Quantum mechanics is a model of the way things work at the atomic scale and below. The key difference between how quantum mechanics works and the way the normal world works is that in quantum mechanics everything is a probability. In the quantum world, things never *are,* they merely have a *probability* of being. Further, *where* something is located is determined by a probability such that something can be everywhere simultaneously. For nanotechnologists, this enables the concept of the *quantum computer,* which could have all possible computational outcomes simultaneously available at the same time. In particular, a quantum computer would depend on the ability of a quantum particle to have more than one state of being at a time. This multistate character would permit a quantum computer to operate billions of times faster than normal computers. Quantum devices, such as single-atom or single-electron memory devices, also become possible thanks to the strange forces of the quantum world.

Another thing worth mentioning at this point is that in quantum mechanics, a particle has the characteristics of both a particle and a wave. What this means is that when a particle bounces off a wall, it does not have to bounce at any particular angle. In fact, a particle can go *through* the wall without disturbing the wall. What this means is that as devices approach the size of atoms, the properties of matter are rather different from what most people are used to. Thus, when you consider investing in some kinds of nanotechnology, it becomes crucial to understand whether the proposed investment has the intellectual capital, the people, who can understand and work with quantum mechanics.

Fortunately, it is not necessary to consider things much smaller than an angstrom. Building things smaller than an angstrom may be possible, but those constructions are the realm of theoretical physicists and science fiction writers. There are enough problems to deal with at this point. Under the rubric of nanotechnology, the sizes of objects that can be considered for investment are as small as 1 angstrom and as large as about 1 millimeter. This is a span of almost seven orders of magnitude, or a factor of 10 million. This is equivalent to describing features that are as small as 1 inch or as long as 160 miles. When dealing with such a range of sizes, the technology issues are different depending on the scale of the device. To help you understand the range of issues caused by scale, Table 8.2 summarizes the dominant effects at different sizes.

NANOMACHINES: A MODEL FOR TECHNOLOGY ASSESSMENT

The core technologies that you need to consider for investment are driven by the vision of microscopic autonomous robots that do useful work in almost any environment. The technologies that will shape these robots have their roots in the biology of the cell. The same mechanisms that are required to give a bacterium life are common to the requirements for functioning

TABLE 8.2 Dominant Effects

Size		Dominant Effects
Centimeter:	0.01 meter	Gravity, friction, combustion
Millimeter:	0.001 meter	Gravity, friction, combustion, electrostatic
Micrometer:	0.000001 meter	Electrostatic, van der Waals, brownian
Nanometer:	0.000000001 meter	Electrostatic, van der Waals, brownian, quantum
Angstrom:	0.0000000001 meter	Quantum mechanics

nanomachines. These mechanisms can be reduced to six fundamental requirements that are common to living organisms and nanomachines:

- Energy
- Movement
- Programming
- Sensing
- Manipulation
- Self-repair (or self-immolation)

Functioning nanomachines need a source of power in the same way that a functioning automobile needs an engine and a gas tank. In order for machines to do work, power must be provided to enable the machines to move, work, and execute their programming. On the very small scale, traditional power systems simply do not work. Novel new forms of power must be created that provide energy on demand in a way that can be sustained for long periods of time.

For a nanomachine to perform work, it has to be in the right place to do the work. A nanomachine must have a means of moving. Traditional locomotion systems, such as wheels or wings, do not work in the land of the small. Solutions must be found that enable a machine to move in a world in which air has the consistency of molasses.

For a nanomachine to do a task, it has to have a guiding program that tells it when to move, when to stop, when to eat, and when to work. If it hits a problem, such as a wall, it has to figure out a way to get around the wall and continue on its assigned task. Most important, the nanomachine must be programmable to do a variety of tasks. In short, the nanomachine needs some kind of brain. Traditional computer-based control systems fall somewhat short in meeting this need. Computers require a constant electrical voltage, and when they have that voltage, they require a lot of real estate to perform the functions they perform. Today's computers, for all their miniaturization, are too large and power-hungry to meet the requirements of nanotechnology. Unique solutions must be found that enable a machine to think in a world in which a normal computer would seem like a minor subcontinent.

For a nanomachine to do anything useful, it has to know where it is. Sometimes, it is enough for it to simply know that it is adjacent to something. If nanomachines are to work in concert, then each machine must know where it is relative to all the other machines working on the same problem. In today's age of global positioning, knowing where you are on the planet to within 3 meters is considered very good. In the nanoworld, if you don't know your location to within one-millionth of a meter, you are hopelessly lost. Similarly, if the nanomachine is lucky enough to find itself next to a target, such as a cancer cell, it has to know which cells are cancerous, and which are not. Solutions must be found that enable a machine to know where it is in a world in which a dust mite seems like Godzilla.

Given that a nanomachine has somehow found its torturous way to where it is supposed to be, it is now ready to do work. Perhaps the work is something basic such as dropping a few atoms in a line. Perhaps its task is to fatally chop into the wall of a cancer cell. Perhaps its task is to fabricate a copy of itself. Whatever the task, there must be some means by which the nanomachine actually does something to create some meaningful change in the world. Once again, traditional lathes, drills, and injection-molding technologies will not work. Ways must be found to enable a machine to grind and hack its way through a realm in which individual electrons can make the world a place of continuous earthquake.

Imagine a nanomachine calmly hacking away at a tumor. In midtask, something breaks and its lifesaving efforts have the tumor-destroying effect of a wet dishrag. It is time for the nanomachine to exit gracefully. Given that it has been dodging the antibody bullets of the immune system for most of its life, there is a growing risk that the nonfunctional machine will malfunction further and actually do more harm than good. Now is the time for the machine to self-destruct without dooming the patient. Nanomachine disposal has to be done in a manner consistent with the body's own means of disposing of normal biological waste. Thus, the nanomachine must somehow convert itself into biological waste before it loses all functionality. With no analog even in the annals of Greenpeace, a means of hari-kari must be found that enables a machine to self-destruct safely and cleanly.

NOTES

1. Robert Hooke ranks behind Isaac Newton and Christopher Wren as one of England's top seventeenth-century scientists. He also wrote extensively on physics, incorporating classic models of springs, a wave theory of light, and some extremely accurate models of orbital mechanics.
2. Antonie van Leeuwenhoek was a Dutch scientist. As a cloth merchant, he was drawn to Hooke's drawings of textiles. He explored the microscopic world and published extensively. He appears several times in this book.

CHAPTER 9

Power Systems

Every machine requires a source of energy. Without energy, a machine is just a limp contrivance, similar at best to a Calder mobile hanging from a ceiling in a museum. Given a source of energy, a machine has the ability to sing, dance, dig, roll, melt, compute, or execute any of the myriad possibilities that have been conceived and fabricated in this industrial age. Of course, energy has to come from somewhere—it does not just happen. Energy, according to the first law of thermodynamics, can neither be created nor destroyed. It can, however, be converted from one form into another. This conversion process frees up some amount of energy for use as the motive force of machines. The efficiency with which energy is converted is of great concern in the design of energy-producing systems. Systems that convert energy with a low efficiency may be wasting 90 percent of the available energy, while systems that convert energy with a high efficiency may waste only 10 percent of the available energy. Efficiencies that waste less than 80 percent are considered good, while efficiencies that waste less than 50 percent are considered outstanding. Efficiency becomes important when you need two different kinds of energy in a system, such as energy for motion and energy for electronics.

One way to think about power systems for nano- and micromachines is to consider the power systems of the conventional automobile. The automobile uses an electrical system powered by a battery to start an internal combustion engine, which converts the chemical reaction of burning gasoline with oxygen into mechanical motion. This mechanical motion propels the car and creates a rotary motion that is used by an electrical generator to convert mechanical motion into electricity, which powers the onboard electronics and recharges the battery. The automobile has a power-conversion system that is used to provide energy for both the mechanical and electrical subsystems of the car. These fundamental capabilities of converting one kind of energy into another use exactly the same principles that are needed to drive the power systems of nano- and micromachines.

In micromachine technology, mechanical motion is required for the machines to go anywhere or do any work. Similarly, the guidance, computational, and sensor systems used by the machines will require electrical energy to control how the mechanical systems are steered and actuated. Although the principles of the automobile are almost identical to those for a micromachine, it is unlikely that anyone will create microscopic autonomous automobiles that go 50 centimeters between fill-ups on a milliliter of gasoline. As noted in Chapter 8, internal-combustion physics do not scale well when parts get much smaller than a millimeter.

A large number of possible technologies can become the power systems that drive micro- and nanomachines. These power systems must satisfy two fundamental requirements to be usable. The first is that the power system must be self-contained within the device. The second is that the power system should have a companion conversion system that can transform electrical to mechanical power, or vice versa.

Being contained within the device means that the power-generating system can produce power without an external tether to the outside world—there are no cables or wires connected to the device. Tethered connections may be possible, but they run the risk of interfering with navigation or being easily broken. It is reasonable, however, to consider power systems that extract their energy from the environment that surrounds them. In the same manner that an automobile relies on oxygen in the air to burn the fuel, micro- and nanomachines may be able to extract fuel from their surroundings.

The requirement for a companion power system means that the onboard power system must be able to provide both mechanical and electrical power. Both types of power are required because no purely electronic device is capable of mechanical motion, and no purely mechanical device is capable of complex computation.[1] Thus, both electrical and mechanical power sources are required, which means there must be a companion system that converts power from mechanical to electrical and back. If one function of the device is to walk on a surface, the device will require some computational ability to figure out a way around the obstacles it encounters. Onboard computer systems will require some means of creating the electrical power necessary to perform the calculations to determine an alternate navigation path around the obstacle. Thus, the power that moves the legs must have the ability to create computational decisions that will, in turn, guide the legs to a new path.

What ideal nanomachines require is a self-recharging power system with an infinite life span. This requirement may be met by the available and proposed power systems that will be fabricated in the near future. Furthermore, there appear to be technologies to create companion power systems similar to those found in an automobile. Of the many kinds of power systems being either studied or developed at this time, six of the most promis-

TABLE 9.1 Power Sources

Name	Type	Source	First Use
Batteries	Electrical	Chemical reaction	Micromachine power source for all applications
Thermoelectric	Electrical	Heat differential	Micromachine power source for extreme-environment technologies
Solar or motion	Electrical	Light	Nano- and micromachine power source for external environment applications
Steam	Motion	Electricity	Micromachine power source for industrial applications
Adenosine triphosphate (ATP)	Motion or electrical	Chemical reaction	Nanomachine power source; ideal for operation within the human body
Brownian motors	Motion	Weird physics	Nanomachine power source; potentially infinite power

ing for potential investment are discussed in this chapter and shown in Table 9.1. These are considered in order, from the more familiar concepts to the more radical.

BATTERIES

As a power source for a micromachine, a battery would be ideal for providing electrical power for movement, sensing, communications, and computation. Electrical power can be used for almost any conceivable task of any machine. The key to using a battery for micro- and nanomachines is to create a small battery with a lot of stored energy that can be easily replaced or recharged when it runs down. The most important element of the battery will be size.

Batteries have a history that may go back to roughly 250 B.C. Earthenware batteries excavated near Baghdad suggest that electroplating technology may have been developed and used well over 2,000 years ago. These batteries may have operated on extreme chemicals such as grape juice or even vinegar. The invention of the battery is more commonly attributed to the Italian inventor Alessandro Volta, around 1793. He was honored for this and other work by the adoption of his name for the standard unit of electrical potential—the volt. Batteries have evolved over time to become one of the most essential elements of industrial society. Virtually all transportation systems, all computers, and a multitude of other devices rely on batteries to provide power. The worldwide consumption of batteries has created an industry valued in excess of $20 billion per year.

The fundamental chemistry that makes batteries work has not changed much in the past century; however, there have been dramatic improvements in size and performance. Batteries are simply devices that release electrons as a result of a chemical reaction. The release of electrons is limited by the degree to which different kinds of chemical reactants can be created, safely contained, and controllably released. The energy storage capacity of batteries has been improving steadily. Improvements in size have been somewhat more dramatic. A Brigham Young University (BYU) team in Orem, Utah, holds the current record for the smallest battery. This team has fabricated batteries the size of a human hair. Other researchers have proposed battery designs that would exploit the voids in nanotubes to create ultrasmall batteries on the order of 10 nanometers in diameter. Regardless of whether batteries are ultimately fabricated at these scales, the materials developed by this kind of research will have a dramatic impact on battery technology, producing lighter and more efficient battery designs for common use.

Investment Synopsis

The advantage of a battery-powered nano- or micromachine is that a compact form of power can be provided at virtually any scale. Batteries can power the onboard systems of the device. Battery technology is available for rudimentary micromachines today, and can be anticipated to be available for nanomachines in the near future. While there are some small companies that may prove to be worthy investments in the near term, the companies that will ultimately be the providers of this technology are the preexisting battery companies such as Panasonic or Energizer Holdings, Inc. Smaller companies such as those affiliated with the BYU technology may have some capability to provide product for some period of time before the pre-existing battery companies acquire them. The key to investment with these companies is to time the investments carefully.

What to Watch

Battery technologies will be the first form of power systems for autonomous micromachines. Nanomaterials may revolutionize existing energy systems for conventional batteries as well as fuel cell technologies. Look for:

- Companies specializing in nanomaterials and nanocomposites
- Companies working with nanostructures and membranes
- Molecular-modeling software companies

THERMOELECTRIC

In 1821, Thomas Seebeck, an Estonian physicist working at the University of Berlin, discovered that if you connect two wires of dissimilar metals in a closed loop and heat one side of the junction while keeping the other cold, a magnetic field is created. What Seebeck did not know was that he had built a device that created a current flow, which *resulted* in a magnetic field. He was focused on magnetism and probably never fully understood what he had discovered. He went on to invent the thermocouple and made important early discoveries about the properties of semiconductors. History knows his work as the *Seebeck effect,* which is the name given to the direct conversion of heat into electrical energy. Devices that use the Seebeck effect to produce electricity are called *thermoelectric generators.*

Thermoelectric generators have been commercial products for decades. The most noted use of thermoelectric generators is in space probes, such as the Galileo mission to Jupiter. Because it uses radioactive material to generate heat, the Galileo probe received a significant amount of press prior to launch on the presumption that if the launch had failed, hundreds of square miles of the Caribbean might have been subjected to a fine dusting of radioactive plutonium-238. Instead of bankrupting cruise lines throughout the Caribbean, Galileo went into orbit and was inserted into a trajectory to Jupiter. Powered by its thermoelectric generators, it became the most dramatically successful space probe of the twentieth century. Other less controversial thermoelectric generators have found more esoteric uses in the production of power on *this* planet, especially in remote locations where power lines or solar cells are not cost effective. These generators are placed where there is a source of heat (i.e., natural gas), and are often used to power transmission and monitoring equipment in remote areas. Power ranges for commercial thermoelectric generators are from 15 to 500 watts, although commercial systems producing up to 5,000 watts have been produced.

Unlike batteries, thermoelectric power systems have the potential to provide power for virtually unlimited periods of time without any of the complications of recharging. For the Seebeck effect to work there must be a temperature difference between one side of the device and the other. As the heat flows from one side to the other, electrons are released, which provides the power from the system. The efficiency of a thermoelectric generator is based on the difference in temperature from one side of the device to the other. An average generator will produce about 30 microvolts for each degree of temperature difference. The higher the temperature difference between the two sides, the more energy is generated. If, however, the temperature on both sides of the generator is the same, there is no production of electricity. These power systems can work only in an environment where one side is hot and one side is cold.

Investment Synopsis

Size reductions of these devices are currently in process for military evaluation. Several thin-film devices (based on semiconductor fabrication methods) that generate power have been developed under contract with the
Office of Naval Research. While the power output is small and depends on
maintaining a temperature differential, these types of devices show great
promise for powering micromachines in certain applications. It is unlikely
that thermoelectric generators will find broad application, primarily
because of the requirement for high temperature differentials.

What to Watch

Thermoelectric systems have historically been the power systems of choice
in extreme environments such as arctic, desert, or outer-space applications.
Look for:

- Companies manufacturing microelectromechanical systems
- Companies specializing in nanocomposites
- Companies manufacturing specialty semiconductors

SOLAR

The sun has long been a source of energy for our planet. As a power source,
the sun predates even the most audacious inventors and therefore is named
after no one. The use of the sun for power has evolved over the past 50
years. Since 1950, the use of *photovoltaic cells,* or *solar cells,* has grown
from an esoteric, expensive endeavor suited only for satellites into a healthy
industry partnered with almost every electrical utility in the world. Since the
1970s, the cost per watt of solar electric power has dropped from approximately $500 to about $5. Solar power materials are improving, and the cost
of manufacturing is continuing its steep decline. As a result, there is a
healthy industry for photovoltaic power. As the technology has matured,
two kinds of solar power have been developed for both micro- and nanomachines. The first involves the reduction in size of conventional solar cells.
The second involves the creation of nanodevices that directly transform
light into mechanical energy.

Reduced-size conventional solar cells have been developed under a
National Science Foundation (NSF) grant. The researchers produced arrays
of individual solar cells that were each approximately 100 micrometers on
each side. The technology they employed in this development is scalable to
produce cell sizes as small as 1 micrometer. The cells developed so far are
capable of producing approximately 1 to 2.3 volts at about 2 milliamps per

square centimeter. This is sufficient power today to provide power to modest computational systems.

Solar power need not produce only electricity. A joint Japanese-Dutch university research team developed a system that produces motion directly from light. This team developed a motor consisting of 58 atoms that spins when it is exposed to light. It utilizes a rather esoteric feature of how two carbon atoms are bonded together, and when a photon of light hits the bond, the bond stretches in a manner that forces rotation of a part of the system. The reported system rotation was a phenomenal one rotation every three minutes, and it only worked above 140 degrees Fahrenheit. Although this is a remarkable solar technology, it clearly lacks the refinements of a commercial product. However, the principle of converting light into motion shows promise for some types of nanodevices.

Investment Synopsis

The technology to generate solar electrical power for micromachines currently exists. If the nano- or micromachine can work in an environment where either the sun or an alternative light source is readily available, solar cell energy systems can be made available in a fairly short time frame. The conversion of light into mechanical motion, however, remains a curiosity for the time being. Micromachine applications for solar power will almost certainly be found in a variety of military and outdoor applications. How extensive these applications are, and how profitable they will be, is highly speculative.

What to Watch

Solar devices will have relatively specialized value in outdoor applications such as mineral extraction or in outer-space applications. Potentially, such power sources can revolutionize mining and construction industries in the distant future. Look for:

- Companies specializing in nanocomposites.
- Companies specializing in thin films.
- Companies specializing in molecular engineering

STEAM

Although steam engines existed as far back as 200 B.C., using them for practical purposes had to wait almost 2,000 years until the late seventeenth and early eighteenth centuries. Early steam engines were used for a variety of locomotion and manufacturing tasks, culminating in the twentieth century with the use of steam engines to generate electricity on a global scale. Today, steam technology is the dominant means of electric power generation. It comes as no surprise that the principles of steam engine technology could prove to be useful in the power-generation systems of micromachine technology.

A steam engine is a rather simple mechanical device. It consists of four elements:

- The first is a source of heat that is capable of heating water to its boiling point.
- The second is a reservoir of water that is attached to the heat source.
- The third is a piston that will move when the water expands.
- The fourth is a condenser that converts the steam back into water through cooling.

There are many variations on steam engines, many of which do not use water. Some do not use condensers. All, however, rely on heat to force the expansion of a gas or liquid that will ultimately move a piston to do mechanical work.

Measuring only a few hundred micrometers, prototype steam engines are currently powered by an electrical source that heats a reservoir of water. Engines developed by Sandia National Laboratory's Microelectromechanical Systems (MEMS) group prove that it is possible to scale mechanical systems and still have some expectation of acceptable performance. While internal combustion engines may be lost to nanotechnology, steam engines may well be practical. This kind of technology might readily support the ability to generate both motion and electricity at the same time. This technology is best used when a steam engine is coupled with a variation of the electrical generator.

One possible means of generating both electrical and mechanical power is the *Stirling engine,* named for the Scottish clergyman named Robert Stirling, who patented a design in 1816 for a totally self-contained engine with no internal combustion or emissions. The Stirling engine, a variation of a steam engine, converts heat into motion through the expansion of a liquid or gas. As with the thermoelectric devices discussed previously, a significant temperature difference must exist from one side of the device to the other. If there is no temperature difference, the device cannot function. A Stirling engine is capable of performing direct mechanical work and could be used to power a small electrical generator. At micromachine scales, however, the generator is not likely to be a conventional generator.

In 1869, a French engineer named Zenobe Gramme invented what is called a *continuous current dynamo.* Although this was not the first device to convert mechanical motion into electricity, Gramme is credited with having developed the first device that did so with sufficient voltage and current to be useful. The basic concept behind a generator of this type is that a mechanical motion moves a magnet through a wound coil, thereby inducing a voltage in the coil. This classic electrical generator consists of a magnet spinning inside a coil. As the magnet spins, the magnetic field induces electrical flow through the coil and thereby generates power. In the simplest sense, all that is required is that a magnetic field passes through a wire, which will result in a flow of current.

When mechanical motion is possible, this motion can be coupled to a generator, which will make electricity. Traditional generators are relatively large devices with many heavy moving parts. However, the concept of magnetic storage, especially that associated with disk drives, has led to the development of a collection of devices that are capable of inducing a current flow at extremely small sizes. The current density of magnetic storage is approximately 10 billion bits per square inch, which means you can squeeze a lot of magnets into a very small space. Rather than using wound coils passing over magnetic fields, current magnetic storage technology uses either thin-film or magnetoresistive devices to determine the magnetic state of a bit. A magnetoresistive device is useless as a power generator; rather than generating a current when it passes through a magnetic field, its resistance changes. A thin-film head, however, has the property of generating a current flow when it passes through a magnetic field, which is exactly what is needed for a generator. Such devices are on the order of tens of micrometers in size, which makes them too large for nanomachines but just about right for micromachines. They could be mated with a Stirling or steam engine to provide electrical generating power, thereby providing a mixed mechanical and electrical power source.

Investment Synopsis

As discussed in the next chapter, hydraulically activated systems such as those provided by steam or Stirling engines are the most likely sources of power for leg-style locomotion. It can be anticipated that these types of power systems will be refined early and will provide a myriad of power-control capabilities for many applications over extended periods of time.

What to Watch

Steam technologies will have limited utility in specialized motion systems where alternative sources of power are readily available. The high efficiency of these systems provides a good means of converting other power sources into mechanical motion. Systems that have, for example, ample electrical power sources could readily utilize steam technologies for supplementary motion-control systems. Look for:

- Companies manufacturing MEMS, especially microfluidic MEMS
- Thin-film production companies, especially those dealing with magnetics

ADENOSINE TRIPHOSPHATE

Adenosine triphosphate (ATP) may be the most popular molecule on the planet. It is the molecule that stores energy for every living thing on this planet. When you suck down a Big Mac, it is ultimately reduced to ATP by the body. All those love handles are just nature's way of keeping ATP around for the proverbial rainy day. When that rainy day comes, ATP conveniently breaks down into adenosine diphosphate (ADP) and releases a fair amount of energy. Interestingly, after ATP releases energy and becomes ADP, if you just add sugar, you can get a reverse reaction and get your ATP back again. This energy cycle is found just about everywhere in living things.

In the case of ATP, nanotechnologists have successfully stolen the energy system from cells and put it to work. This theft owes its legacy to a strong interest in sex. As you will recall, van Leeuwenhoek was the first person to describe microorganisms when he first turned his attention to the microscope. He hesitated less than a year before wondering how it was that human babies came into being. Using a sample of his own sperm, he saw the classic oval head and tail structure. He also noted that the tail seemed to move or *flagellate*. This tail later became known as a *flagellum*. For about three centuries, it was presumed that the motion of the flagellum was analogous to the motion of a tail of a dog—that it was something that simply undulated back and forth. One day, an unknown microscopist was examining a population of bacteria that propelled themselves with flagella. He or she noticed that for some reason, several of the tails had become stuck to the slide. While this wasn't unusual in itself, what was unusual was that with their tails stuck in place, the heads of the bacteria were spinning. This prompted several biologists to deliberately stick the tails of a variety of bacteria to a variety of surfaces. Universally, if the flagellum was stuck to something, the body of the cell would merrily spin like a top. The obvious implication was that common bacteria use a *rotary* motor to rotate a fixed tail. Those who were taking pride that humans invented the wheel had to return to the mount for reeducation.

Nature probably invented the rotary motor at the beginning of bacterial life on this planet. What is even more interesting is that the bacterial motor that drives the flagellum is a system that converts ATP directly into rotary motion. Now *this* is an idea worth stealing from nature. What is most fascinating about the ATP reaction is that it is accomplished by a direct conversion of voltage into mechanical motion. When ATP becomes ADP there is a voltage potential of about 0.158 volt.[2] In theory at least, ATP could be used either as a source of electricity or as a source of mechanical motion.

Some nanotechnologists have changed hats to briefly become genetic engineers to study ATP as a source of power. Using gene-splicing techniques, several groups have successfully created ATP rotary-motor systems derived from the *Escherichia coli* (*E. coli*) bacteria that usually contribute to the digestion of food. One enterprising researcher came up with a small rotary-motor system that spins a tiny lever at several revolutions per second. His system is based on genetically modifying *E. coli* mitochondria. Although the first system took about four years to fabricate, subsequent batches produce about 10^{24} (1 septillion) little rotary-motor systems per fabrication run, all of which would fit in a beer can.

Clearly ATP power sources are possible, provided there is a source of ATP. In devices intended to work within the human body, ATP can be extracted from glucose, which exists in large quantities in the blood and every cell in the body. Using a variation on the Krebs cycle,[3] ATP-based devices could have an unlimited supply of energy as long as the host is alive.

Investment Synopsis

The practical use of ATP outside living organisms is limited. At this point, there is no commercial activity focused on using ATP to power any devices outside of a laboratory setting. One can, however, anticipate that ATP motors will provide both mechanical and electrical power to future devices. For the long-term investor, ATP technologies will probably prove the most valuable for diagnostic and medical practice.

What to Watch

Technologies based on ATP power sources would have almost universal applications in biomedical and other intrusive medical systems. When technologies are developed that can actively operate within the human body, ATP systems may prove to provide them with almost unlimited power. Look for:

- Molecular engineering companies
- Bioengineering companies
- Software companies specializing in molecular engineering

BROWNIAN MOTORS

Of all the free lunches available to nanotechnology, the brownian motor will probably be the most sought after and difficult to achieve of all power sources. The concept behind the brownian motor is that, with a proper mechanical design, it is possible to extract energy from normal brownian motion and thereby get a free infinite supply of energy (provided the temperature of the whole system doesn't drop to zero). Richard Feynman first published the concept of a brownian motor when he proposed the brownian ratchet in 1963.[4] Consider a lever pinned at one end, with the other end placed on a ratcheted wheel. If the lever is pushed by brownian motion against the ratchet wall, the lever stops. If the lever is pushed the other way, over the ratchet wall, it will slip into a new position and force the ratchet to move. Brownian motion should move the lever both ways on a random basis; however, one direction is preferred because of the ratchet. Eventually, the wheel might turn, producing free energy.

Feynmann noted that it might be a violation of the second law of thermodynamics for such a motor to actually work, but it was something to think about.[5] In fact, without violating the second law, a number of brownian motor prototypes have been fabricated, but with the predicted result that they do not quite spin as hoped. However, there are models that suggest that brownian motors can be used effectively provided the entire system does not violate the second law. It is presumed that some kind of brownian motor is used to push ions through cell membranes, although ATP conversion to ADP is also implicated in this instance. At this time, brownian motors are a far-fetched but potentially valuable candidate among the power systems available for nanotechnology. Brownian motors remain on the bleeding edge of technology and are probably best funded by tax dollars.

Investment Synopsis

The investment strategy for brownian motors can be summarized in a single word: *Beware*. There is no certainty that brownian motors can be made to work. However, if they can be made to work, they will provide almost unlimited energy for indefinite periods of time. This is definitely a technology to watch, albeit with intense caution.

What to Watch

Brownian power systems may or may not violate physical laws. The potential of these systems is unknown at this time. If they prove to be practicable sources of power, they will operate in the most advanced nanotechnologies and could be a source of power for nanomachines that operate at the atomic and molecular scales. Look for:

- Companies specializing in quantum structures
- Companies specializing in molecular engineering

SUMMARY

This chapter presents a brief overview of six different types of energy production systems. There are many other types of systems that have been and will be proposed for the production of power. In reviewing the systems presented here, it is important to note that preexisting technology is probably the best guide to predicting how these newer technologies will develop. For example, there are existing industries that are already supporting the development of batteries. Choosing to extend the size of batteries into the range of micro- and nanomachines is the kind of decision a battery company can make based on whether it wants to accept the market risk. At the other extreme, there is the brownian motor concept, where no industry exists today. Without that preexisting industry, it is difficult to make the big leap of faith necessary to face the investment required to take on the second law of thermodynamics and expect to win.

NOTES

1. This deliberately discounts the possible use of either fluidic or brownian computers, primarily because only fluidic logic devices have ever been built, and those that have been built are many orders of magnitude slower and larger than electronic devices.
2. Alternate ATP reactions are possible in the range of up to 1.1 volt. Overall efficiencies are on the order of about 42 percent, which is excellent by any standard.
3. The Krebs cycle is named after Sir Hans Krebs, who described this cycle in 1937. Basically, this is a sequence of ordered chemical reactions by which the body breaks food products down into energy supplies that can be used by the cell, such as ATP. This cycle also demonstrates how the body consumes oxygen and how carbon dioxide is excreted.
4. R. P. Feynman, R. B. Leighton, and M. Sands, *The Feynman Lectures on Physics,* vol. 1 (Reading, MA: Addison-Wesley, 1963).

5. The second law of thermodynamics basically says, "The entropy of the universe increases." What this means is that order tends to disorder, heat tends toward cold, and dense concentrations tend to diffuse. In this discussion, what it basically means is that you cannot create more energy than there is, and you are forbidden from creating perpetual motion machines or infinite power supplies.

CHAPTER 10

Locomotion Systems

For a machine to do useful work, it has to be at the place where it can do the work. A hammer is of no value if it is wrapped in a box under the Christmas tree. It has to be out of the box in your hand poised to strike a nail before it can be counted as ready to do work. Simply put, the machine has to be directed to a place where it is productive. The solution is easy for a hammer, but a little more difficult for a micromachine. This chapter explores the various mechanisms of locomotion that are available to get a micro- or nanomachine to the place where it can punch a time clock and be counted among the employed robots of the twenty-first century.

When objects get into the micrometer range or smaller, friction is no longer one of the dominant forces of nature, and motion control becomes difficult. One way of dealing with motion is to draw analogies from the biological world, where creatures swim, walk, and fly. Biological solutions vary widely among creatures and indicate a wide range of solutions that can be designed into machines. For devices that swim, analogs can be found in the tails of fish and the flagella of microorganisms. For devices that walk, analogs can be found in the legs of dogs or spiders. For devices that fly, analogs can be found in the wings of insects. Each of nature's creatures has come up with robust and powerful solutions for moving in its world. Most of these solutions can be scaled to meet the requirements of moving nano- and micromachines to their place of work.

A dust mite, for example, measures about 300 micrometers from side to side. Its leg systems permit it to walk on almost any surface, including its common home on the skin of most humans. What is clear from this example is that nature's solutions scale amazingly well from very large creatures to very small ones. The same system that works for the Alaskan king crab works equally well for the lowly dust mite. In exploring the technologies of locomotion, this chapter borrows from nature at almost every step along the way (see Table 10.1).

TABLE 10.1   Locomotion Systems

Type	Useful Application Range	Biological Counterpart
Legs	Micro- and nanomachines; propulsion in almost any environment	Spiders
Wings	Micromachines; propulsion in airborne environments	Insects
Rockets	Micromachines; propulsion in outer space	Octopuses
Tails	Micro- and nanomachines; propulsion in liquid, environments, including within the human body	*Escherichia coli*

LEGS

Approximately 560 million years ago, during the end of the Proterozoic era, animals started crawling around in the ancient mud, assisted by leglike structures. Although not terribly different in locomotion from the flatworm of today, these creatures appear to have started the long march to sentience with some kind of articulated appendages similar to legs. What is commonly called the *Cambrian explosion* (544 million years ago) resulted in at least 35 different animal phyla, many of which had clearly articulated limbs. Over time, most of the 35 phyla became extinct, joining 99.9 percent of all species that have ever lived. However, the basic leg patterns that emerged during the Cambrian explosion have remained basically unchanged to the present day. The leg patterns that have evolved appear to have morphological features that are suited to the terrain traversed by the creature. Most animals in the mammalian, reptilian, and amphibian families function with four legs, although two-legged systems go back almost 230 million years. Most members of the insect family function with six legs. A small minority of the insect family, the millipedes, functions with more than 6 legs, sometimes as many as 200. The arachnid (spider) family operates on a system of eight legs.

The advantages and disadvantages of leg counts depend on the terrain and locomotion requirements of the animal. While almost every leg design works on land or in water, as animals decrease in size there seems to be a tendency to have a six- or eight-legged preference. The overarching design of nature is one of balance, resulting in symmetrical designs in which pairs of legs are situated to balance the center of mass around the stationary support points of the legs. In robotics research, there are indications that computational power (or brainpower) is reduced as the leg count increases. However, the energy efficiency of legs tends to increase as the leg count decreases. The balance between energy efficiency and computational requirements for motion seems to direct nature's design for selecting leg counts and locomotion styles that work with these leg counts. As leg counts exceed four, there is sufficient redundancy that the loss of a leg does not end the animal's ability to move. In one sense, the spider represents the optimum balance between computational requirements, center of gravity management, and redundancy.

In the development of leg systems for micro- or nanomachines, initial leg counts will probably be based on either six- or eight-leg designs. A variety of university robotics models have successfully demonstrated that six- and eight-leg designs require less centralized control (computational power) than designs with fewer legs. In fact, enterprising readers may wish to explore six-legged robotics designs by purchasing a commercial hexapod kit.[1] There is no better way to understand how legs work than by watching the difference between a cat and a hexapod kit.

The Massachusetts Institute of Technology (MIT) Leg Lab has been studying leg designs since the 1980s. The lab has simulated and built a variety of robotic prototypes that walk, hop, and run on one, two, and four legs. The crucial outcome of this research has been an engineering definition of what it means to walk and how walking algorithms are developed. Thanks to the Leg Lab and other researchers, the physics of walking is relatively well understood.

For researchers building nano- and micromachines, the primary concern in using legs for locomotion involves the selection of a muscle system for leg motion. One outcome of current research indicates that electrical motion systems may be less robust and efficient than motion systems that are based on pneumatic or hydraulic systems. Electrical systems, for all their ecological promise, may operate too slowly at small scales when compared to alternative systems. This implies that early designs may be based on the steam or Stirling-cycle designs described earlier. However, there are several unique possible alternatives for motion control, based on recent research focused on the development of artificial muscles.

Two distinctive lines of research show promise in providing musclelike motion for small legs. The first is the use of polyelectrolite gels. These gels are a family of polymers that contract when subjected to a voltage, in almost exactly the same way as a muscle would contract. When the voltage is removed, they return to their original state. A model arm that raises and lowers has been fabricated using a gel called *polyacrylonitrile* (PAN). This gel operates at the same speed as a muscle with almost twice the strength. The second is the use of sheets of nanotubes with embedded electrolytes. In recent work by a team at Allied Signal (a Honeywell company), researchers demonstrated that a sheet of nanotubes could have a musclelike contraction when subjected to a voltage. These devices, if made practical, promise to work at extremely low voltages and very high temperatures.

Investment Synopsis

Leg systems are well understood at this time and can scale easily into the realm of micromachines, but it is unclear whether legs can scale to the sizes required for nanomachines. Significant research has been done on leg design at both obscure research labs and industrial giants such as Honda. The technology is advanced enough to go into production for products that can benefit from the use of legs. For example, logging systems currently exist that can operate on a variety of terrains where no roads can be found. Similarly, prototype military transport systems that can move through almost any obstacle course without stumbling or getting a flat tire have been demonstrated. At this time, there are no identified companies that are scaling legs to micro- or nanomachines. If commercial decisions require legs as part of a larger system, the legs themselves will pose a tremendous technological hurdle. Companies that specialize in leg designs could be good investment targets. Ultimately, such companies could be envisioned as ancillary component providers to the micro- and nanotechnology industries in the same way that tire companies are ancillary component providers to the automotive industry.

What to Watch

Early robotics systems will utilize leg technology for motion. In principle, leg systems will work in any environment and will permit both micro- and nanomachines to move freely to their destinations. Look for:

- Companies specializing in biomimetics
- Companies specializing in micro- and nanostructures

WINGS

The idea of an aircraft the size of an insect that can fly into a room and send back live video and sound is something that has excited military planners for years. Two general directions have evolved for these types of vehicles—the micro air vehicle (MAV) and airborne smart dust. The MAV project is funded by the Defense Advanced Research Projects Agency (DARPA) and has very specific goals suited toward a military environment. The basic requirement of the DARPA MAV program is to create reconnaissance aircraft with a maximum size of 15 centimeters. The airborne smart dust is a more academic approach that scales flying objects to a size of about one cubic millimeter. Between MAV and smart dust is a project at Berkeley that is focused on creating a micro flying insect (MFI) based on the body and wing plan of the blowfly. The acronyms alone may be worthy of analysis for investment.

The key problems faced by devices of this type are the problems that airfoils face when wings are small and speed is low: The traditional method of generating lift with a wing begins to fail. A simple experiment you can conduct yourself is to make two identical paper airplanes—one with a normal 8.5- by 11-inch sheet of paper, and one with a Post-it Note. You will find almost immediately that the flight characteristics of the Post-it Note airplane are extremely poor compared to the conventional paper airplane. This is because the conventional wing characteristics that generate lift are less effective as the wing gets smaller. Simply put: To fly when you are small requires a different view of aerodynamics.

Insect flight designs rely less on the lift characteristics of conventional wings and more on the turbulence characteristics of oars. From an insect's point of view, lift is much less relevant than rowing through the thick gooey mess that is air at the scale of an insect. The range of insect wing performance spans from 28 centimeters for the wingspan of the *T. agripina* dragonfly down to the *Dicopomorpha echmepterygis* wasp, which has a body length of about 0.2 millimeters, or about one-fifth the size of the proposed smart dust. As insects get smaller, the speed of the wing beat gets faster. While a dragonfly wing may beat several times per second, smaller insects can have wing-beat speeds in excess of 1,000 beats per second. If small flying devices are going to mimic insect flight systems, this kind of beat performance is an interesting challenge.

The high repetition rate required of wings tends to select different kinds of motion technologies than those required by leg systems. Legs have relatively low motion rates, especially when four or more legs are used. Wings, however, especially insect wings, have extremely high motion-rate requirements. A leg could work well at rates measured in steps per minute. A wing could require rates measured in beats per second. Therefore, drive systems for wings may require different kinds of motion actuation than those described previously for legs. One type of device that can support these high motion rates is a *piezoelectric crystal*. A piezoelectric crystal is one of 30 types of crystal, including quartz, that have the ability to expand and contract when a voltage is either applied or removed. Piezoelectric crystals are in common use in home speaker systems, where they are often used to drive the tweeter at rates up to 20,000 cycles per second. Such devices may be appropriate for driving small wing structures for insect-style flight. Unfortunately, piezoelectric devices have relatively small total expansion, which means that although they expand or contract very fast, they do not expand or contract very much. For use in insect-style wings, piezoelectric devices have some way to go.

Investment Synopsis

The first use of wings in micromachines will be in the DARPA-funded MAV arena. A variety of prototypes exist today and will evolve into operational use within the next few years. These wings will be scaled down from conventional wings and will be used to provide lift based on forward motion from propellers driven by electric motors and small batteries at the scale of micromachines (see Figure 10.1). Nanotechnology will play virtually no role in early MAV designs, although micromachine technology may play a significant role. Both large and small aerospace companies will provide MAV systems, and there is some opportunity for emergent start-up companies to play in this pond.

The use of wings for devices such as smart dust is still some years off. To date, only conceptual models exist. Insect-type devices will remain laboratory curiosities until federal agencies such as DARPA look toward advanced military applications. Opportunities will exist for small and large companies to develop a variety of technologies associated with tiny flying devices, such as spy devices, weather observation devices, or traffic-monitoring devices. The early markets, however, will be limited to the military uses that fund the research at this time.

What to Watch

Most of the early applications of the devices will be in the military sector. However, monitoring of agricultural systems and weather systems has

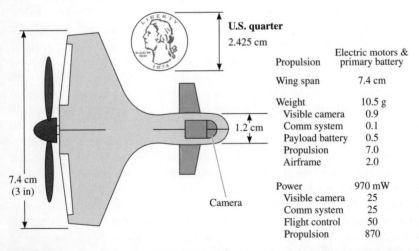

FIGURE 10.1   Massachusetts Institute of Technology Lincoln Laboratory's micro air vehicle (MAV) concept. *(Reprinted with permission of MIT Lincoln Laboratory, Lexington, Massachusetts.)*

great potential value and promise for these systems. As these technologies emerge from university settings and military research and development labs, look for:

- Companies specializing in biomimetics
- Companies specializing in micro- and nanostructures
- Companies specializing in piezoelectric devices

ROCKETS

Rockets have a biological history that goes back to the Cambrian explosion. The cephalopods belonged to one of the 35 phyla that came into the world about 538 million years ago. The cephalopods include about 700 distinct species, including the venerable octopus family. The octopus has a jet propulsion system that sucks in water and forces it out, resulting in forward motion. While the efficiency of the jet propulsion used by the octopus is a far cry from that necessary to enter low earth orbit, the system is extremely effective in escaping predators and sprint swimming. Rockets of human manufacture are first attributed to the Chinese, as early as 1045. Accounts from the era indicate that hollow bamboo rods filled with gunpowder were used in military tactics, and by the thirteenth century, rockets were an established part of the Chinese military arsenal. Although few fundamental changes have been made since the thirteenth century, development since then has focused on more efficient designs of larger rockets with greater lift capabilities. Rockets have tended to be the playground of the military and aerospace industries, and consumer uses of rockets are virtually nonexistent.

In 1979, when Ronald Reagan was on his presidential election campaign, he visited NORAD headquarters under Cheyenne Mountain, in Colorado. While there, he was informed that the United States had absolutely zero capability to intercept an incoming nuclear warhead launched from the Soviet Union. Being somewhat aghast at the national defense concept of the time, mutually assured destruction (MAD), Reagan made a concerted effort to understand the issue and its alternatives. Two studies of a potential ballistic missile defense system were completed in 1983. In January 1984, President Reagan announced to the world that the United States would embark on a program called the *Strategic Defense Initiative* (SDI), which would, upon completion, make the United States invulnerable to nuclear attack. As billions of dollars were poured into the SDI program, it became apparent that there were no easy technical solutions to stopping a swarm of incoming Soviet warheads. Simple rockets designed to shoot down simple warheads could easily be overwhelmed by the complex process of determining which of thousands of targets to aim for. In 1988, the Lawrence Livermore National

Laboratory came up with the "brilliant pebbles" concept, in which thousands, or even tens of thousands, of small autonomous space stations would encircle the globe, each with the mission of immolating itself in a kamikaze dive into the nearest Soviet warhead. When the Soviet Union self-destructed in the early 1990s, the SDI program lost significant support and went into fiscal decline.

Brilliant pebbles languished for several years before the National Aeronautics and Space Administration (NASA) revitalized the notion while examining the possibilities mandated by the "cheaper-better-faster" requirements of administrator Daniel Goldin. Suddenly, brilliant pebbles became a plausible means of creating small inexpensive satellites for a variety of purposes. At the epicenter of this research are small propulsion systems, and while none of the systems in development can qualify as nanotechnology, two types of rocket systems certainly qualify as micromachine technology. The first system is the digital rocket. The second is the ink jet.

The digital micropropulsion project, funded by DARPA, is attempting to develop extremely small rockets for propulsion and spacecraft stabilization. The intent of this program is to develop an array of small one-time-use rocket motors that can operate under digital control to provide precise increments of thrust for precision maneuvering and control of spacecraft. Several tests have already been conducted on this technology, with a high degree of success. Current plans are to increase the thrust by a factor of 10, and to increase the array size from 15 solid-fuel motors to several hundred.

A less exciting but equally promising technology is used in commercial ink-jet printers. In ink-jet printing technology, an extremely small droplet of ink is expelled with great force from a nozzle; the ink droplet then hits the paper, leaving a splotch. While the thrust potential of an ink jet is not phenomenal, it is greater than zero. If you steal some concepts from the venerable bombardier beetle, it would be feasible to use ink-jet technology to shoot droplets of a catalytic fuel into a microchamber for combustion, delivering digital thrust similar to that envisioned by the DARPA project. Several variations on ink-jet technology could prove competitive to the microrockets currently under development.

Investment Synopsis

Rockets, because they tend to have short-term use and are throwaway devices, are likely to remain the exclusive toys of the military and national space programs. While a disposable product is a virtue in companies that make razor blades, rockets will remain outside of consumer interest for the foreseeable future. Within the purview of military and space applications, microrockets clearly have a future. There is also strong interest in developing *swarms* of small spaceborne vehicles for a variety of applications. The companies that work on these technologies will predominantly be large aerospace conglomerates, although there is the potential for some university programs to spin off into specialty providers of some technologies. If spin-off companies succeed, they will ultimately be acquired or absorbed by the large aerospace companies. In most cases, these companies will be limited in their ability to be profitable by the terms of their military and government contracts.

What to Watch

Rocket systems will have value almost exclusively in outer-space applications. In cases where swarms of hundreds or thousands of satellites are needed (i.e., in missile defense systems), these types of systems will prove invaluable. Most likely, large aerospace companies will look for subcontractors to provide these capabilities. Look for:

- Companies specializing in microelectromechanical systems, especially microfluidics
- Companies working with piezoelectric materials, especially microfluidics

TAILS

When it comes to swimming, nothing works better than a tail, an instrument that has thrived in nature for at least 500 million years. And even prior to that, there is evidence of soft-bodied creatures that may have used tail-like structures to get from place to place. Early fish-type creatures used designs similar to those found on some single-celled protozoa of the era. The protozoa family of one-celled animals includes two groups—ciliates and flagellates—that utilize tails or a related structure called *cilia* for their locomotion. As seen in Chapter 9, flagella are rotary engines that burn adenosine triphosphate (ATP) for fuel, rotating at up to 6,000 revolutions per minute, providing forward or backward motion in a substance like water or blood. A spinning tail operates in much the same way as a propeller, except that at the scale of a bacterium, it is more efficient and reliable than a propeller. The hydrodynamics of flagellum-based swimming have been studied extensively, and several mathematical models exist to describe how a flagellum's rotation results in motion.[2] Tail structure, tail length, rotation speed, and flex are all factors in the success of the tail in swimming. Think of it this way: From the viewpoint of the flagellum, it is like turning a screw through Jell-O.

A flagellar propulsion system is of particular interest when considering possible micro- and nanomachines that will operate inside the human body. The ability to maneuver forward or backward is a critical component of motion. Flagella handily do forward and backward motion depending on whether they rotate clockwise or counterclockwise. Changing direction, however, requires more than the ability to go forward or backward. Going left or right or up or down is also required in the three-dimensional world of immersible micromachines. Nature provides several methods for attaining directional control. One of the simplest is to give a protozoan several flagella that are offset at angles, which permits steering to occur if one rotates at a different speed from the others. This gives directional control by providing unequal thrust to the body of the organism. An alternate means is to provide the organism with cilia. Cilia are a variation of flagella with a radically different motion system. While flagella are rotational propulsion systems, cilia function more like fins or oars, with a repetitive back-and-forth motion. In one direction, the cilia are rigid, imposing a slight thrust away from the direction of motion. When returning to the starting position, the cilia become limp and impart only a minor reverse thrust. Thus cilia, can be used for motion, although with somewhat less efficiency than flagella. However, when one places cilia on the sides of an animal or micromachine, they become an extremely effective steering mechanism.

The practical implementation of flagellar motion may hinge on stealing more from bioengineering techniques than from micro- or nanofabrication techniques. Most of the work to this point has focused on the development of flagella systems based on the genome of *Escherichia coli*.[3] The *E. coli* is a single-celled animal that finds residence in many organisms, but most commonly in your digestive tract. *E. coli* also have the honor of being in the nation's genome database. The genetics of *E. coli* have been so well mapped that the motor from the *E. coli* can be considered a prospective locomotive device for hybrid systems that use both biological and nonbiological system components.

Nonorganic systems can also create motion systems based on the flagella. Work at the Sandia National laboratory has produced prototype rotary motors that in principle can be used as a drive system for any rotary motion function, including flagellum propulsion (see Figure 10.2). These systems, although several orders of magnitude larger than flagella, and larger than the ATP engines discussed in Chapter 9, show a definite capability to provide locomotion capabilities at extremely small sizes.

Investment Synopsis

The ability to put a quasi-intelligent machine inside the human body is a high-priority objective of both micro- and nanomachine development. Locating that machine to do effective work will require submersible propulsion systems such as the tail. Flagella are the best-understood propulsion systems that will work at the sizes necessary to navigate through the human body. Chapter 9 describes how the use of ATP sparked a variety of research

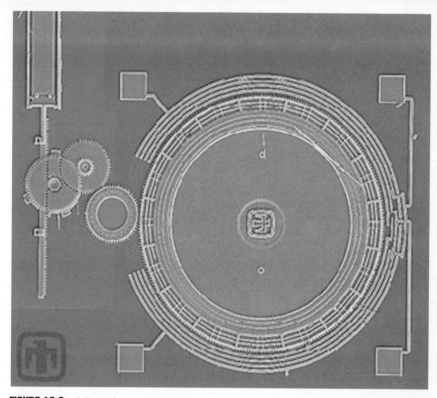

FIGURE 10.2 Microelectromechanical rotary motor. *(Courtesy of Sandia National Laboratories, MEMS and Novel Si Science and Technology Department, SUMMiT Technologies, www.mems.sandia.gov.)*

directions, including the fabrication of motors at the nanometer scale. Grafting larger flagellum motors from bacteria is definitely a relatively short-term expectation. At this time there is no corresponding industry that works with either micromotion systems or with the mixed technologies required to create tail-type propulsion systems. These technologies will emerge as a result of either university or federal research dollars or investment by intrepid souls who provide venture funds for technology start-ups. Investing in companies that provide tail motion systems for micro- and nanomachines will be risky but potentially profitable.

What to Watch

Micromachines that operate within the human body, or any fluid environment, will probably include some element of a flagellum-based tail system.

By the time these technologies are capable of being inserted into the human body, the most effective locomotion systems will likely be based on tail or flagellate structures. Look for:

- Companies specializing in biomimetics
- Companies specializing in molecular and biological engineering
- Companies specializing in molecular engineering software

NOTES

1. Hexapod kits are available from Lynxmotion, Inc, Perkin, Illinois.
2. See especially work by James Lighthill, who described the hydrodynamics of flagellum locomotion; "Flagellar Hydrodynamics," *SIAM Review* 18:161–230 (1976).
3. *Escherichia coli (E. coli)* is named for the German pediatrician Theodor von Escherich, who described the bacteria in 1879. This bacterium plays a prominent role in many discussions in subsequent chapters.

Control Systems

Choosing a brain for a small machine is not going to be an easy exercise. Not that it will be difficult to determine the *form* of the brain—what will be difficult will be figuring out the content of the software that goes *into* the brain. As any parent knows, it is not whether you *have* a brain that counts; it is whether you *use* the brain.

There is an interesting theory about why the dinosaurs became extinct. This theory is so ancient that it even supposes that dinosaurs were cold-blooded and were just a big kind of reptile. This theory of extinction is based on the interesting observation that the brontosaurus had two brains. If you examine the vertebrae of a brontosaurus, you find that the spinal column becomes suddenly enlarged just at the point above the hind legs. In fact, the space reserved for this enlargement is as large as the space reserved for the brontosaurus's main brain about 40 feet forward on the spinal column. Many paleontologists wondered why a brontosaurus would have a need for two brains. One speculation suggested that if the brontosaurus was like a lizard, then the nerve impulses traveled at about 3 feet per second, which meant that directions from the front brain to the hind legs could take 10 or 15 seconds to arrive. For a beast weighing upwards of 30 tons, it could be somewhat difficult to manage a stubbed toe, given a round-trip time of 20 or 30 seconds from the time the hind leg tripped on a tree and the time the brain registered the *ouch* and directed the foot to move up rather than forward. However, if the hindbrain had sufficient authority, it could respond to the stubbed toe and get that leg back on track before the brontosaurus caused itself significant injury. But this only explains why it would make sense to have a front brain and a hind brain. What it doesn't explain is why two brains could result in the extinction of dinosaurs.

Two brains could turn out to be fatal. Consider the idea of a cooperative system whereby the front brain controls everything forward of the stomach, and the hind brain controls everything from the stomach rearward. Normally, the front brain would send minor messages to the rear brain and vice versa, and life in the animal would be good and somewhat companionable. The front brain would get the vision and smell systems, and the rear brain would get the digestive and tail systems.

Consider, however, the following problem between two coequal brains.

A brontosaurus is walking along the Jurassic savannah idly looking for lunch. The front brain says to the rear brain, "I see a cliff up ahead, it's time to stop and consider a different direction."

Fifteen seconds pass. The rear brain having no sense of vision, but being acutely aware of an empty stomach replies, "My priority is getting a good meal. We're making good progress. I don't know why we have to stop. What's a cliff? You know I can't see. You have to explain yourself better."

Fifteen seconds pass. The front brain says, "A cliff is a sudden end to flatness. If we don't stop, we'll go over the cliff and fall to our death."

Fifteen seconds pass. The rear brain replies, "That seems kind of ridiculous to me. I've never heard of anything so silly. Are you sure we have to stop? I'm really hungry."

Fifteen more seconds pass, but by now the brontosaurus has probably wandered over the cliff into extinction.

Nature has generally limited most creatures to either one or zero brains. Perhaps the experience of the brontosaurus repeated itself many times over geologic time, but in the end, life seems to do extremely well with a brain count of less than or equal to one. In fact, when measured by the pound, the biomass of the animal kingdom has a greater preponderance of creatures without brains than creatures with them. This could bring one to conclude that a brain is not necessary in performing the functions of purposeful living; anyone who has taught several classes of college sophomores might subscribe to this opinion.

When it comes to building nano- and micromachines, however, you do need some mechanism that enables these things to do useful work. Chapter 9 discusses giving the machines the power to drive motion-control systems. Chapter 10 discusses giving the machines the locomotion ability to go places. Now, this chapter has to consider how to control where these machines go, how they get there, and what they do when they get there, without casually walking over any cliffs.

This chapter explores some of the most likely control systems that will evolve in the next few years to operate as the brains of the first nano- and micromachines. The systems are summarized in Table 11.1. The first system type, the microprocessor, is relatively well understood and is similar in concept to the desktop personal computer. The second, the analog control system, is typified by the thermostatic control systems found in houses. The third is the qubit system, which is based on the consequences of quantum mechanics.

TABLE 11.1   Control Systems

System Type	Computational Means
Microprocessor	Turing machines; computation through a series of steps with a small set of instructions
Analog control	Control systems; computation through dynamic seeking of equilibrium through continuous measurement of status
Qubit	Quantum mechanics; computation by having multiple simultaneous outcomes with a means to select the desired outcome

MICROPROCESSORS

Intel is generally credited with creating the first microprocessor in 1971—dubbed the 4004, which had a modest set of 50-plus instructions and had the ability to execute approximately 100,000 instructions per second on its 2,300 transistors. Although destined to be the workhorse of calculators, a 4004 found its way into the Pioneer 10 spacecraft that toured the outer solar system, returning the first pictures of Jupiter in 1973. As evidence for the long life of the 4004 microprocessor, the Pioneer 10 was last found broadcasting on April 28, 2001, at a distance of approximately 7 billion miles from earth. The 4004 processor is ancient by today's standards, and it covered approximately 23,000 square micrometers, with feature sizes of about 10 micrometers per transistor. Using Intel's 0.18-micrometer technology, this same 4004 capability could be placed in a space of approximately 9 by 9 micrometers, about the width of the leg of a dust mite. The current technology for microelectronics points to a clear capability to put significant computing power in extremely small spaces. The Intel 8088 microprocessor, which started the personal computer revolution, could be placed in a space of approximately 30 by 30 micrometers. Several 8088s could be placed on the back of a dust mite.

There are proposals to migrate existing circuit designs into a concept called *molecular computing*. Molecular computing is based on the idea that the individual electronic components can be fabricated from single molecules without losing any of the design rules that are used to create current microprocessors. If such a technology can be harnessed, reductions in size of another factor of a million could be seen.

At least for micromachines, computing devices have already been reduced to a reasonable size to provide the programmable capabilities required of such systems. Many current microelectromechanical system (MEMS) designs incorporate modest microprocessing capabilities along with their mechanical functions. There are, however, two fundamental issues that remain unresolved. What software do you put into these systems? And how do you link these computers to the outside world for reprogramming?

From a software point of view, there are approximately 1,000 companies worldwide that specialize in the development and sale of software for robotics and machine-vision applications. The proliferation of industrial robotics has resulted in the development of a number of standards for the implementation of software destined for motion-control systems associated with repetitive-function robots. There is, in fact, a mature software industry dedicated to industrial robotics that can, in principle, work with the processor typologies ultimately selected for nano- and micromachine controls. Most of the control-system methods appropriate for industrial robotics will scale to the robotic control requirements of nano- and micromachines. There will, of course, be additional algorithms required to reflect time-scale differences and management of motion at scales where van der Waals forces may dominate over gravity. However, within the constraints of software engineering, there are no significant issues pending regarding software for nano- and microrobotic control systems.

Reprogramming of control systems poses interesting problems. One of the fundamental issues in putting software into a computer is how to load the software. You are probably comfortable with the idea of inserting a CD or a floppy disk, or executing an Internet download to bring up a new application program. Obviously, there will have to be alternative means of getting software into the brains of microprocessors when about 1.1 million processors would fit in the same space as a conventional 3.5-inch floppy disk.

The ideal mechanism for sending software to a computer is to have another computer that downloads the software via a connected cable. This is likely to be a nasty problem for micro- and nanomachines. First, there is the issue of taking a commercial connector that has typical connector separations of about 1 to 2 millimeters, and downscaling these connectors by a factor of 1,000 to interface with the logic circuits of a current generation microprocessor. Perhaps the closest analog to this would be taking a steel I-beam, the kind used in the fabrication of the Golden Gate Bridge, and trying to plug it into your cable TV connector. Needless to say, there are some problems of scale. The issue becomes even more complex when you assume that the nano- and micromachines are actually mobile and not destined to sit still while you try to plug them in for reprogramming.

Ultimately, interconnection between the onboard computer system and the master programming system will probably require electromagnetic rather than physical connections. Use of pulsed light, radio, or magnetic fields would readily be detectable by the sensor technologies discussed in the next chapter. The protocols that enable devices to accept programming in this manner have already been developed for the universal remote-control devices sold to manage the varied equipment some folks have stacked up in the name of home entertainment. Such protocols for micromachines would probably be unidirectional. This means that while it is possible to alert a micromachine that it is time to accept and implement new programming, it will be extremely difficult for the device to let you know that it has in fact received and executed the new instructions. This will ultimately lead to a careful definition of the apoptosis (self-destruct) requirements of these machines, as is discussed in Chapter 14. Initial programming of these devices will probably have to include some set of instructions that direct that if new programming has not been received within a certain time frame, the device must go though a self-destruct sequence rather than execute potentially outdated programming. This problem is akin to that of a ballistic missile submarine patrolling out of radio contact, with only the capability to receive one-way extremely low frequency radio communications.

Investment Synopsis

Microprocessor technology is probably the best understood of all technologies associated with nano- and micromachines. For almost 40 years, the technology has followed Moore's law, which states that capabilities double approximately every 18 to 24 months.[1] While capabilities have increased, the feature sizes have simultaneously decreased. Much of this decrease in feature size has resulted in the technologies that are currently being used to fabricate micromachine capabilities. From an investment point of view, certain specialty niches exist that will be interesting to watch. For example, companies such as Microchip Technologies, Inc., that specialize in embedded control processors may be better situated to be responsive to the requirement for the smaller, less sophisticated processor designs that are required for current MEMS-based devices. The future of molecular electronics is more vague at this time. Although many molecular electronics designs exist at present, the fabrication means have yet to be found to create most of these devices. In any event, the entry barriers to marketing these technologies may be extremely costly. Typical silicon foundries required to produce state-of-the-art microprocessor designs are now exceeding $1 billion per facility. While molecular electronics may be less expensive, the absence of functioning devices of any utility does not clearly indicate that major cost savings will occur with this approach. However, current opportunities do exist in the emerging software companies that provide and will provide robotic control systems. Additional opportunities also exist in smaller companies that have software or algorithms that could be used to develop high-reliability one-way communications protocols.

What to Watch

Generally speaking, all of these technologies will evolve in the normal course of semiconductor development and research. The key investment opportunities, however, will be found in novel approaches such as those promised by molecular electronics and novel nanolithography technologies. The number-one problem for all of these technologies is how to connect these microprocessors to the human-scale systems that provide the software that must be downloaded to ensure proper computational functioning. The ultimate investment opportunity is with companies that develop technologies that interconnect devices developed at the atomic scale to devices that can interface with humans. Simple wiring systems may be the key to value as these systems evolve. Look for:

- All semiconductor manufacturing equipment suppliers
- All semiconductor materials manufacturers
- Companies manufacturing nanowires and quantum dots
- Companies manufacturing functioning molecular electronics
- Companies that manufacture MEMS with onboard microprocessors
- Companies manufacturing nanoscale electronics interconnection devices
- Companies providing software for molecular electronics modeling
- Companies manufacturing nanolithography equipment

ANALOG CONTROL

The author's father became an electronics technician during World War II at Los Alamos, New Mexico. Over the next 45 years, he became a very effective electrical engineer, managing a variety of projects, and he earned a patent or two. One day he was discussing how the industry had reengineered itself many times during his career. When he started, the standard design component was the vacuum tube. The miniature form of the vacuum tube, the nuvistor, followed this. Following the nuvistor, there was the transistor. After the transistor, there was the integrated circuit. After the integrated circuit, there was the microcontroller. After the microcontroller, there was the microprocessor. That was about the time he decided to retire. He had been through too many changes in the industry, and it was not until perhaps 20 years into his retirement that he finally got the idea of what programmability was all about.

One of the things that he used to wonder about was why the younger engineers were writing software programs to perform fairly simple control functions. Reflecting training that was unique to his generation, he wondered how it was that German V-2 rockets landed on London during the last year of World War II without a single digital circuit. The point he was making was that many control and guidance circuits exist that can perform simple functions without relying on either software or microprocessors. These functions were attained with analog feedback systems.

The concept of an analog feedback system, or guidance control system, is based on the presumption that it is possible to design and create a circuit that simulates the real world so well that the circuit operates as a complete and self-contained control system. For simple behaviors such as phototropism (which is attraction to light), circuits can be easily designed and fabricated that will control a device to the goal of seeking out light. Simple circuits like this were developed by the Germans during World War II and were later adapted for use in the guidance systems of the famous Sidewinder missile.[2] A basic guidance system can be constructed using as few as 15 components and can provide as complete a control system as any software-guided microprocessor. Similar basic control circuits have been developed for controlling leg motion, obstacle avoidance, and other biomimetic behaviors.[3] Several of the hexapod systems developed for leg-motion control use simple circuit guidance systems that contain no digital or computational components.

In the absence of a brain, nature tends to provide other decision-making means that do not require a nervous system to get things done. A white blood cell (phagocyte) does quite well in attacking and destroying bacterial invaders simply by having a chemical control system that attracts it to certain antibody chemical markers. There is no brain in a phagocyte, yet humans owe their existence to the remarkable diligence, discrimination, and constant patrolling behavior of the millions of phagocytes in the body.

When considering the concept of controlling nano- and micromachines, you do not need a microprocessor to define purposeful behavior. Rather, you need to understand what kinds of control systems are required to create desired behavior. Purposeful behavior is any behavior that delivers a known output for a known input as a result of physical design. By design, for example, a phagocyte will attack and engulf anything that has the appropriate antibody markers—the phagocyte responds to the input of the antibody marker, with the output being the attack and engulfment.

Harry Nyquist, a Swedish émigré to the United States, developed the first steps to a theory of control systems. Working with AT&T and Bell labs for most of his career, Nyquist made significant contributions to information theory and communications theory. One of his projects, in 1932, was the development of a basic model of control systems involving feedback. Nyquist's work ultimately evolved into a branch of the engineering sciences called *control theory*. Control theory is a discipline that attempts to determine the mathematics of how systems perform based on their inputs and outputs. To the degree control theory has evolved, it is a quite complete mathematical discipline. As it applies to the control systems of nanomachines and bacteria, it lacks some elements of practicality. However, control theory provides a means of determining how designers will program or motivate nano- and micromachines to perform useful work.

The easiest way to grasp control theory is to think of the thermostat in your home that turns the heat on and off during winter. The thermostat has two possible outputs—heat on, heat off. The decision to make the heat go on or shut off is determined by a calibrated coil of wire that expands or contracts as the temperature goes up or down. This system is called a *closed-loop feedback system*. When the wire contracts and turns the heat on, the increase in temperature is the feedback that expands the wire, which turns the heat off, which ultimately results in the temperature going down, which . . . you get the idea. The most important thing to keep in mind about a system like a thermostat is that Intel manufactures none of the parts. In fact, control systems need not have any computational components. Computational components are available, but they are optional. In fact, there are over 16,000 discrete circuits in the public domain that control specific kinds of behavior.

Investment Synopsis

This is an arena in which a one-person shop can make a significant breakthrough that benefits an entire industry. Many of the control systems that will be used have been developed and placed in the public domain in the past century. Novel requirements, such as coordinating leg motion or phototropic or other attractive behaviors, can be defined, designed, and patented with extremely low investment. Over time, these types of control systems will migrate from the electronic into the biochemical domain as designers mimic the complex simplicity of unicellular control systems.

What to Watch

Analog control system designs are in many respects like the length of women's skirts. One year long skirts are in, the next, out. Relatively few electrical engineers are trained in analog control systems. However, companies that recognize the value of these control systems over digital systems will be able to provide cheaper, better, and faster solutions for well-defined problems and repetitive tasks. Look for:

- Analog-design specialty companies
- Analog system fabricators
- Control systems software companies

QUBITS

One of the more interesting concepts for control systems is the quantum computer, which features the hypothetical ability to operate a billion times faster than current electronic computers, with virtually no power, in a space in which individual atoms operate as functional computational units. A quantum computer would be based on the idea that the individual components would have all possible calculations available simultaneously, due to the quantum characteristics of the components. In many respects, a quantum computer would work like a traditional digital computer. However, there are some significant differences that make a quantum computer very appealing.

Normal computer functions are based on the principles of boolean algebra, named of course after George Boole, the British mathematician who invented it and first published it in his 1854 text, *An Investigation of the Laws of Thought.* It turns out that Boole had invented the basic logic by which digital computers would ultimately operate. The basic idea in boolean algebra revolves around the notion of a *bit*, which represents either true or false. In the conventional language of computer junkies, the bit is a 0 if *false*, and a 1 if *true*. Whether the bit is true or false is referred to as the *state* of the bit; that is, if the bit contains a 1, the state of the bit is true. The next thing that is important in boolean algebra is that you can change the state of a bit from true to false, or false to true. To change the state of a bit, you perform an *operation* on the bit. The operation is usually done with a function called a *gate*. A simple example of a gate is shown in Figure 11.1.

A NOT gate turns a *true* into a *false* and a *false* into a *true*. So, if you have the value 0 presented at *A*, you get the value 1 presented at *Q*. Conversely, if you have the value 1 presented at *A*, you get the value 0 presented at *Q*.

A slightly more complex form of an operation is defined by a gate that compares two bits simultaneously. The comparison results in a single bit that represents the comparison between the two bits. Figure 11.2 shows an example of an AND gate. Here, if both values are true (1) at the inputs *A*

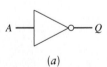

(a)

Input	Output
A	*Q*
1	0
0	1

(b)

FIGURE 11.1   NOT gate: (*a*) gate, (*b*) logic table.

Inputs		Output
A	B	Q
0	0	0
0	1	0
1	0	0
1	1	1

(a)   (b)

FIGURE 11.2   AND gate: (a) gate, (b) logic table.

and B, then the output is true (1) at Q. Otherwise, if either or both are false (0) at the inputs A and B, then the output is false (0) at Q.

The final example is a function represented by an XOR gate (also called an exclusive OR gate). The idea behind this gate is that if the inputs are different, then the output is true. If both inputs are the same, then the output is false. There is one rather special thing about the XOR gate. Although it may not be very efficient, any boolean circuit can be designed by using combinations of XOR gates. In fact, every computer design that has ever been created could be defined in terms of interconnecting XOR gates. (See Figure 11.3).

In quantum mechanics, it turns out that it is relatively easy to create an XOR gate using quantum devices. In fact, a simple two-bit quantum computer was tested in 1998 at the Massachusetts Institute of Technology.

One reason a quantum computer is supposed to operate faster than a conventional computer is because the state of the computer for a given set of inputs represents all possible inputs and outputs simultaneously. In a sense, the logic of the system is massively parallel. Rather than having a single bit of information represented by either a 0 or a 1, in quantum computer designs, the quantum computer bits (or qubits) have the characteristic of being *both* a 0 and a 1. In the context of the XOR gate shown in Figure 11.3, rather than presenting the possible combinations of A and B one at a time to determine the outcomes at Q, a quantum computer has all possible states simultaneously presented at once, with the corresponding outcomes

Inputs		Output
A	B	Q
0	0	0
0	1	1
1	0	1
1	1	0

(a)   (b)

FIGURE 11.3   XOR gate: (a) gate, (b) logic table.

also simultaneously represented at the same time. This, in theory at least, makes computational operations extremely fast.

It turns out that although quantum computers would normally be conceived to exist at the size of an atom or smaller, it is not actually the case that quantum devices *will* be that small. There is, in the realm of the nonquantum world, the ability to create relatively large objects that behave in quantumlike ways. In July 2000, a team of Dutch and American physicists reported the creation of a small quantum device holding the equivalent of one qubit of information.[4] This device may represent the first generation of quantum storage devices.

Investment Synopsis

It is unclear whether quantum computing will play a significant role in providing brains for nano- and micromachines, or whether quantum computing will itself be considered one of the accomplishments of nanotechnology. What is clear is that achieving quantum-computing capabilities is going to take a long time and a significant amount of capital. There are many small breakthroughs that are required to bring this technology to market, and few of these breakthroughs can be afforded by any but the largest research institutions and companies. Companies such as IBM, Hitachi, and NEC have ongoing research programs to develop quantum computers, and, in time, they will undoubtedly produce something fantastical. Smaller research institutions may produce some modest intellectual property, but it is unlikely that investment into this type of technology will have any payoff except for already existing computation giants.

What to Watch

Whether quantum computers are possible is still not certain. Given that the electronics can be fabricated, programming a quantum computer may be an extremely difficult task. However, if these obstacles can be breached, quantum computers could easily be the next generation of computing. Because of the highly esoteric and specialized nature of the associated physics, most breakthroughs are likely to emerge from individuals in university settings. Investors with an eye to these opportunities would be well advised to focus on university technology transfer offices and the companies that they create. Look for:

- Companies manufacturing quantum devices (memory, logic, and systems)
- Companies manufacturing nanowires and nanodots

NOTES

1. Moore's law is named after Intel founder Gordon Moore, who noted in 1965 that the capacity of Intel's products appeared to double every 18 to 24 months. The law became formulated as "Capacity doubles every 18 to 24 months." This observation has been an accurate description of the integrated circuit and microprocessor industry through the present day. It is anticipated that this will remain true at least until the year 2010.

2. The Sidewinder, originally designated the AIM-9A, was the first heat-seeking missile developed for air-to-air combat. Operationally released in 1956, the heat-seeking circuit of the AIM-9A is a model of simplicity.

3. *Biomimetic* refers to the concept that biological materials or behavior can be duplicated with nonbiological systems. For example, a plant's biological behavior of presenting the most leaf surface area to the available sunlight can be duplicated with a light-sensing circuit that drives an actuator, giving equivalent results. Such a circuit would be biomimetic. The ability to produce spider silk without a spider would be biomimetic as well.

4. van der Wal, et al., "Quantum Superposition of Macroscopic Persistent-Current States," *Science* 290(5492):773.

CHAPTER 12

Sensor Systems

When James Stockdale, Ross Perot's running mate, attended his first presidential debate, his opening words were "Who am I? Why am I here?" What was missing was the final question—"Where am I?" Perhaps Stockdale knew where he was, but knowing where one is in the world is one of the wonderful problems of epistemology. A branch of epistemology, memetics, addresses this problem. According to memeticists, you can know where you are only by sharing what you know with others who are nearby. Where you are depends on where you want to be, where you're going, and who is available to provide directions. Memetics teaches that where you are depends on your ability to interact with the people you see around you. Thus, at least philosophically speaking, to know where you are, you must be able to see.

Seeing is one of the ways that people interact with the world to determine where they are. People are presumed to have five senses—vision, hearing, touch, taste, and smell. Enterprising neurologists can come up with more than 20 senses, based on specific neurons that respond to different kinds of stimuli. Sight itself could be assigned four different senses, based on the distinct nerves used to distinguish red, green, blue (the cones in the retina), and low light levels (the rods in the retina). Seeing is not the only sense that helps people locate themselves. Other senses can tell people where they are. Touch can let them know when they have hit a wall. Hearing can help them judge distance and location to obstacles. Smell can lead them to the ancient pizza that has been left too long in the refrigerator. How many senses exist, and how they are used to guide humans through the world, is still a pending and active part of neurological research. However many senses there are, they all contribute to people's awareness of who they are, how they are doing, and where they are.

As you move away from the human experience, you find that other creatures use unusual senses to determine their location. Birds, turtles, and even some kinds of microbes may respond to subtle changes in the earth's magnetic field, guiding them in accurate migrations on a planetary scale. Other creatures, such as bees, respond to parts of the electromagnetic spectrum unseen by the human eye. A bee's ability to see in near ultraviolet detects colors on flowers that are invisible to humans but guide the bee to rich supplies of honey for the hive. Sharks can feel the electromagnetic fields of other fish and determine the pulse rate and general health of the prospective sushi.

Most senses are linked to specific kinds of nerve cells that can detect specific changes in the environment. But not all creatures see their world through their nervous system. Euglena, a single-celled animal with plantlike characteristics, will consistently move towards the light without having a single nerve cell. Phagocytes, the white blood cells in the human body, will find and attack invading bacteria and viruses without the use of a single nerve. What is common to all senses, with or without the use of nerves, is that when the sense is stimulated, there is a biochemical change that either triggers a nerve cell or causes some other action, such as digesting an invader. A sense is the means by which a stimulus evokes a response. In deference to the philosophy of B. F. Skinner, it does not take nerves or the makings of a mind to respond to the environment. The lowly amoeba would happily respond to the ancient behaviorist chantey: "What is mind? Doesn't matter. What is matter? Never mind."

Senses have a degree of complexity that can vary from extremely simple to extremely complex. A single nerve associated with the sense of touch (typically a Meissner corpuscle) is capable of sending a message of pressure. The millions of nerves in the retina are integrated to produce the sense of vision, which identifies objects and changes in the scene seen by the organism. When designers choose to create senses in machines, those senses will lack the billion-year sophistication of evolutionary history. They will, however, be very similar in many respects to the senses that have evolved over time.

Some of the senses considered in this chapter (shown in Table 12.1) have explicit biological analogs. Others *may* have biological analogs. One or more of these senses will ultimately be required for the machines to find their way to their place of work and perform the tasks for which they have been programmed. In all cases, the senses considered are those that are sufficient to answer the most basic question a machine can ask itself, "Where am I?"

VISION

Machine vision is the term used to describe the attempt to teach computers to see and act on what they see. This industry encompasses hundreds of companies offering thousands of products. Over the last 40 years, machine vision has evolved from an esoteric fad in computing science labs to a powerful aid to many manufacturing and quality-control processes. The birth of machine vision probably dates back to the early 1960s when the first efforts

TABLE 12.1 Senses

Name	Sense Equivalent	Type
Vision	Vision	Photoelectric or photochemical; usable in most microelectro-mechanical systems (MEMS) environments
Chemical gradient	Smell or taste	Chemical; usable in MEMS or nanotechnology environments, especially in medical diagnostic and repair devices
Atomic force	Touch	Various; limited primarily to precision atomic or molecular manufacturing or research

were made to manipulate images with computers. While it is difficult to determine precisely when computers started dealing with images, it is probably safe to state that around 1960, when Digital Equipment Corporation introduced the PDP-1, it became possible for computers to accept video images as input. This generation of computers included interface boards operating at up to 10 megahertz, which for the first time supported the speeds required to convert video signals into digital signals in real time. By the early 1970s, a variety of companies were working in the machine-vision marketplace to develop video-camera-based image-processing systems. These companies developed systems and software that enabled computers to look out into the world and act on the things that they could see.

Although it proved relatively easy to get computers to see pictures, it has proved extremely difficult to get computers to understand what they are looking at. For the past 30 years, most of the developments in machine vision have focused on the development of software approaches that attempt to tell computers what they are looking at. Early approaches to machine vision focused on developing algorithms that could extract knowledge from the scene that the machine was looking at.[1] These first approaches tried to determine features of a scene by finding the edges of objects and deriving shapes and locations from perspective models of possible geometric representations of the real world. More sophisticated variants of scene analysis evolved to include stereooptic analysis, in which two cameras would attempt to determine object locations derived from the parallax vantage equivalent to what would be seen by a pair of eyes (see Figure 12.1).

While significant progress has been made in developing machine-vision systems that can determine where they are in the visual world, there are laws of physics that will limit the degree to which these systems will function in the world of micro- and nanomachines.

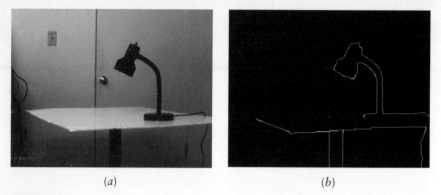

(a)   (b)

FIGURE 12.1   Stereovision reconstruction of a scene: (a) one of two stereo pairs, (b) reconstructed scene objects. Produced at the Stanford Vision Laboratory. (*From Stan Birchfield and Carlo Tomasi*, International Journal of Computer Vision 35[3]:269–293 [December 1999]. *Reprinted by permission.*)

Imaging devices are familiar in the consumer market as the chips used in digital cameras; they consist of an array of individual photodetectors. The arrays can include a few hundred to several million photodetectors. The chip is typically either a charge coupled device (CCD) or a complementary metal oxide semiconductor active pixel sensor (CMOS APS)—an integrated circuit device that includes the array of photodetectors. A conventional photodetector has an area of about 8 by 8 micrometers. Each photodetector generates a voltage proportional to the amount of light that has been absorbed. The efficiency of this conversion is called *quantum efficiency*, which is a measure of how much of the energy of a photon is converted into electrons. Typical quantum efficiency today is on the order of about 20 percent. The efficiency varies as a function of the wavelength of light hitting the detector—ultraviolet light tends to release more electrons than visible or infrared. Electrons that are released are transferred into a small capacitor underneath the photodetector, where they will later be examined for their net voltage. A typical capacitor will contain between 40 and 70,000 electrons at the end of an exposure. As the size of the pixel decreases, the number of electrons available to register information also decreases. Using Intel's current semiconductor technology, a photodetector *could* be constructed on the order of 0.2 by 0.2 micrometers in size. However, the proportional charge available after exposure, with current quantum efficiencies, would be between 0 and 40 electrons. If one somehow got perfect measurement of the voltage, the measurement would yield about 15 percent of the dynamic range used by conventional image-processing algorithms.[2]

Assuming that a detector can be made at the 0.2- by 0.2-micrometer scale, and assuming that image-processing algorithms can be constructed that work with a highly restricted dynamic range, the quantum efficiency will ultimately drop to unusable levels. A detector that is only 200 nanometers across is too small to respond to a photon of light with a wavelength of 600 nanometers.[3] The detector must be larger than the wavelength of the light to which it is intended to respond; otherwise, the probability of photoelectric conversion from photon to electron drops rapidly. It is a characteristic of the world of light that there is a limit as to how small a camera can be and still see something. Thus, conventional machine-vision approaches will work only for micromachines of relatively large sizes.

Fortunately, nature can come to the rescue again. At the micrometer scale, there are eye systems that function quite well without using conventional camera optic systems. The most interesting system is the compound eye. The compound eye shows up in the fossil record with the venerable trilobite at the beginning of the Cambrian explosion, 540 million years ago. The compound eye works by using a small array of highly directional light sensors. Each sensor is pointed at a slightly different angle, so the collection of angles covers a wide field of view to render a scene. A modern example of a compound eye is the eye of the honeybee.

The bee's nervous system is capable of operating successfully with its view of the world in spite of the fact that no single element of the compound eye sees more than a tiny portion of the total scene. Thus, a compound eye demonstrates the ability to take a picture without using the conventional lens optics of a camera. One other minor but important point about a compound eye is that it does not have to respond to light, or any electromagnetic energy. *Any* form of energy can be used to stimulate the elements of a compound eye, provided there are some data that indicate the direction of the energy source. This opens up a wide range of possible imaging capabilities. For example, at the extreme limit of nanotechnology, there is a technology called the *carbon-fiber nanotube*. In one mode of operation, a carbon-fiber nanotube can operate as a conductor that transports individual electrons from one end to the other. It is conceivable that one could construct a compound eye from carbon-fiber nanotubes that would derive an image of an electrostatic field adjacent to the eye. In the molecular realm, the proton transport mechanisms of the cell wall could be clustered together into a compound eye that would derive an image of the immediate chemistry adjacent to the eye. These examples point to the possibility that imaging can be scaled down to the smallest nanomachines, although it is unlikely that light could be used to create images with these eyes.

Systems that see with light need not be based on semiconductor-based photodetectors. Biology has provided several alternative means that are used by plants and in the light sensors embedded in eyes. These chemical means of detecting electromagnetic radiation are demonstrated by the proteins chlorophyll and rhodopsin. *Chlorophyll* is the protein that is the basis for photosynthesis. In photosynthesis, chlorophyll initiates the release of energy into the adenosine triphosphate (ATP) system of the cell by absorbing light and releasing electrons. *Rhodopsin* is a similar detector that is used in the retinas of many eye systems. Rhodopsin, like chlorophyll, releases electrons when it absorbs light. In both cases, it is possible to generate either a chemical or electrical output when the proteins absorb light at their respective resonant frequencies.[4] Mixing biological subsystems such as rhodopsin with mechanical systems may be an effective approach for some vision systems.

Investment Synopsis

At the scale of micromachines, existing vision systems can be scaled to be functional for devices that are about several hundred micrometers in size. Below that size, conventional imaging systems will not work well. Imaging systems smaller than a few tens of micrometers will be based on more esoteric technologies, some of which are only theoretical at this time. While there are reasonably sophisticated, albeit computationally expensive, methods for deriving scene information for conventional imaging systems, there are few that are more than theoretical for smaller systems. The dependence of vision on light will ultimately fail as system sizes decrease. Some techniques developed for scanning near-field optical microscopy (SNOM) have indicated that there are tricks that permit optical imaging of objects as small as 20 nanometers. These approaches may hint at the possibility of using light in nanoimaging systems. It just may prove possible to equip nanomachines with real-time imaging, provided there are significant breakthroughs in other energy-sensing areas. For the near term, however, investors would be wise to focus on micromachine vision systems rather than nanomachine vision systems.

What to Watch

While there is substantial ongoing research on systems that perform imaging, there is relatively little research as yet on the types of systems that would provide images for self-propelled devices. The commercial value at present is in delivering pictures for human use, and scaling issues are focused on bringing the data to the human eye. However, the most likely emergent technologies will derive from attempts to perform quality-control checks in semiconductor fabrication. Look for:

- Companies specializing in photonic devices
- Software companies specializing in image analysis and enhancement
- Companies specializing in microscopy, especially optical microscopy

CHEMICAL GRADIENT

The idea behind a chemical-gradient sensor is that it is possible to smell your way to your goal. Using the sense of smell to find one's way is not an unusual concept in nature. Many hunters rely on the ability of their dogs to follow a scent trail to locate game animals. A variety of sharks use scent to find their way to their prey. Ants use scent to follow the path laid down by other ants, directing them to caches of food. Most creatures that rely on scent to find their way use a single technique. When animals need to derive directional information from scent, they systematically change the orientation of their noses. If you watch a dog search for a bone, you will notice that it waves its nose back and forth in an effort to sense the direction with the strongest scent. Sharks and ants perform similar head waving in their efforts to target their food. While the details of a picture are lacking in this approach, it is extremely successful at gauging distance and direction to a target.

Successfully sniffing your way to your goal depends on being able to detect a diffusion gradient. Assume that there is an open bottle of perfume sitting in the middle of a dark room. The perfume is diffusing through the air from the bottle. Near the bottle, the smell of the perfume is very strong. As you move away from the bottle, the smell becomes weaker. The strength of the smell drops off rapidly in a uniform way from the center of the room. As you enter the room, if you have a good sense of smell, you can turn your head through an arc in an effort to determine where the smell is coming from.

In the case of perfect diffusion, as you get closer to the center, the smell gets stronger. As you move, continual testing of the odor to each side of the head will provide continuous guidance to the bottle. This technique is very effective for animals with an extremely sensitive sense of smell. Some sharks can use this technique to zero in on a target 100 meters distant, from a point where the scent—blood—has a density of 1 part in 1.5 million.

The ability to detect scent is nothing more than a biological capability to discriminate between the chemistry of various compounds. At the neurological level, a single olfactory nerve is tipped with perhaps 10 small hairs called *cilia*. Several hundred to several thousand genes, each of which represents a protein that responds to a particular chemical, encode the nerves. When a gene-selected chemical binds with the matching protein in the cilia, the nerve is triggered, producing the sensation of a particular smell.

One of the early successes of micromachine technology has been the development of chemical detectors. Chemical detectors are based on two approaches, mass spectrometry and chromatography.

The basic idea in mass spectrometry is that every chemical compound has a specific weight, determined by the weight of the atoms that make up the compound. For example, water consists of two hydrogen atoms and one oxygen atom and has an atomic weight of approximately 18.[5] This is because the weight of each of the two hydrogen atoms is about 1, and the weight of the oxygen atom is about 16. Although there is an infinite range of possible molecular weights, most molecules have a unique weight. If you have a table of molecular weights, and you can find the weight of an unknown molecule, then you can look in the table and identify which molecule you have weighed.

In chromatography, a different characteristic of molecules—their adsorption rate—comes into play. *Adsorption* is the process by which a molecule will be taken up by and moved some distance across the surface of a solid or liquid. Different molecules will be adsorbed and moved at different rates. When this happens, molecules end up at different places over time, and their location is used to uniquely identify them. Researchers at Cornell University have used semiconductor fabrication techniques to develop prototype devices that use chromatography to identify molecules and even strands of DNA. The objective of their research is to develop a "lab on a chip." The lab on a chip could consist of an array of tiny chromatographs. Each sensor in the array would be designed to respond to a different chemical. Such an array could simultaneously test for the presence of thousands of chemicals. These arrays would perform the same function as the olfactory nerve, and thereby become a micromachine's sense of smell.

The major advantage of this type of technology—nanonoses, if you will—is in the construction of machines that travel through the human body. In much the same way that phagocytes use antibodies to identify invaders, nanonoses could be the guidance systems. Devices could be programmed to detect the unique scent of cancers and follow the scent trails to the cancerous tumors. Unlike the bloodhound and shark, nanonoses will probably be placed laterally along the body of the machine to permit directional data to be generated without the head-tossing motion of biological trackers.

Investment Synopsis

Although nanonoses are likely to be years away from implementation, the techniques that will evolve into these capabilities are on the verge of useful commercialization now. The prospect of a lab on a chip has excited a number of companies that are already playing in the chromatography, gas sensor, and the DNA genome marketplaces. The ability to detect toxic gases and bacteria has a strong appeal to the military, resulting in significant funding from the Defense Advanced Research Projects Agency and other federal agencies. Commercialization of this kind of technology will probably be more useful in other arenas of chemical analysis long before it plays a role in the guidance of microbots through the human body.

What to Watch

Systems that detect smell have immediate value in military, chemical, and biological sensing applications. The entire lab-on-a-chip concept in production by some biochip companies is a direct precursor of this kind of technology. At present, however, the technology is in the single-use (use one time, then throw away) stage, except for some specialty gas-sensing devices. Multiple-use devices—that is, those that can repeatedly sample fluids without degrading—will be the most valuable targets for investment in these technologies. Look for:

- Microelectromechanical systems companies, especially microfluidics
- Biochip companies

ATOMIC FORCE

One of the dreams of nanotechnology is to fabricate devices one atom at a time. The ability to fabricate atom by atom hinges on knowing where an atom is, and where it is going to be. To fabricate at this scale, it is necessary to have some way of seeing individual atoms. Seeing an individual atom is a routine task for the atomic force microscope (AFM). An AFM uses one of two general techniques to take a picture. The first technique is called the *contact mode*. The second is called the *noncontact mode*. Contact mode is based on actually touching the surface to be imaged. Noncontact mode is based on not *quite* touching the surface to be imaged. The physics employed by AFMs includes van der Waals, electrostatic, magnetic, and capillary forces; ionic repulsion; and, in the near future, antibody biophysics. Whichever mode is used, the basic idea is to bring an extremely small probe to within about 10 to 100 angstroms of a surface. The probe is moved in a raster pattern over the surface. As the probe moves, the atomic forces either push the probe up and down or hinder its motion. The push or hindering is measured, and that measurement creates the value for a single pixel. When the scanning is complete, a composite picture of the surface emerges. An AFM can operate in virtually any domain. It can function in liquids, in vacuums, in gasses, and at extreme temperatures. The only major drawback to AFMs is that they operate more like the sense of touch than a sense of sight. The requirement to be in contact or nearly in contact with the object being imaged means that an AFM will never be able to look at anything that is just out of reach.

Investment Synopsis

Atomic force microscopes are widely accepted and come in a wide variety of flavors for specific applications. Regardless of whether AFMs are used in imaging applications for small machines, the AFM industry is growing at a modest pace and will support an ever-increasing array of applications. The ability to create embedded AFMs within micromachines is probably a near-term prospect. Since most of the technologies used to create AFM probes are based on conventional semiconductor fabrication techniques, it is a reasonable expectation that a complete AFM will be fabricated as a stand-alone chip in the near future. In the world of micro- and nanomachines, the AFM is the Braille approach to getting around.

What to Watch

There are presently a large number of companies producing AFMs and AFM-related products. As surface-imaging technology evolves, there will be increased demand for cheaper and faster AFM approaches. Technologies that would be of immediate value would be those that perform scanning of large areas at high speed. In particular, AFM arrays with hundreds of AFM probes operating in tandem would have extreme value in next-generation semiconductor testing and quality assurance. Look for:

- Microscopy companies, especially AFM companies.
- MEMS companies, especially with AFM production capabilities.
- Semiconductor fabrication equipment companies

NOTES

1. *Scene* is nothing more than a machine-vision expert's term for a digital picture. Early scenes consisted of a digital image that was 512 by 480 pixels with 256 shades of gray per pixel. The word *pixel* comes from the contraction of the words *picture* and *element*. A pixel is the smallest component composing an image.
2. *Dynamic range* is the range of signals from the weakest to the strongest. Typical gray-scale image-processing algorithms utilize an 8-bit range that has 256 possible signal strengths.
3. A relatively new technique called *scanning near-field optical microscopy* (SNOM) may be capable of producing optical images of features as small as 20 nanometers. However, the physics behind SNOM is not well understood. Further, the technique is a scanning process, and it requires that the sample be within a few tens of nanometers of the camera aperture. While SNOM can generate pictures, it cannot be used like a conventional camera.
4. Resonant frequency is the basis for color. When a material absorbs light, it does so because the wavelength of light matches the electron

wavelength in the atom or molecule. When the two frequencies match, the photon is absorbed, and the electrons are excited to a higher energy state. Photons that are reflected rather than absorbed become the visible color.

5. The unit of measure for atomic weight is also known as a *dalton*, named after John Dalton, a British physicist of the late eighteenth and early nineteenth centuries, who articulated the concept of atomic weight and introduced the principles of the first mass spectrometer.

CHAPTER **13**

Actuator Systems

To understand what a tiny machine is going to do when it gets to where it is going, you have to know what tools it has to get things done. To shape its world, the machine needs an actuator system that makes real changes happen in a real world—a way of constructing, growing, or destroying. In short, it needs some hands and a tool kit designed to work with those hands.

Approximately 2 million years ago, the ancestors of modern humans foraged on the plains of North Africa. Later they would be disparaged as being uncivilized ape-people and perhaps even cannibals but for their time, they were the most sophisticated technologists this planet had ever seen. They, like us, modern humans, learned to invest in the future, and they demonstrated this by carrying handmade tools that were carefully crafted in anticipation of tasks yet to be done. The most common and sophisticated tool was the hand axe—an early version of the Swiss Army knife. This general-purpose tool was used for cutting meat, scraping skins, chopping wood, and keeping unfriendly neighbors at a safe distance. It had no moving parts and a limited lifetime warrantee, and it came in an assortment of colors. The hand axe was a better companion than a dog, and infinitely more useful. The hand axe was so amazingly advanced for its time that after its early use by *Australopithecus africanus* (over 2 million years ago), it continued to be used in almost unaltered form by at least four species of early humans.

Tools, like species, evolve over time. A knife's evolutionary path can be traced directly back to the hand axe. In fact, it is common for archaeology field students to be handed a rock from which they must first make a hand axe, then a knife. Today's knives are not usually fabricated by chipping rocks. However, there may be a dozen variations of the knife in the family kitchen, and thousands more are available for purchase. A recent review of the Swiss Army knives revealed at least 89 different kinds of knives. There are also families of knives bearing the Swiss Army name that are dedicated to chopping, cleaving, shaping, skinning, filleting, sticking, boning, slicing, and other specialty functions. That several hundred knives are available from a single company is certainly a sign of evolutionary radiation from the venerable hand axe of our ancestors.

Early tools performed a simple function. They were created to extend the grasp of the hand and permit the shaping of the world more efficiently than can be done with fingers. Each tool was custom-made by hand, one loving chip at a time. Tools have changed a lot since the day of the hand axe. Most histories of tools focus on tools that have evolved since the industrial revolution. The industrial revolution is a relatively easy discriminator for tools because earlier tools were made by hand and were unique. After the industrial revolution, tools were made by mass-production techniques and looked pretty much the same.

History says that an American engineer named Eli Whitney invented mass production. One of Whitney's claims to fame was the cotton gin, which brought tremendous wealth to the southern states before the Civil War. Whitney's other claim to fame was the invention of mass production for manufacturing guns with interchangeable parts. In the late 1790s, the United States was on the brink of a war with France. France had undergone nearly a decade of revolution—the king was dead, democracy had come and gone, and Napoleon was about to conquer Europe. Louisiana was a French territory, secretly ceded to France by Spain, and the French had just sent troops to beef up their military might in the New World. Thinking relations with France might be somewhat shaky, the U.S. government decided to increase its military readiness by purchasing arms. Historians suggest that the U.S. government contracted with Whitney to produce 10,000 muskets. Whitney then manufactured 10,000 muskets, using the first mass-production assembly line. History usually stops at this point and moves on to other industrial giants.

What is less well known (and a good lesson for investors) is that Whitney borrowed the concept from a French gunsmith named Honoré Blanc at the specific request of Thomas Jefferson. Blanc had demonstrated this concept for the French government in 1790, showing the interchangeable parts of the 1,000 muskets he had made. Jefferson was suitably impressed and realized that in any arms race with France, muskets with interchangeable parts would be the latest technology and could determine the final victor in the coming war. Thus, he encouraged Whitney to do what Blanc had done in 1790. Whitney, unlike Blanc, did not have a working mass-production system. He staged a demonstration for Jefferson, showing that you could assemble a Whitney musket from parts selected at random from a bin, just as Blanc had done. What Jefferson did not know was that Whitney had meticulously hand-finished each part so that it was interchangeable with all the other parts in the bin. With this slight of hand—and Jefferson's failure to perform proper due diligence—Whitney got the contract and started production. Needless to say, Whitney had some difficulties. When he finally started delivering his muskets, a long eight years after being awarded the contract, the parts were not interchangeable as advertised. Fortunately, the threat of war with France had long since passed, and the muskets were never needed. Although Whitney is often credited with the first mass production, the honor rightly belongs to Blanc, as well as others who copied what they *thought* Whitney had achieved. The publicity surrounding Whitney's success convinced others that mass production was a real technology. Thus, others developed the techniques that Whitney never quite mastered, and the concept of developing tools to make tools to make interchangeable parts became standard manufacturing practice throughout the world.

With this cautionary tale in mind, the universe of tools can be divided into three categories that make the most sense for assessing the technologies of micro- and nanomachines. (Table 13.1). Because these tools will be designed to work in an automated fashion, the proper word to describe them is *actuator,* meaning a mechanism that performs a function automatically. Three kinds of actuators are of interest for investors, differentiated by how these tools make changes to their environment:

- The first type of change is *erosion,* which is comparable to the method employed by the common hand axe. By hitting, rubbing, slicing, and etching, many common manufacturing processes can be scaled down to the level of individual atoms.
- The second type of change is *genetic assembly,* which is based on the techniques employed by growing organisms. For more than a decade, biologists have been shaping new organisms from old, creating drugs and organisms that have high economic value. As their practices improve, they will create a wide variety of hybrid biological and mechanical systems.
- The third type of change is that performed by the *atomic assembler,* the ultimate dream of nanotechnologists. The assembler is a machine that actually fabricates something, one atom at a time.

Variations on these three kinds of actuators will be the hands of micro- and nanomachines.

TABLE 13.1 Actuators

Name	Use	Physical Effect
Erosion	Drilling, cutting; production of micro-channels and specialty semiconductors	Friction, etching
Genetic assembly	Enzyme and protein expression; chemical means of assembling valuable molecules and expressing or changing genetic traits	DNA and RNA modification
Atomic assembler	Nanofabrication; building something one atom at a time	Unknown

EROSION

Erosion is the process of shaping something by removing material through friction or chemical action. In the common household tool chest, a saw and drill are devices that work with friction to shape materials. In friction shaping, a cutting edge is brought into contact with the material to be shaped, and the tool is moved across the surface. As the tool moves, the friction compresses the material, forcing it to heat up and lose its internal cohesion, which pops chips of the material away from the cutting tool. When things are large (several hundred micrometers), friction works reasonably well as a shaping device. When things are smaller, on the scale of micrometers or nanometers, abrasion becomes a much more difficult process. Trying to scrape something that has a thickness of a few atoms is not a trivial enterprise. At that scale, the atomic forces become a significant obstacle to the normal process of friction. Processes that work at this scale are called *micromachining*.

Micromachining covers a wide assortment of processes that are used to fabricate parts at the micrometer and nanometer scales. This chapter describes three processes:

- The first is chemical erosion, in which a chemical (usually an acid) dissolves away the stuff you do not want, leaving the stuff you do want. The most common form of chemical erosion is a process called *photolithography.*
- The second is based on the erosion that happens when you blast a surface, blowing away the parts you do not want—*ablation.* Ablation is most often controlled by focusing an intense beam of light or ions and using the focused energy to blast away atoms from the surface until the part achieves its final shape. The most common focused-energy process uses the electron-beam ablator.
- The third process features the return of the venerable hand axe. Hitting, cutting, scraping, and chopping still have a future for humankind at the atomic scale, through technologies based on superhard materials.

Photolithography owes its roots to a Czech actor named Aloys Senefelder. Born in Prague in 1771, Senefelder failed to succeed in his father's profession of acting and resolved to become a dramatic writer. Failing to find a publisher, he started looking for an inexpensive way to publish his own work at low cost. In 1798, after many years of neither acting nor writing for a living, he discovered that he could take a flat slab of limestone, mark it with a waxy material in the pattern he wanted to print, and then use the resulting plate to selectively absorb ink, which he could then transfer to paper. He sustained himself with faith rather than royalties until his death in 1834.

A French citizen named Joseph Niepce became incredibly interested in the new and revolutionary lithographic process. Among other desires, he wanted to be an artist but lacked the talent to draw. Merging photography with lithography turned out to be his talent. In 1816, he started development of a technique by which, 10 years later, he ultimately etched a photograph onto a pewter plate from which copies could be printed. Photolithography took off at that point; over the last 175 years, it has evolved to become the methodology of choice in the production of virtually every electronic device. Today's photolithography bears little resemblance to the work of Niepce, and in many respects bears little resemblance to photography at all.

Photolithography starts by depositing a thin layer of material on a flat substrate or wafer. The layer is then coated with a liquid film of light-sensitive material called a *photoresist*. After coating, the photoresist is exposed to light in a pattern that represents the ultimate pattern desired. The photoresist is then developed in much the same way film is developed, leaving a coating where the photoresist was *not* exposed to light. The entire surface is then washed in an acid that etches away those parts of the layer where the photoresist is absent, thereby creating a pattern in the material. The photoresist is then washed off. This process is repeated many times until the final intended structure is created.

Objects of almost any conceivable complexity can be fabricated in this manner. Objects as small as 0.18 micrometers are routinely created with current photolithographic technology. The major issue in the semiconductor industry is the smallest size at which a feature can be made. Because the process is photographic, the minimum feature size is limited by the wavelength of light used to expose the photoresist. Because short wavelengths of light become more and more difficult to work with, the wavelengths ultimately become so small that you move from the ultraviolet into the X-ray range. Moving to ever-shorter wavelengths has proven to be extremely difficult. This has opened the door to alternative ways of eroding surfaces.

One alternative method is called *electron-beam lithography*. The wavelength of an electron is approximately 0.1 angstrom—at least a few thousand times shorter than the wavelength of light. This short wavelength makes the electron an excellent candidate for focusing energy in extremely small places. Electrons also can be directed and focused with a high degree of precision. A focused collection of electrons is called an *electron beam*. In the most common practical use of electron beams, the beam is focused on a region as small as 20 nanometers, where it exposes a layer of photoresist in virtually the same manner as would light. The drawback is that the transparent film used in photolithography cannot control where the electron beam exposes the photoresist. In order to expose a surface at different intensities, the beam must be swept in a raster pattern across the surface to be exposed. Sweeping a beam takes time, resulting in exposure times that are extremely long and expensive.

A variation of electron-beam lithography is *electron-beam ablation*. In this process, rather than using an electron beam to expose a photoresist, the power of the electron beam is increased to the point at which it literally blasts the target, in much the same way that a water jet cuts into a material. Again, the electron beam is swept across the surface in a raster pattern. Instead of exposing a photoresist, the beam gouges the surface until the intended pattern or structure remains. Needless to say, there are myriad alternative and related ablative approaches to fabricating small structures. However, the devices required to perform these kinds of micromachining cost hundreds of thousands to millions of dollars and tend to occupy the same space as an automobile. Clearly this is not what is needed for actuator systems. Worse, many of these processes work only in a vacuum, potentially a very unhealthy environment, which limits their applicability in many real-world situations.

Essentially, what is missing at this level of fabrication is the trusty hand axe. Something like a paring knife is needed to whittle away material and shape objects. One possible version of the hand axe is something called *diamonoid*. Diamonoid is a theoretical material made of carbon. In a diamond, the constituent carbon atoms are bonded tetrahedrally to each other. In this configuration, each carbon atom bonds to four other carbon atoms, forming an incredibly strong structure. A diamonoid is a really small diamond with more than 50 times the strength of titanium. It may be possible to fabricate a diamonoid cutting tool with remarkable strength and durability. If a means can be found to fabricate diamonoids, they could be used for a variety of purposes, including saws, drills, routers, and cutters. If you put a diamonoid tip on one of the motion-control devices described earlier, it would become a cutting tool that could precisely duplicate the functions of common machine tooling in virtually any environment. In this configuration it would be relatively easy to cut, rout, mill, drill, and saw objects into useful shapes in much the same way that a machine shop fabricates parts today. Like the hand axe of old, a single diamonoid tool would rapidly evolve into a family of other specialty tools.

Investment Synopsis

One practical achievement of existing technology is the mass production of machined parts that can be incorporated into fully assembled devices. Sandia National Laboratory maintains a lab where many of the devices discussed in this book are routinely made by photolithography. The mass fabrication of micro- and nanocomponents starts with the highly successful photolithography techniques developed for the semiconductor industry.

This industry has enjoyed hundreds of billions of dollars of development funding and has a wide breadth of experience in both operational and future technologies. At the same time, the increasing cost and technical difficulty of producing ever-smaller components are approaching both their financial and physical limits. Employing micro- and nanofabrication technologies will potentially increase the density of components while simultaneously reducing the start-up costs required to build the factories. Investing in existing semiconductor companies such as Intel offers an excellent long-term potential return. Companies that are focused on producing micrometer- and nanometer-sized components using variations on traditional machine tools may show explosive growth potential when the reality of tooling catches up with theory.

What to Watch

Most activity at this time is focused on electron-beam technologies. The major problem with these technologies is that the beam can shape only one point at a time, whereas photolithographic techniques can shape large areas with a single exposure. Electron-beam arrays are likely to be an early development; their market value is yet to be validated. Alternative lithography approaches that have the exposure times of photolithography but the precision of electron beams would be of tremendous value. Look for:

- Companies specializing in lithography, especially nanolithography
- Companies manufacturing electron- and ion-beam systems
- Thin-film production companies, especially those with diamond capabilities

GENETIC ASSEMBLY

One of the most productive assembly systems on the planet is life. The *Escherichia coli* (*E. coli*) bacterium gives one a good sense of the assembly capabilities of life. An *E. coli* will split in half and create two *E. coli* every 20 minutes if the environment is perfectly suited for growth. In a perfect bacterial environment, you would have four E. coli in the next 20 minutes, then 20 minutes later, you would have eight, and so on. If you were able to keep things going for a day or two, 45 hours after you started, the *E. coli* population would weigh as much as the earth. Fortunately, things are rarely perfect in the world of bacteria. However, the point is that the manufacturing potential of life is tremendous. Under the right conditions, a single bacterium has the potential to fabricate something the size of a planet in less than two days. If it were possible to manufacture something other than bacteria at the speed at which bacteria manufacture themselves, you might have an incredibly valuable tool. The field dedicated to achieving just these results is *genomics*. Genomics is a branch of genetics that focuses on manipulating the DNA (deoxyribonucleic acid) of organisms for commercial purposes. Genomics is of such tremendous potential that it already represents a rapidly growing $13-billion-per-year industry.

Genomics focuses on understanding and exploiting the DNA found in every living cell. Everything that lives comes with an instruction book that explains how to make each and every part, and how to put each part together. This book is written into one or more structures called *chromosomes*. The chromosome is the cover of the book; it keeps the DNA in place. A single strand of DNA is shaped like a helix; it is about 24 angstroms across and may extend up to 5 feet in length. The DNA molecule consists of an outer backbone of sugar and an inner collection of the four letters of the genetic alphabet: *adenine* (A), *guanine* (G), *thymine* (T), and *cytosine* (C). On the backbone, adenine is always bonded with thymine, and guanine is always bonded with cytosine. The coding used by DNA is the order in which the letters occur. A simple DNA fragment is read by following along one side of the helix. As you read along the helix, you come up with an ordered list of bases, such as AGTCAAGTCCA; each letter corresponds to one of the four bases. A long sequence of letters is the complete coding instructions for manufacturing a protein.[1] With this coding system, DNA does two things: It makes copies of itself, and it makes proteins.

Proteins are the good stuff. Proteins are the bricks and mortar of everything that lives. If you have to build a person or a frog, your raw materials for that construction project are going to be the proteins. Proteins are the girders, the heating system, the stoves, the closets, the water pumps, the walls, the waste disposal system, and every other constituent part of your construction project. Proteins themselves are made from combinations of about 20 amino acids.[2] Just as you can stack Legos into incredibly complex structures, amino acids can be stacked into proteins of incredible complexity. A protein can consist of a few tens of atoms or a few hundreds of thousands of atoms. The range of possible proteins and what they can do is almost unlimited. Every bizarre and interesting feature of every living creature exists because DNA made some proteins that put it all together.

What is important about DNA as an assembler is that it is a routine practice to alter the instructions on a strand of DNA and reinsert that altered strand into an organism to create new proteins. What this means is that if a protein might be a critical component of a micromachine, it is possible to modify an organism's DNA to produce that protein. Alternatively, if there is a structure that can be fabricated by a cell that can be used in a micromachine, it may be possible to alter the cell's DNA to fabricate that structure.

Investment Synopsis

Genetic engineering is of sufficient breadth to be an investment arena that stands on its own. When one searches for upcoming revolutions of the twenty-first century, genetic engineering usually tops the list of most significant. Because of the tremendous progress made by geneticists, their tools are finding their way into the labs of nanotechnologists. It is a certainty that the overlap between genetic engineering and nanotechnology will become blurred over time as both fields grapple with the same microassembly issues. In the development of actuator systems for micromachines, the hybridization of mechanical and biological components will happen only because of the successes of the genetic engineers. Investments in these technologies are generally good, provided that the specific products have reasonable markets. Keep in mind, however, that the start-up costs to get into the genomics game are high, and not every brilliant genomic concept translates into a product that will meet approval by the Food and Drug Administration.

What to Watch

There are many university programs working with mixed genetic and semiconductor technologies. At this time, there is no clear indication whether these types of technologies will result in valuable products. However, because the diversity of living organisms is so high, it is likely that novel and exciting technologies may result. Applications in mineral and metal extraction, waste management, and even generic chemical manufacturing are likely to emerge suddenly. Look for:

- Genetic and bioengineering companies
- Molecular engineering companies
- Companies providing software for genetic and molecular engineering

ATOMIC ASSEMBLER

The ultimate dream of the nanotechnologist is to create a device that can fabricate objects one atom at a time. The name given a hypothetical device with such a capability is the *atomic assembler*. This device is the touchstone of the dreams and hype of nanotechnology. Before venturing into the hows of such a device, it is important to take a look at its raw capabilities.

Assume for the moment that an atomic assembler is capable of operating at a rate comparable to the speed at which DNA replicates. This is a good starting point because the DNA replication occurs at the same atomic scale as the assembler operates, and the problems are of comparable complexity. For example, under good conditions an *E. coli* bacterium will make a copy of itself every 20 minutes. The DNA helix that is the core of the *E. coli*'s genetic material contains approximately 3.6 million nucleotides on each of the two sides of the helix. For one *E. coli* to split into two, the DNA helix must unwind and fabricate a copy of each side. This means that 7.2 million nucleotides[3] must be synthesized to create two complete copies of the DNA helix. Assuming the replication can consume the full 20 minutes, this means that DNA must be assembled at approximately 6,000 nucleotides per second. A typical nucleotide might consist of 9 carbon atoms, 12 hydrogen atoms, 2 nitrogen atoms, and 6 oxygen atoms. Thus, with a typical total of about 30 atoms per nucleotide, DNA replication operates at a rate of approximately 180,000 atomic assemblies per second, with an error rate that is astonishingly low. Now consider one of the basic concepts in chemistry, the mole, a standard number of molecules. A mole of carbon weighs about 0.012 kilograms (about 0.4 ounces) and contains about 6×10^{23} atoms. That's about 600 sextillion atoms. With an assembly rate of 180,000 atoms per second, the high-speed assembler in DNA could make about half an ounce of carbon in about 105,699,306,612 years. A billion assemblers could make that half-ounce in about 105 years. That is a long time to wait for something you can barely touch. It is pretty clear that building things an atom at a time is not going to put a nanofabricated Ferrari in every garage any time soon. The only chance an assembler has to build macroscale objects is if the assembler can be replicated at the same speed and manner as the *E. coli*. Then, perhaps, you could get enough assemblers in one place to make something large, provided the assemblers could find the raw materials.

The real value of the atomic assembler is not in its ability to build objects that can be touched or felt, but in the ability to build devices that take advantage of the quantum physical properties of individual atoms. This book often touches on the strange and wonderful things that happen in quantum physics. Computers that operate a billion times faster than today's computers are just one family of devices that could be fabricated by an atomic assembler. When the capability exists to create quantum devices out of single atoms, there must also be a means of assembling these units into functioning devices that compute—and, more important, that can communicate their answers to the plodding giants who are more comfortable with a hand axe than multistable quantum states. This means will be provided by the atomic assembler.

One of the more intriguing possibilities for the atomic assembler is the fabrication of new molecules by assembling them from their constituent atoms. The traditional approach of chemistry is to take a substance and force reactions with other substances until the target molecular structure is achieved. This is not a hit-or-miss process, but one that requires meticulous care and a rather devious ability to solve complex puzzles. If, for example, you want to make water out of hydrogen and oxygen, there are certain constraints as to how you can go about it. You cannot just put some hydrogen and oxygen in a container and expect water to pour out the bottom. You have to initiate a chemical reaction to get the water. If you initiate the reaction by, say, lighting a match, you will find yourself in an emergency room, having pieces of container plucked from your torn and mangled body. More complex compounds require even more extensive preparation and care to get the final compound. If it were possible to stick atoms to each other, one at a time, it would be possible to create a wide variety of new compounds that might otherwise be impossible to produce. An atomic assembler—or in this case, a molecular assembler—would be a powerful tool for exploring and exploiting new chemistries.

Investment Synopsis

At this time, there are a few companies focused on the issues of creating atomic assemblers. Prototype work using atomic force microscopes has proven the viability of moving individual atoms into specific patterns. The number of companies taking the assembler concept seriously can be counted on the fingers of one hand. The most prominent company, Zyvex, calmly reports that investors should have no expectations for products in less than a decade. One of the more amusing or interesting aspects of assembler work is that a number of companies and universities are developing software that will simulate the operation of assemblers. This computer-aided design (CAD)[4] software is being developed with the intent of guiding future engineers in the actual development of nanodevices. As such, the industries that should be followed consist of:

- The preexisting companies that invest in assembler capabilities
- The companies that are working on actually creating assemblers
- The companies that are developing the CAD software

The concept behind the assembler, of building objects one atom at a time, is, in the final analysis, the way nature started the universe. There is no question that the power of reducing the steps of fabrication to the individual atoms provides a precision and exactitude that simply cannot be equaled. As for investing in this kind of technology, consider that the proper role of government.

What to Watch

This is a technology that should be monitored but is unlikely to result in investment opportunities in the short term. Technologies that are developed will probably find niche markets selling to other researchers. However, when the first atomic or molecular assembler is successfully brought to market, those companies will have astounding potential. Look for:

- Companies working on self-assembled structures
- Companies working on atomic and molecular assemblers
- Companies providing software for CAD and molecular assembly

NOTES

1. A protein is a large molecule consisting of amino acids. Proteins represent 50 percent of the dry weight of a typical organism. They are the essential building blocks of everything living. In the human body, there are an estimated 30,000 different proteins.
2. Amino acids are simple molecules that are based on small molecular groups called *amino* (NH_2) and *carboxyl* (COOH) groups. Each amino and carboxyl group attaches to a single carbon atom. The carbon atom also attaches to something else, which gives the amino acid a unique character. Life appears to have about 20 variations of amino acids.
3. A nucleotide consists of three components. The first is a sugar called *deoxyribose*. The second is a phosphate group. The third is one of the four bases that make up the code: *adenine, guanine, thymine,* or *cytosine.*
4. The concept in computer-assisted design (CAD) is that a computer can completely model a physical object and all the operations that the object can perform. Such models simulate entire automobiles long before any manufacturing begins. Similarly, factory processes that manufacture automobiles are prefabricated and simulated in the computer. The CAD software for nanotechnology operates in exactly the same way as conventional CAD software, except that the units that are simulated include individual atoms.

CHAPTER 14

Disposal Systems

One of the things archaeologists love to find is a garbage dump. A garbage dump contains fragments of almost everything that comprises a civilization. Searching through the piles of junk and debris, a good detective can reconstruct a diet, study a religion, and evaluate a technology from the scraps left at the bottom of a pile of gnawed chicken bones, broken crockery, and dog-worn issues of *USA Today*. Most of the time, the archaeologists' task is to carefully map the location of every scrap and keep detailed catalogs for future analysis. Sometimes, archaeologists face more sinister and dangerous challenges. During digs through medieval ruins in London, several cases of the plague occurred when archaeologists opened the tombs of plague victims that contained still-virulent bacteria. These toxic landfills from medieval times are nowhere near as toxic as the landfills adjacent to today's modern metropolis. As modern civilization has discovered new and novel technologies, new and novel toxins have been dumped into the city landfills. As these snapshots in time are excavated, future archaeologists will know with certainty that today's garbage is more than a cross section of contemporary civilization. They will know that the care with which this society treated its landfills is a clue to the way that its people treated their bodies and themselves.

When nanotechnologists provide doctors with tiny healing machines that are inserted into human bodies, traces of these machines will be rambling around within people to the end of their days. Their bodies, in a sense, will be massive cities with waste disposal problems similar to those faced by today's landfill operators. What *do* you do with the garbage? What do you do with machines that are broken, are defective, no longer function, or have begun to malfunction? If a machine is broken, you cannot assume it will somehow work its way to a place where it can be safely disposed of. A broken machine is like a no-legged dog. Where do you find a no-legged dog? Exactly where you left it.

You cannot take for granted that every component of every micromachine is nontoxic and harmless if left to drift inside your body. Neither can you take for granted that every piece of software loaded into the brain of a micromachine is bug-free and capable of dealing with all possible contingencies. History is full of the dire consequences of software that was never fully tested. Similarly, when a swarm of micromachines is activated to perform a task and you suddenly change your mind, how do you make them stop whatever they are doing and undo whatever tasks they have already started? And how do you deal with the inevitable unforeseen accidents? What do you do when you stub your toe and crush the functional life out of scores of micromachines that were previously patrolling for rhinoviruses? How do you clear all those smashed micropower plants and brains and legs and sensors and actuators out of your body before they do you serious damage?

The nightmare possibilities of what can happen when things go wrong has been and will be the subject of books and movies for generations to come. The possibilities of converting people into neat piles of organic raw materials, or unleashing nanotermites that consume entire cities in hours, will certainly be a specter to think about. Even if you assume benevolent uses for this technology, and the highest of engineering standards, there will always be Murphy to remind you that if anything can go wrong, it will.[1] Machines go awry, parts break, programming fails, and accidents happen. When the number of possibilities is virtually infinite, trying to find solutions to handle them can be a fruitless effort. There are an infinite number of things that can go wrong with micromachines. Fortunately, designers do not have to invent what has already been invented. Once again, nature faced these kinds of problems and solved them eons ago. Nature has an incredible array of processes to manage, repair, and recover from things that go wrong. For every living thing that has a multicellular structure, there is some form of immune system. An immune system is more a strategy than a particular set of things. It is a means by which possible threats to an organism will be evaluated and attacked. The immune system can be incredibly complex, but the problems it is designed to deal with are complex, too. This planet is home to trillions of creatures, many of which are dedicated to dining on each other. If you do not not want to be someone's lunch you need a means of fighting back—an immune system.

One element of the immune system is *apoptosis,* a process in cellular biology that causes specific cells in the body to commit suicide. Apoptosis serves at least two functions. The first is in the growth of an organism from sperm and egg to fully formed infant. At various times during development, certain groups of cells become obstacles to the continued development of the organism. They conveniently self-destruct to ensure that the body develops normally. The second purpose is in the maintenance of the health of an organism. Sometimes a cell gets in trouble or becomes old or sick. When this happens, the cell—like a broken micromachine—is more of a hazard than an aid to the organism. Cells are ingeniously designed to recognize many of their own failure modes. When they enter a failure mode, in most cases cells will self-destruct. The principles of this self-destruction are simple to describe, albeit poorly understood. When a particular cell's DNA program decides that the time has come to leave this world, it may simply self-destruct, or, in a more ritualistic manner, it may activate a family of proteins called *caspases,* which initiate a complex process of suicide. One of the outcomes of a cell's decision to die is that it releases a number of "eat me" flags that signal to the outside world that it is time for lunch, and *it* is the lunch.[2] The phagocytes, otherwise known as the white blood cells, swarm around the "eat-me"-encoded cells and promptly engulf and digest them.

While the immune system is clearly incapable of dealing with all possible invaders and agents of destruction, the immune system is a model by which you can control the possibly errant effects of broken or badly programmed machines. In order to manage these processes, you need to develop three kinds of technologies:

- The first is a *taggant* technology, which is analogous to the antibody system except that it is developed for families of micromachines and permits them to identify each other and their current state of repair.
- The second is a manufacturing technology that ensures that most if not every component of a micromachine is truly *biodegradable.*
- The third is a *scavenger* technology that sweeps the body and completely excretes machine parts.

The required technologies and their biological analogs are shown in Table 14.1.

TAGGANTS

One of the problems with micromachines is that it is extremely difficult to communicate with them. In the normal world, you can communicate with

TABLE 14.1 Apoptosis Technologies

Technology Type	Utility	Biological Equivalent
Taggants	Identifying targets of disease or locations to be sought by nano- or microdevices	Antibodies
Biodegradation	Eliminating aberrant machines or machine parts from inside the body	Digestion
Scavengers	Eliminating aberrant machines or machine parts from inside the body	Phagocytes

machines with a variety of remote control devices and systems that seem to operate easily and without great expense. You can control your television without touching it, make an automobile start itself from across a crowded parking lot, or even watch remotely piloted vehicles crash into the walls and roofs of the military enemies of the day. This is old and proven technology, and one would think that you could simply make it smaller so it would fit inside a micromachine. But you cannot.

Consider a remote-control system based on radio. The problem with radio is that the wavelengths used in radio are extremely long. The wavelengths are sometimes measured in meters. To receive a radio signal, the receiver must have an antenna. An antenna is a device that resonates with a particular wavelength of electromagnetic radiation and produces a small current whenever a radio wave of the proper frequency passes through it. A radio antenna is designed for a particular range of wavelengths. A single design will not work well for *all* wavelengths. There are many different designs for antennas, depending upon the wavelength and intended use. For example, one kind of design is called a *quad antenna*. A quad antenna looks a lot like a half dozen clothes hangers bent into squares and strung along a small pipe. The size of the antenna is very important. If you want to make a quad antenna that will respond at 100 megahertz (in the middle of the FM radio dial), the ideal design that best picks up this signal is about 123 inches long. This is obviously a bit large for a micromachine. The design rules for antennas allow you to reverse the process and ask the question, at what frequency do you have to operate for a given antenna size? Suppose you want an antenna that is one-thousandth of an inch long, the size that is ideal for a micromachine, yet far too large for a nanomachine. Antenna design rules tell you that for an antenna that is one-thousandth of an inch long, the transmissions must be at about 10 million megahertz (about 10 terahertz), which is far-infrared light. At these frequencies, you are not really talking about radio; you are talking about light. The problem with light is that, unlike radio waves, it tends to be blocked by most parts of the body. Designing and building a device that is sensitive to infrared is no problem. Having it see a transmission while inside the human body is a big problem. It will not work. It is easy to conclude that radio is not going to be on the short list of technologies for roadside emergency broadcasts for micromachines.

What is needed is something that can go anywhere, night or day, and deliver a message without worrying about the frequencies of light. This something must contain all the information necessary to take action. The concept was invented thousands of years ago on early Neolithic battlefields. This traditional military information system was called the *runner*—your basic messenger. To make this concept work for micromachines, the old biological technology of the antibody must be merged with a relatively new technology called *taggants*.

Taggants were originally conceived as a way to identify the original source of an explosive by examining the residue left at the site of an explosion. The idea was that if you could find out which company made the explosive, you could trace the explosive to the person who made the bomb that caused the explosion. As a device to track explosives, taggants have a rather limited history. Switzerland is the only country that has actively embraced taggant technology for its explosives industry. Few people are as aware of Swiss explosives as they are aware of Swiss chocolates. The principle behind the taggant is that it is possible to manufacture an object that uniquely encodes an identification tag and can survive just about anything short of a nuclear explosion.[3] With a taggant, you come up with a few million particles (about $350 per pound) approximately 20 to 600 micrometers in size, all of which have the same unique pattern that can easily be recognized under a microscope. You add a bunch of taggants to a particular batch of explosive. When you make a new batch, you add taggants with a different unique pattern. When the explosive detonates, though most of the taggants will be destroyed, some will survive to be found in the residue of the explosion, telling investigators exactly who made the explosive and when. The U.S. explosives industry claims that taggants affect the performance of explosives and suggests that the destruction of an Arkansas explosives factory in 1979 was due to the effects of adding taggants to a batch of explosive called HMX. Because of this controversy, the fledgling taggant industry has migrated away from the use of taggants to identify explosives. The evolving use of microscopic taggants is in uniquely identifying other products for security and tracing purposes. A taggant in a bucket of paint sold to an automobile manufacturer, for example, can uniquely identify whose paint failed if corrosion problems occur before the car's warranty expires. Taggants can be used in a variety of manufacturing processes to provide lot traceability and material accountability. Because taggants can be encoded with a wide variety of possible patterns, each can be the key to unlock a unique set of information.

Antibodies are the biological equivalent of the taggant. Antibodies, like most things that drift through the body, are complex proteins. Their primary purpose is to stick to something—like crazy glue. With *great* oversimplification, an antibody works in three steps:

- First, the antibody wanders around in the bloodstream, bounding hither and yon.
- Second, it bounces into something that it has been designed to mate with such as a virus, and it sticks to the surface.

- Third, the fact that it is stuck to something tells phagocytes that whatever the antibody is stuck to must be bad and therefore must be destroyed.

Describing how antibodies work is beyond the scope of this book; however, there are two concepts inherent to their function that are important to understand. The first is that an antibody is a *signaling device*. It is a flag to any passing phagocyte that something is going on that needs to be investigated. The second is that an antibody works through *diffusion*. Just as a perfume spreads through the air, antibodies originate from one place and then spread throughout the body. Antibodies have no motive force; they are specially tailored molecules that wander completely at random. They become part of the immune response only when, at random, they bind to the surface of an invading object.

Now, what happens when you mix the concepts of a taggant and an antibody? A taggant is nothing more than a message with millions of possible codes. An antibody is nothing more than a scent that says "Here I am, see what I'm stuck to." At least two possible scenarios can be envisioned when the two ideas are merged. In one scenario, you have a means of reprogramming a micromachine. In the other, you have a means of identifying a defective micromachine for destruction.

As a reprogramming device, a taggant can operate like the military runner. If a micromachine sniffs out a particular antibody-like structure while coursing through the body, it can be programmed to find out what is attached to the antibody and decode and execute the message embedded in the taggant. The complexity of the taggant can vary greatly. It can be a numeric instruction keyed to activate one of the machine's sets of predefined programs. Alternately, it can be a completely new set of programs instructing the machine to perform a new task. To reprogram a host of micromachines, you would simply dump a few million tailored taggants with an attached message and let them diffuse through the body, knowing that each micromachine would eventually get reprogrammed to follow the new set of directions.

Another taggant opportunity is the case for a machine that is no longer working properly. If a machine is defective, or needs to be destroyed, the machine itself can be encoded with antibodies that can be sniffed out by other machines. The exterior of the machine can be encoded with antibody structures so that scavenger machines can uniquely identify it and destroy it if required. In the case of a defective or broken machine, the interior surfaces, which normally would not be exposed, could be coded with antibody structures that would advise scavenger machines to find and destroy the parts attached to the antibody. In the case in which the machines consist of organically digestible parts, the antibodies could actually consist of normal antibodies that would trigger the body's immune system and instruct phagocytes to find and digest the component.

Investment Synopsis

It is clear that as medical technologies evolve, finding and controlling medical tools placed in people's bodies will become increasingly important. The technologies that help doctors find and communicate with invasive machines and their parts may evolve from studies of the immune system and the diseases associated with immune-system failures. There are numerous priority disorders, including acquired immunodeficiency syndrome (AIDS), arthritis, Crohn's disease, lupus, and multiple sclerosis, which are being intensely investigated to determine how the immune system fails in each case. Understanding these failures will lead to diagnostic procedures and devices, which, in turn, will evolve into the communication systems that will lead to new investment opportunities. Investments in the related biotechnologies may be warranted, but it will be some time before direct investment in the related nanotechnology will be warranted.

What to Watch

Early commercial applications for taggant technologies are in explosives tracking and certain types of inventory and identification systems. Many of the technologies being developed for cancer, however, show promise in developing generalized approaches to marking diseased cells for attack. Indirect technology investments (i.e., targeted to markets other than nanotechnology) are the most likely investment opportunities for the next decade. Look for:

- Microelectromechanical systems companies, especially fluidics
- Taggant manufacturing companies
- Bioengineering and molecular engineering companies

BIODEGRADATION

The industrial revolution has created an aura around the machine as the basic tool of modernization. When one thinks of machines, there is a mental image of gears and motors and wires. Most of the interest in micro- and nanomachines is based on a mechanistic view of the world. People *like* the idea of tiny motors and tiny feet and tiny computers doing tiny things.

Organic things are not so interesting. People see organic things all the time. People *eat* organic things. Originally, organic chemistry dealt with chemistry that was derived from living creatures, with the corollary that inorganic chemistry dealt with the chemistry of nonliving things. Today, organic chemistry deals with just about anything that includes hydrogen and carbon in the molecule. The lines between organic and inorganic are fuzzy everywhere except in the state of California, where legislators have defined the chemistry of what is organic and what is not.

One of the assumptions about organic things is that they are biodegradable. Originally, the concept of biodegradability made sense. One thought of something as being biodegradable if it would ultimately vanish as the result of biological action. Unfortunately, this idea lost clarity when the McDonald's corporation introduced a styrofoam cup that degraded when exposed to sunlight. Matters became worse when geologists started intimating that the vast deposits of iron throughout the world may have been the direct result of the biological action of MV-1 bacteria.[4] Iron is not supposed to be organic.

For the purposes of this book, something is biodegradable if lysosomal enzymes can destroy it. A *lysosomal enzyme* is one of the constituents of the brew used to digest those varied things that are ingested by a phagocyte, or white blood cell. The trick of digestion is done with peculiarly named sacks. When a phagocyte eats an invading bacterium, it places the invader in a sack called a *phagosome*. Once inside the sack, a bundle of chemicals kept in a different sack, called a *lysosome*, merges with the phagosome sack. When the lysosome merges with the phagosome, lysosomal enzymes are released that promptly surround and destroy the bacteria. These lysosomal enzymes include noxious things like hydrogen peroxide, peroxidase, lysozyme, and a collection of other chemicals called *hydrolytic enzymes*. This concoction of enzymes will destroy just about anything that reacts with oxygen, which is just about everything. After whatever is in the phagosome sack has been reduced to organic sludge, the whole mess is dumped out of the cell.

One of the early problems of having machines roving about inside human bodies is that the immune system will be inclined to attack and destroy these machines. Initially, they will have to have *histocompatibility*, meaning they will have to be chemically inert to such a degree that the body's immune system will not immediately attack and destroy them. If you choose to make these machines from organic substances (carbon-hydrogen-based compounds), then it is possible that when you want to throw the machines away, the disposal system could be the body's own immune system. This could operate in a relatively simple way. Consider the fate of a misfortunate machine that breaks in half, or determines that its days are numbered. To trigger the digestion of this machine and its component parts, you simply have to coat the parts with antibodies. Any phagocyte that encounters an antibody-coated machine part will promptly attempt to engulf and digest the part. If lysosomal enzymes can destroy the part, then the part will in fact be destroyed.

The choice of materials used to create machine components can be deliberately directed toward materials that can be destroyed by lysosomal enzymes. It is not clear, however, whether all components required of a micromachine could be fabricated from such materials. Specialized materials such as the rare earths used in some computer components or the materials used in batteries might have no organic substitutes.

Investment Synopsis

Bioengineering companies are the primary focal point for biodegradable and histocompatible materials. Starting with dissolving stitches, these companies have been working on the development of graft and transplant materials that survive within the human body without being attacked by the immune system. Larger pharmaceutical companies have directed most of the research in these arenas, with a high degree of commercial success. A few outlying companies have started work on some of the foundations of materials research that will ultimately be used in the membranes and surfaces of micro- and nanomachines. While there is no short-term likelihood of major advances in biodegradable materials for nanotechnology, investment in companies working on histocompatibility issues has proven to be fruitful and will probably prove quite valuable over the long term.

What to Watch

It is unlikely that nanotechnology investment opportunities will be available for these technologies in the short term. However, related technologies in medical and pharmaceutical markets have extremely good upside potential. Look for:

- Companies specializing in nanomaterials and nanocomposites
- Companies specializing in molecular engineering, especially biomimetics
- Software companies specializing in chemical and molecular engineering

SCAVENGERS

Earlier, this chapter discussed the possibility that there would have to be a class of scavenger machines whose function is to remove broken or defective machines. Given that there is a means of identifying a broken machine through its release of a taggant or an antibody, there must exist some means of grabbing and disposing of the machine. There must be some kind of scavenger that can course through the body, picking up broken machines, machine parts, and any toxic residue, and not only store this garbage, but physically transport it *outside* of the body without releasing the toxic waste or injuring the host.

Perhaps one way to define a scavenger's capabilities is to duplicate the capabilities of a nematode worm. In fact, one worm in particular comes to mind, the *Caenorhabditis elegans*. *C. elegans* is a member of the nematode worm family. Fully grown, at 1 millimeter in length, it has 959 cells, of which 300 are nerve cells (some of which respond to taste, smell, touch, and temperature) and 81 are muscle cells. It has all the characteristics of a higher organism, including the ability to eat, learn, mate, and produce both eggs and sperm. Not bad for 959 cells. Its genetics consist of about 17,000 to 18,000 genes, and its genome of 100 million bases is mapped. This is an organism in which every cell is described from the moment of conception to the end of its two- to three-week life span. *C. elegans* is a venerable member of a family of some 10,000 different kinds of nematodes, many of which are parasitic in humans and other creatures. *C. elegans* normally lives in rotting soil, dining on bacteria.

Larry Niven proposed a rather unsavory idea in *A Gift from Earth* (New York: Del Rey, 1968). The idea was to genetically engineer a rotifer,[5] that would course through the human circulatory system, finding and dining on cholesterol plaques. His idea was that because a rotifer is a reasonably good swimmer and is small enough to fit in most blood vessels, it was not a big stretch to think about genetically altering a rotifer to live in blood and have it perform productive work. Where the target is a biodegradable material, a rotifer-style solution will work fine. However, if a nanomachine contains toxic materials—and a battery is a typical example of a toxic material—digesting the toxin will not remove the toxin. All the rotifer could do in such a case would be to encapsulate the toxin until the rotifer itself died and rereleased the toxin.

However, parasitic worms have a radically different lifestyle from that of a rotifer. Like Niven's rotifer, some worms are happy running around in the body's arteries. Some of these worms ultimately end up lodged in the intestinal wall, where they can find a rich supply of food. They both dine and excrete through the holes they create in the intestines. At low levels of infection, the body tolerates these invaders without any adverse consequences. Some of these worms are close relatives of *C. elegans*. They are routinely found in the digestive tract, dining and excreting material that ends up in the fecal deposits of the host organism.

This is exactly what is needed. Something that can swim through the human body, suck up all the toxic material, bore through the large-intestinal wall, and dump the waste. Whether the toxic contents might have a downstream impact on sewage-treatment facilities is beyond the scope of this work. There are members of the nematode family that could do this scavenging task, with a bit of bioengineering. An alternative approach is simply to design a micromachine that duplicates all the processes of a nematode. In this case, flipping a coin probably delivers the best long-term investment option.

Investment Synopsis

Scavenging is in roughly the same domain as the brownian motor discussed in Chapter 9. The concept borders on real science and real science fiction. Clearly, scavenging capabilities will be required before the first micromachine is injected into the first human. How the scavenger will come into being, and whether it will be a variation of a micromachine or a fully organic creature, is difficult to ascertain. From an investor's point of view, it is not even possible to invest in this kind of technology at this time, so it is safe to caution against investment in these technologies. However, the bioengineering side of the equation is a different story. In that market, research and development is approximately 30 to 50 times greater than on the nanotechnology side. Investment advice in bioengineering is not the focus of this book, but the general prognosis for investment is favorable.

What to Watch

These types of technology suffer from the chicken-or-egg problem—which comes first? Since no nanomachines are running lose in the world, there is no immediate need to find a means of controlling them. Thus, the development of technologies for their disposal has no immediate commercial value. However, the concept of bioengineering organisms has led to the development of several valuable products. As this engineering migrates, farther, from plant to animal species, the opportunities to create valuable organisms without mechanical components may provide profound and incredibly valuable products within a few years. Look for:

- Bioengineering companies
- Companies focused on genetic engineering

NOTES

1. Among the humorous tenets of engineering are Murphy's laws. Oral history suggests that these laws originated with Captain Ed Murphy, a developmental engineer for Wright Field Aircraft Lab in 1949. Oral his-

tory also suggests that Murphy's law was not actually coined by Murphy, but by another man of the same name. Examples include:

- If anything can go wrong, it will.
- If there is a possibility of several things going wrong, the one that will cause the most damage will be the one to go wrong.
- If anything just cannot go wrong, it will anyway.

2. "Eat me" flags are specialized proteins that signal to a nearby phagocyte in much the same way that an antibody directs the phagocyte to invading bacteria. There are a number of proteins used in apoptosis, including phosphatidylserine and C1q, which is used in the *complement* system of defense. Complement is a collection of nine families of proteins (C1 through C9) that the autoimmune system uses in identifying and destroying cells.

3. A typical taggant is a tiny piece of layered plastic wherein each layer is a different color. Millions of combinations of colors and layer patterns are possible.

4. The MV-1 is a strain of magnetotactic bacteria. These bacteria actually create small crystals of magnetized iron, which they use to orient themselves along the earth's magnetic field in their migratory search for food. There is persistent speculation and evidence that these bacteria created many of the earth's rich deposits of iron over the past billion years. There is also evidence that the famous Martian meteorite AHL 84001 contains hexaoctahedral iron crystals previously associated only with these magnetotactic bacteria.

5. A rotifer is a small (1 millimeter or less) waterborne animal found in most ponds and streams. It generally feeds on algae and bacteria.

Epilogue

While investment in nanotechnology may bring fantastic rewards, there is no such thing as a free lunch. Since I first started exploring the world of nanotechnology, I have followed more than 260 companies with a commitment to this field. Since 1998, 80 of these companies either have ceased to exist or have changed their focus to other markets. Those who invested in these 80 companies learned the hard way that the path of the pioneer is not always easy. While this corporate attrition rate is not unusual for a new technology, it is important to track what is happening across a wide range of opportunities and markets. New companies are always emerging. Some will become household names, while others will vanish. If this book has done its job well, you now have a body of information and a basic tool kit in hand to make an informed judgment about opportunities that did not exist a few short months ago.

As companies come and go, so do the technologies that draw the investor's focus to opportunity. When I started writing Chapter 10, the concept of an ATP-powered motor was relatively new and mostly theoretical. I was forced over a period of a few months to revise the chapter several times as new developments transformed theory into not one, but several implementations. In a field where $1 billion is spent annually developing knowledge and capabilities, change comes very rapidly and must be monitored closely.

As I put the final edits to bed, I saw a research report in the latest issue of *Science* indicating that a new form of microscopy based on quantum magnetic effects is opening the door to research on developing, and ultimately fabricating, magnetic memory devices that have bits only 5 nanometers in size (O. Pietzsch, et al., "Observation of Magnetic Hysteresis at the Nanometer Scale by Spin-Polarized Scanning Tunnel Spectroscopy," *Science* 292[5524]:2053–2056). If such a technology can be brought to market, it will be possible to store 25 *trillion* bits per square inch—the equivalent of over 5 million books in the space the size of a postage stamp. The investor must remember, however, that capability does not equate to market. Keeping a level head regarding what is possible and what can be brought to market is the crucial challenge of informed investing in growth technology.

I am certain of only one thing. Each and every human being on this planet will benefit from the technologies described in this book. Each of us will live longer and healthier lives as a direct result of investments in these technologies. In the most altruistic sense, investing in nanotechnology is investing in the future of us all. The returns will be far greater than wealth.

Excerpts from the National Nanotechnology Initiative

The following excerpt summarizes the operational plan of the U.S. National Nanotechnology Initiative (NNI), which operates under the control of the National Science and Technology Council (NSTC) and reports directly to the office of the President of the United States. With a budget of $422 million in fiscal year 2001, the NNI is responsible for coordinating federal research programs directed toward the development of nanotechnology. The proposed budget for fiscal year 2002 is $518 million.

1. INITIATIVE OVERVIEW

The "National Nanotechnology Initiative (NNI)—Leading to the Next Industrial Revolution" is part of the President's proposed fiscal year (FY) 2001 Federal budget. The initiative supports long-term nanoscale research and development leading to potential breakthroughs in areas such as materials and manufacturing, nanoelectronics, medicine and healthcare, environment and energy, chemical and pharmaceutical industries, biotechnology and agriculture, computation and information technology, and national security. The impact of nanotechnology on the health, wealth, and lives of people could be at least as significant as the combined influences of microelectronics, medical imaging, computer-aided engineering, and man-made polymers developed in this century. This new Federal investment will lead to a near doubling of the government's total investment in nanoscale R&D. The NNI incorporates fundamental research, Grand Challenges, centers and networks of excellence,

National Science and Technology Council (NSTC), Subcommittee on Nanoscale Science, Engineering, and Technology (NSET), *National Nanotechnology Initiative: The Initiative and Its Implementation Plan* (Washington, DC: U.S. Government Printing Office, July 2000).

and creating a research infrastructure—activities that are high risk, high pay-off, and broadly enabling. This initiative also addresses development of novel approaches to the education and training of future nanotechnology workers, the ethical, legal and social implications of nanotechnology, and rapid trans-fer of knowledge and technology gained from the research and development efforts. The National Science and Technology Council Committee on Tech-nology's Interagency Working Group on Nanoscience, Engineering and Tech-nology (IWGN) prepared a few publications, as listed in Appendix C [of the original NTSC NSET report], that form the foundation for the evolution of the NNI.

In 1999, the President's Committee of Advisers on Science and Tech-nology (PCAST) established a PCAST Nanotechnology Panel comprised of leading experts from academia and industry to provide a technical and budgetary review of the proposed NNI. Upon review, the PCAST strongly endorsed the establishment of the NNI, beginning in Fiscal Year 2001, say-ing that "now is the time to act." PCAST also noted the NNI has "an excel-lent multi-agency framework to ensure U.S. leadership in this emerging field that will be essential for economic and national security leadership in the first half of the next century." PCAST's endorsement to the President is attached in Appendix D [of the original report].

The Administration is currently evaluating the mechanisms to establish a national nanotechnology coordination office that would support the NNI and an external review board of experts that would annually monitor the NNI goals.

2. DEFINITION OF NANOTECHNOLOGY

The essence of nanotechnology is the ability to work at the molecular level, atom by atom, to create large structures with fundamentally new molecular organization. Compared to the behavior of isolated molecules of about 1 nm (10^{-9} m) or of bulk materials, behavior of structural features in the range of about 10^{-9} to 10^{-7} m (1 to 100 nm—a typical dimension of 10 nm is 1,000 times smaller than the diameter of a human hair) exhibit important changes. Nanotechnology is concerned with materials and systems whose structures and components exhibit novel and significantly improved physi-cal, chemical, and biological properties, phenomena, and processes due to their nanoscale size. The goal is to exploit these properties by gaining con-trol of structures and devices at atomic, molecular, and supramolecular levels and to learn to efficiently manufacture and use these devices. Main-taining the stability of interfaces and the integration of these "nano-structures" at micron-length and macroscopic scales are all keys to success.

New behavior at the nanoscale is not necessarily predictable from that observed at large size scales. The most important changes in behavior are caused not by the order of magnitude size reduction, but by newly observed phenomena intrinsic to or becoming predominant at the nanoscale. These phenomena include size confinement, predominance of interfacial phenomena and quantum mechanics. Once it becomes possible to control feature size, it will also become possible to enhance material properties and device functions beyond what we currently know how to do or even consider as feasible. Being able to reduce the dimensions of structures down to the nanoscale leads to the unique properties of carbon nanotubes, quantum wires and dots, thin films, DNA-based structures, and laser emitters. Such new forms of materials and devices herald a revolutionary age for science and technology, provided we can discover and fully utilize the underlying principles.

3. A REVOLUTION IN THE MAKING: DRIVING FORCES

In 1959 Richard Feynman delivered his now famous lecture, "There Is Plenty of Room at the Bottom." He stimulated his audience with the vision of exciting new discoveries if one could fabricate materials and devices at the atomic/molecular scale. He pointed out that, for this to happen, a new class of miniaturized instrumentation would be needed to manipulate and measure the properties of these small—"nano"—structures.

It was not until the 1980s that instruments were invented with the capabilities Feynman envisioned. These instruments, including scanning tunneling microscopes, atomic force microscopes, and near-field microscopes, provide the "eyes" and "fingers" required for nanostructure measurement and manipulation. In parallel, the expansion of computational capability enabled sophisticated simulations of material behavior at the nanoscale. These new tools and techniques have sparked excitement throughout the scientific community. Traditional models and theories for material properties and device operations involve assumptions based on "critical scale lengths" that are generally larger than 100 nanometers. When at least one dimension of a material structure is under this critical length, distinct behavior often emerges that cannot be explained by traditional models and theories. Thus, scientists from many disciplines are avidly fabricating and analyzing nanostructures to discover novel phenomena at the intermediate scale between individual atoms/molecules and hundred of thousand of molecules where the novel phenomena develop. Nanostructures offer a new paradigm for materials manufacture by utilizing submicron-scale assembly to create entities from the "bottom up" rather than the "top down" ultra-miniaturization method of chiseling smaller structures from larger ones. However, researchers are just beginning to understand some of the principles to use to create "by design" nanostructures and how to economically fabricate nanodevices and systems. Even when fabricated, though, the physical and chemical properties of those nanostructured devices are just beginning to be uncovered. Models developed for micron-size and larger devices only work at scale lengths greater than the 100+ nm range. Each significant advance in understanding the physical, chemical, and biological properties of nanostructures, and in the development of principles and predictive methods to fabricate and control them, will increase researchers' ability to design, fabricate and assemble the nanostructures and nanodevices into a working system.

Federal support of the nanotechnology is necessary to enable the United States to take advantage of this strategic technology and remain competitive in the global marketplace well into the future. Focused research programs on nanotechnology have been initiated in almost all industrialized countries in the last five years. Currently, the United States has a lead on synthesis, chemicals, and biological aspects; it lags in research on nanodevices, production of nano-instruments, ultraprecision engineering, ceramics, and other structural materials. Japan has an advantage in nanodevices and consolidated nanostructures; Europe is strong in dispersions, coatings, and new instrumentation. Japan, Germany, U.K., Sweden, Switzerland, and EU all are creating centers of excellence in specific areas of nanotechnology.

4. NANOTECHNOLOGY'S IMPACT

The potential benefits of nanotechnology are pervasive, as illustrated in the fields outlined below:

Materials and Manufacturing

Nanotechnology is fundamentally changing the way materials and devices will be produced in the future. The ability to synthesize nanoscale building blocks with precisely controlled size and composition and then to assemble them into larger structures with unique properties and functions will revolutionize segments of the materials manufacturing industry. Some of the benefits that nanostructuring can bring include lighter, stronger, and programmable materials; reductions in life-cycle costs through lower failure rates; innovative devices based on new principles and architectures; and use of molecular/cluster manufacturing, which takes advantage of assembly at the nanoscale level for a given purpose. Researchers will be able to develop structures not previously observed in nature. Challenges include synthesis of materials by design, development of bio- and bio-inspired materials, development of cost-effective and scalable production techniques, and determination of the nanoscale initiators of materials failure. Applications include (a) manufacturing of nanostructured metals, ceramics and polymers at exact shapes without machining; (b) improved printing brought about by nanometer-scale particles that have the best properties of both dyes and pigments; (c) nanoscale cemented and plated carbides and nanocoatings for cutting tools, electronic, chemical, and structural applications; (d) new standards for measurements at nanoscale, and (d) nanofabrication on a chip with high levels of complexity and functionality.

Nanoelectronics and Computer Technology

The Semiconductor Industry Association (SIA) has developed a roadmap for continued improvements in miniaturization, speed, and power reduction in information processing devices—sensors for signal acquisition, logic devices for processing, storage devices for memory, displays for visualization, and transmission devices for communication. The SIA roadmap projects the future to approximately 2010 and to 0.1-micron (100 nm) structures, just short of fully nanostructured devices. The roadmap ends just short of true nanostructure devices because the principles, fabrication methods, and the way to integrate devices into systems are generally unknown. The SIA roadmap explicitly calls for "sustained government support if this industry is to continue to provide for strong economic growth in the U.S." The lead time for science maturing into technology is approximately 10 to 15 years; now is the critical time for government investment in the science and technology of nanostructures for the hardware necessary to satisfy continuing demands in information technology. Further, the investment will have spin-offs that enable the attainment (or acceleration) of other SIA roadmap goals. The area of magnetic information storage is illustrative. Within ten years of the fundamental discovery of the new phenomenon of giant magnetoresistance, this nanotechnology completely replaced older technologies for disk computer heads, leveraging a market worth $34 billion in 1998. Other potential breakthroughs include (a) nanostructured microprocessor devices that continue the trend in lower energy use and cost per gate, thereby improving the efficacy of computers by a factor of millions; (b) communications systems with higher transmission frequencies and more efficient utilization of the optical spectrum to provide at least ten times more bandwidth, with consequences in business, education, entertainment, and defense; (c) small mass storage devices with capacities at multi-terabit levels, a thousand times better than today; and (d) integrated nanosensor systems capable of collecting, processing, and communicating massive amounts of data with minimal size, weight, and power consumption. Potential applications of nanoelectronics also include affordable virtual reality stations that provide individualized teaching aids (and entertainment); computational capability sufficient to enable unmanned combat and civilian vehicles; and communication capability that obviates much commuting and other business travel in an era of increasingly expensive transport fuels.

Medicine and Health

Living systems are governed by molecular behavior at nanometer scales where the disciplines of chemistry, physics, biology, and computer simulation all now converge. Such multidisciplinary insights will stimulate progress in nanobiotechnology. The molecular building blocks of life—proteins, nucleic acids, lipids, carbohydrates and their non-biological mimics—are examples of materials that possess unique properties determined by their size, folding, and patterns at the nanoscale. Recent insights into the uses of nanofabricated devices and systems suggest that today's laborious process of genome sequencing and detecting the genes' expression can be made dramatically more efficient through utilization of nanofabricated surfaces and devices. Expanding our ability to characterize an individual's genetic makeup will revolutionize the specificity of diagnostics and therapeutics. Beyond facilitating optimal drug usage, nanotechnology can provide new formulations and routes for drug delivery, enormously broadening their therapeutic potential. Increasing nanotechnological capabilities will also markedly benefit basic studies of cell biology and pathology. As a result of the development of new analytical tools capable of probing the world of the nanometer, it is becoming increasingly possible to characterize the chemical and mechanical properties of cells (including processes such as cell division and locomotion) and to measure properties of single molecules. These capabilities thus complement (and largely supplant) the ensemble average techniques presently used in the life sciences. Moreover, biocompatible, high-performance materials will result from controlling their nanostructure. Proteins, nucleic acids, and lipids, or their nonbiological mimics, are example of materials that have been shown to possess unique properties as a function of their size, folding, and patterns. Based on these biological principles, bio-inspired nanosystems and materials are currently being formed by self-assembly or other patterning methods. Artificial inorganic and organic nanoscale materials can be introduced into cells to play roles in diagnostics (e.g., quantum dots in visualization), but also potentially as active components. Finally, nanotechnology-enabled increases in computational power will permit the characterization of macromolecular networks in realistic environments. Such simulations will be essential in developing biocompatible implants and in the drug discovery process. Potential applications include (a) rapid, more efficient genome sequencing enabling a revolution in diagnostics and therapeutics; (b) effective and less expensive health care using remote and in-vivo devices; (c) new formulations and routes for drug delivery that enormously broaden their therapeutic potential by targeting the delivery of new types of medicine to previously inaccessible sites in the body; (d) more durable rejection-resistant artificial tissues and organs; (e) enable vision and hearing aids; and (f) sensor systems that detect emerging disease in the body, which will ultimately shift the focus of patient care from disease treatment to early detection and prevention.

Aeronautics and Space Exploration

The stringent fuel constraints for lifting payloads into earth orbit and beyond, and the desire to send spacecraft away from the sun (diminished solar power) for extended missions, compel continued reduction in size, weight, and power consumption of payloads. Nanostructured materials and devices promise solutions to these challenges. Nanostructuring is also critical to design and manufacture of lightweight, high-strength, thermally stable materials for planes, rockets, space stations, and planetary/solar exploratory platforms. Moreover, the low-gravity, high-vacuum space environment may aid development of nanostructures and nanoscale systems that cannot be created on Earth. Applications include (a) low-power, radiation-tolerant, high performance computers; (b) nano-instrumentation for microspacecraft; (c) avionics made possible by nanostructured sensors and nanoelectronics; and (d) thermal barrier and wear-resistant nanostructured coatings.

Environment and Energy

Nanotechnology has the potential to significantly impact energy efficiency, storage, and production. It can be used to monitor and remediate environmental problems; curb emissions from a wide range of sources; and develop new, "green" processing technologies that minimize the generation of undesirable by-product effluents. The impact on industrial control, manufacturing, and processing will be impressive and result in energy savings through market driven practices. Several new technologies that utilize the power of nanostructuring but developed without benefit of the new nanoscale analytical capabilities, illustrate this potential: (a) a long-term research program in the chemical industry into the use of crystalline materials as catalyst supports has yielded catalysts with well-defined pore sizes in the range of 1 nm; their use is now the basis of an industry that exceeds $30 billion/year; (b) the discovery of the ordered mesoporous material MCM-41 produced by oil industry, with pore sizes in the range of 10–100 nm, is now widely applied in removal of ultrafine contaminants; (c) several chemical manufacturing companies are developing a nanoparticle-reinforced polymeric material that can replace structural metallic components in the auto industry; widespread use of those nanocomposites could lead to a reduction of 1.5 billion liters of gasoline consumption over the life of one year's production of vehicles and reduce related carbon dioxide emissions annually by more than 5 billion kilograms; and (d) the replacement of carbon black in tires by nanometer-scale particles of inorganic clays and polymers is a new technology that is leading to the production of environmentally friendly, wear-resistant tires. Potential future breakthroughs also include use of nanorobotics and intelligent systems for environmental and nuclear waste management, use of nanofilters to separate isotopes in nuclear fuel processing, of nanofluids for increased cooling efficiency of nuclear reactors, of nanopowders for decontamination, and of computer simulation at nanoscale for nuclear safety.

Biotechnology and Agriculture

The molecular building blocks of life—proteins, nucleic acids, lipids, carbohydrates and their non-biological mimics—are examples of materials that possess unique properties determined by their size, folding and patterns at the nanoscale. Biosynthesis and bioprocessing offer fundamentally new ways to manufacture new chemicals and pharmaceutical products. Integration of biological building blocks into synthetic materials and devices will allow the combination of biological functions with other desirable materials properties. Imitation of biological systems provides a major area of research in several disciplines. For example, the active area of bio-mimetic chemistry is based on this approach. Nanoscience will contribute directly to advancements in agriculture in a number of ways: molecular-engineered biodegradable chemicals for nourishing the plants and protecting against insects; genetic improvement for animals and plants; delivery of genes and drugs to animals; and nanoarray-based testing technologies for DNA testing. For example, such array-base technologies will allow a plant scientist to know which genes are expressed in a plant when its is exposed to salt or drought stress. The application of nanotechnology in agriculture has only begun to be appreciated.

National Security

The Department of Defense recognized the importance of nanostructures over a decade ago and has played a significant role in nurturing the field. Critical defense applications include (a) continued information dominance through advanced nanoelectronics, identified as an important capability for the military; (b) more sophisticated virtual reality systems based on nanostructured electronics that enable more affordable, effective training; (c) increased use of enhanced automation and robotics to offset reductions in military manpower, reduce risks to troops, and improve vehicle performance; for example, several thousand pounds could be stripped from a pilotless fighter aircraft, resulting in longer missions, and fighter agility could be dramatically improved without the necessity to limit g-forces on the pilot, thus increasing combat effectiveness; (d) achievement of the higher performance (lighter weight, higher strength) needed in military platforms while simultaneously providing diminished failure rates and lower life-cycle costs; (e) badly needed improvements in chemical/biological/nuclear sensing and in casualty care; (f) design improvements of systems used for nuclear non-proliferation monitoring and management; and (g) combined nano and micromechanical devices for control of nuclear defense systems.

Other Potential Government Applications

Nanoscience and technology can benefit other Government agency missions, including (a) lighter and safer equipment in transportation systems; (b) measurement, control, and remediation of contaminants; (c) enhanced forensic research (Department of Justice, DOJ); and (d) printing and engraving of high quality, forgery-proof documents and currency (Bureau of Engraving and Printing, BEP).

Science and Education

Advances in nanoscale science, engineering, and technology will require and enable advances in many disciplines: physics, chemistry, biology, materials, mathematics, and engineering. The dynamics of these interdisciplinary nanoscale research efforts will reinforce educational connections among disciplines and give birth to new fields that are only envisioned at this moment. The interdisciplinary nature of nanoscale science, engineering, and technology requires changes in how students and professionals are educated and trained for careers in these fields.

Future U.S. Competitiveness

Technology is the major driving factor for growth at every level of the U.S. economy. Nanotechnology is expected to be pervasive in its applications across nearly all technologies. Investment in nanotechnology research and development is necessary to maintain and improve our position in the world marketplace. A national nanotechnology initiative will allow the development of critical enabling technologies with broad commercial potential, such as nanoelectronics, nanostructured materials and nanoscale-based manufacturing processes. These are necessary for U.S. industry to take advantage of nanotechnology innovations.

5. INVESTMENT OPPORTUNITIES

Need for Investment

Nanoscale scientific, engineering, and technical knowledge is exploding worldwide. It is being made possible by the availability of new investigative tools, synergies created through an interdisciplinary approach, rapid dissemination of results, and driven by emerging technologies and their applications. With sustained investment, the number of revolutionary discoveries reported in nanotechnology can be expected to accelerate in the next decade; these are likely to profoundly affect existing and emerging technologies in almost all industry sectors and application areas. Over the past few years, it has become evident that there is a clear need for Federal support to create a balanced infrastructure for nanoscale science, engineering, technology and human resources development, and to address critical areas of research. The field is highly competitive and dynamic in the international arena. The time now appears right for the nation to establish a significant R&D initiative to support nanotechnology.

Federal Government expenditure for nanotechnology in FY 1997 was approximately $116 million, according to the 1998 WTEC report *"R&D Status and Trends in Nanoparticles, Nanostructured Materials, and Nanodevices in the United States"* (NTIS Report PB98-117914). Nanotechnology as defined there only included work to generate and use nanostructures and nanodevices; it did not include the simple observation and description of phenomena at the nanoscale. Utilizing the broader definition, the Federal Government expenditure is estimated to be about $270 million for FY 2000. A much greater investment could be utilized effectively. There are signs of a significant increase in interest within the research community. For example, the funding success rate for the small-group interdisciplinary research program, FY 1998 NSF "Functional Nanostructures" initiative, was about 13% (lower, if one considers the limitation of two proposals per university). The success rate for the DOD 1998 MURI initiative on nanostructures was 17% (5%, if one starts with the number of white papers submitted to guide proposal development). In both instances, the level of funding available limited the funding success rate. There were more meritorious proposals than could be supported at that time.

The promises of nanotechnology can best be realized through long term and balanced investment in U.S. infrastructure and human resources in five R&D categories in particular: (1) Nanostructure *properties:* Develop and extend our understanding of biological, chemical, materials science, electronic, magnetic, optical, and structural properties in nanostructures; (2) Synthesis *and processing:* Enable the atomic and molecular control of material building blocks and develop engineering tools to provide the means to assemble and utilize these tailored building blocks for new processes and devices in a wide variety of applications. Extend the traditional approaches to patterning and microfabrication to include parallel processing with proximal probes, self-assembling, stamping, and templating. Pay particular attention to the interface with bionanostructures and bio-inspired structures, multifunctional and adaptive nanostructures, scaling approaches, and commercial affordability; (3) Characterization *and manipulation:* Discover and develop new experimental tools to broaden the capability to measure and control nanostructured matter, including developing new standards of measurement. Pay particular attention to tools capable of measuring/manipulating single macro- and supra-molecules of biological interest; (4) Modeling *and simulation:* Accelerate the application of novel concepts and high-performance computation to the prediction of nanostructured properties, phenomena, and processes; (5) Device *and system concepts:* Stimulate the innovative application of nanostructure properties in ways that might be exploited in new technologies.

International Perspective

The United States does not dominate nanotechnology research. There is strong international interest, with nearly twice as much ongoing research overseas as in the United States (see the worldwide study *Nanostructure Science and Engineering,* NSTC 1999). Other regions, particularly Japan and Western Europe, are supporting work that is equal to the quality and breadth of the science done in the United States because there, too, scientists and national leaders have determined that nanotechnology has the potential to be a major economic factor during the next several decades. This situation is unlike the other post-war technological revolutions, where the United States enjoyed earlier leads. The international dimensions of nanotechnology research and its potential applications implies that the United States must put in place an infrastructure that is equal to that which exists anywhere in the world. This emerging field also creates a unique opportunity for the United States to partner with other countries in ways that are mutually beneficial through information sharing, cooperative research, and study by young U.S. researchers at foreign centers of excellence. A suitable U.S. infrastructure is also needed to compete and collaborate with those groups.

5. HIGH-LEVEL RECOGNITION OF NANOTECHNOLOGY'S POTENTIAL

The promise of nanoscience and engineering has not passed unnoticed. Dr. Neal Lane, currently the President's Advisor for Science and Technology and former NSF director, stated at a Congressional hearing in April 1998, "If I were asked for an area of science and engineering that will most likely produce the breakthroughs of tomorrow, I would point to nanoscale science and engineering." In March 1998, Dr. John H. Gibbons, Dr. Lane's predecessor, identified nanotechnology as one of the five technologies that will determine economic development in the next century. Several federal agencies have been actively investigating nanoscience R&D. NSF started the Nanoparticle Synthesis and Processing Initiative in 1991 and the National Nanofabrication User Network in 1994, and has highlighted nanoscale science and engineering in its FY 1998 budget. The Defense Department identified nanotechnology as a strategic research objective in 1997. NIH identified nanobiotechnology as a topic of interest in its 1999 Bioengineering Consortium (BECON) program.

More recently, on May 12, 1999, Richard Smalley, Nobel Laureate, concluded in his testimony to the Senate Subcommittee on Science, Technology, and Space that "We are about to be able to build things that work on the smallest possible length scales. It is in our Nation's best interest to move boldly into this new field." On June 22, 1999, the Subcommittee on Basic Research of the Committee on Science organized the hearing on "Nanotechnology: The State of Nano-Science and Its Prospects for the Next Decade." The Subcommittee Chairman Nick Smith, of Michigan, concluded the hearings stating that "Nanotechnology holds promise for breakthroughs in health, manufacturing, agriculture, energy use and national security. It is sufficient information to aggressively address funding of this field."

6. PROPOSED FEDERAL CONTRIBUTION TO THE NNI

Government's Role in Nanoscience and Technology

While nanotechnology research is in an early stage, it already has several promising results. It is clear that it can have a substantial impact on industry and on our standard of living by improving healthcare, environment and economy. But investments must be made in science and engineering that will enable scientists and engineers to invent totally new technologies and enable industry to produce cost-competitive products. Since many of the findings on nanostructures and nanoprocesses are not yet fully measurable, replicable, or understood, it will take many years to develop corresponding technologies. Industry needs to know what are the principles of operation and how to economically fabricate, operate, and integrate nanostructured materials and devices. Private industry is unable in the usual 3–5 year industrial product time frame to effectively develop cost-competitive products based on current knowledge. Further, the necessary fundamental nanotechnology research and development is too broad, complex, expensive, long-term, and risky for industry to undertake. Thus, industry is not able to fund or is significantly under-funding critical areas of long-term fundamental research and development and is not building a balanced nanoscience infrastructure needed to realize nanotechnology's potential.

Thus far, Federal and academic investments in nanoscale science, engineering, and technology have occurred in open competition with other research topics within various disciplines. This dynamics is one reason that U.S. nanotechnology research efforts tend to be fragmented and overlap among disciplines, areas of relevance, and sources of funding. It is important to develop a strategic research and development and implementation plan. A coordinated national effort could focus resources on stimulating cooperation, avoid unwanted duplication of efforts, capture the imagination of young people, and support of basic sciences. The government should support expansion of university and government laboratory facilities, help to build the workforce skills necessary to staff future industries based on nanotechnology and future academic institutions, encourage cross-disciplinary networks and partnerships, ensure the dissemination of information, and encourage small businesses to exploit the nanotechnology opportunities.

Nanotechnology R&D Require Long-Term Federal Investment

Nano-science and engineering R&D will need a long-term investment commitment because of their interdisciplinary characteristics, the limitations of the existing experimental and modeling tools in the intermediate range between individual molecules and microstructure, and the need for technological infrastructure. The time from fundamental discovery to market is typically 10–15 years (see for instance the application of magnetoresistance, and of mesoporous silicate for environmental and chemical industry applications). Historically, industry becomes a major player only in the last 3–5 years, when their investments are much larger than in the previous period, but the economic return is more certain. Industry is frequently reluctant to invest in risky research that takes many years to develop into a product. In the United States, the government and university research system can effectively fill this niche.

Government leadership and funds are needed to help implement policies and establish the nanotechnology infrastructure and research support in the next decade. Since major industrial markets are not yet established for nanotechnology products, it is proposed that the government support technology transfer activities to private industry to accelerate the long-term benefits. The enabling infrastructure and technologies must be in place for industry to take advantage of nanotechnology innovations and discoveries. The increasing pace of technological commercialization requires a compression of past time scales, parallel development of research and commercial products, and a synergy among industry, university, and government partners. The government role will be on crosscutting, long-term research and development nanotechnology areas identified in this report.

Universities Performing Research in Nanotechnology

Arizona State University

http://invsee.asu.edu/Invsee/invsee.htm
www.eas.asu.edu/~nano/index.html

Interactive Nanovisualization in science and engineering education
- Remote operation of advanced microscopes and nanofabrication tools
- Surface characterization methods.

Nanostructures Research Group
- Ultrasmall semiconductor devices.
- Nanolithography
- Physics of nanostructures and ultrasmall semiconductor devices
- Modeling of these structures and devices
- Study of very large scale implementations of novel device architectures

Baylor College of Medicine

http://public.bcm.tmc.edu/pa/tomorrow.htm

Molecular biology

Brown University

http://en732c.engin.brown.edu

Experimental, computational and conceptual study of nanomechanics and micromechanics of materials

California Institute of Technology

www.wag.caltech.edu/research.html

Nanotechnology
Self-organization

Clemson University

http://virtual.clemson.edu/groups/NANOTECH/index2.htm

Organic technologies and device physics
- Optical sourcing based on organic matrix nanocomposites
- Electroactive, piezoactive, and photoactive nanocomposites
- Optical sensing and photovoltaics based on organic matrix nanocomposites

Nanophotonics and near-field physics
- Synthesis of novel nanostructured materials for optical applications
- Pulsed-laser deposition inorganic photonic heterostructures
- Nonlinear optics of passive organic-matrix nanocomposites
- Nonlinear optics of electroactive organic matrix nanocomposites

Nanoelectronics
- Quantum effects in topologically complex systems with reduced dimensionality
- Molecular electronics and self-assembly
- Quantum contact dynamics

Quantum computing
- Nanotube mediated quantum entanglement of luminescent species
- Spin injection systems and superexchange in inorganic thin films

Columbia University

http://research.radlab.columbia.edu/mrsec

Interparticle interactions in self assembly
Real-time monitoring of organic surface ligands and solvent during the self-assembly of nanocrystal arrays.
Self-assembly of starburst dendrimers

Cornell University

www.nbtc.cornell.edu

Member of the Nanobiotechnology Center, a close collaboration between life scientists, physical scientists, and engineers.

Darmstadt University of Technology
www.tu-darmstadt.de/fb/ms/fg/ds/work.html

Nanocrystalline ceramics
Gas sensors
Magnetosensors
Ion-beam techniques
Diffusion in amorphous metals

Dartmouth College
www.dartmouth.edu/~dmmg

Ultrafast tunneling microscopy and millikelvin force microscopy
Fluorescence lifetime imaging microscopy and spectroscopy
Nanocluster synthesis theory of polymer blends
Fabrication and transport properties of ligand-stabilized nanoparticle
Langmuir-Blodgett(L-B) thin films
Assembly of macromolecular arrays
Thin-film chemistry statistical mechanics of fluids and fluid mixtures
Structure-property relationships in polymers

Delft University of Technology
www.tudelft.nl/matrix/home.cfm

Nanotechnology applied to computing, especially quantum computing
   devices

Duke University
www.duke.edu/~eom/research.html

Semiconductor research
Thin films
Nanomembranes

Eidgenössiche Technische Hochschule
www.nanophys.ethz.ch/projects.html

Metal-insulator transition in two-dimensional systems
InAs/AlSb quantum wells transport
Measurements with parabolic quantum wells
Fabrication of nanostructures with atomic force microscope techniques

Georgia Institute of Technology

www.physics.gatech.edu/research/whetten/#goals

Synthesis and characterization of nanometer scale crystalline molecules (nanocrystals), and highly oriented molecular (Au, Ag) nanocrystalline arrays

Institut für Neue Materialien, University of Saarland

www.inm-gmbh.de/inm-research.html

High-tech materials on a large scale. The research center is a nonprofit limited liability company (GmbH) with institutional sponsorship. This structure affords great entrepreneurial flexibility.

Interuniversity Microelectronics Center

www.imec.be/mcp/Welcome.html

Microelectromechanical system components for telecommunication, information technology peripherals, and instrumentation

Iowa State University

http://cmp.ameslab.gov/cmp

Modeling large molecular systems

Kaunas University of Technology

www.microsys.ktu.lt/LABS/Mst.htm

Piezo and ultrasonic actuators for nanopositioning
Actuators for scanning probe microscopy
Microsensors based on micromechanical cantilevers
Micro- and nanotribology
Application of atomic force microscopy for the investigation and structures formation on the surface

Kyushu University

www.ed.kyushu-u.ac.jp/ed3E.html

Integrated circuits and computer-assisted design for integrated systems
Quantum electron devices and vacuum electronics

Ultrathin films, superlattice, and surface and interface control
Plasma processing, photon processing, and microbeam machining
Nanofabrication technique and atomic manipulation
Microelectromechanical systems

Massachusetts Institute of Technology

http://nanoweb.mit.edu

Scanning-electron-beam lithography
Spatial-phase-locked electron-beam lithography
X-ray nanolithography
Zone-plate-based X-ray and ultraviolet projection lithography
Improved mask technology for X-ray lithography
Nanometer-level feedback-stabilized alignment and X-ray exposure
    system
Interference lithography
Fabrication of optical Sources in III-V materials using photonic crystals
Patterned magnetic materials for data storage
Magnetic random access memories (MRAMs)
50 nm low-threshold-voltage MOSFETs: questions of ultimate MOS-
    FET performance
CMOS technology for 25-nm channel length
Deep-ultraviolet contact photolithography
Fabrication of three-dimensional photonic bandgap structures
Development of fabrication techniques for building integrated optical-
    grating-based filters
Design of integrated Bragg-grating-based filters for optical commu-
    nications
High-dispersion X-ray transmission gratings for space research
Supersmooth X-ray reflection gratings
Ultraviolet-blocking transmission grating filters for neutral atom
    imaging
Field-emitter array flat-panel displays for head-mounted applications
High-accuracy assembly of X-ray foil optics

Michigan State University

www.pa.msu.edu/cmp/csc/nanotube.html

Carbon nanotubes
Modeling the self-assembly and electronic properties of these systems

Middle Tennessee State University
www.mtsu.edu/~chem

Nanotechnology design tools

New Jersey Institute Of Technology
http://megahertz.njit.edu/~vijaya/nanopage.html

Nonlinear optical properties of semiconductor nanostructures

New York University
www.nyu.edu/projects/nanotechnology

Chemical modification and functionalization of carbon nanotube
Solid- and solution-phase combinatorial and robotic synthesis
Fluorous fullerene and carbon nanotubes
Water-soluble fullerenes, fullerene antibody

North Carolina State University
www.ncsu.edu/chemistry/facrespro.html

Self-assembled monolayers
Nanometer-scale materials properties and engineering
Development of nanostructured materials and studies of their properties
Use of scanning probe microscopes for investigating nanoscale processes
Molecular photonics
Inorganic materials at the interface of molecular and solid-state chemistry
Molecular magnetism
Design, synthesis, and characterization of organic molecules
Analysis of scanning tunneling and atomic force microscopy images
Heterogeneous catalysis by transition metals and surface reactions on electronic materials
Impurities and hot atom reactions in semiconductors

Northwestern University
National Nanofabrication Institute
www.nanotechnology.northwestern.edu/index.html

The role of the Institute is to support meaningful efforts in nanotechnology, house state-of-the-art nanomaterials characterization facilities, and nucleate individual and group efforts aimed at addressing and solving key problems in nanotechnology.

Nottingham Trent University

www.domme.ntu.ac.uk/pec/Res1.html

Layered-silicate nanocomposites
Metallic-nanoparticle-reinforced polymers
Graphite/polymer nanocomposites
Other inorganic/polymer nanohybrids

Osaka University

http://surf5.mat.eng.osaka-u.ac.jp/nano

Metallic nanoparticles encapsulated into carbon

Pennsylvania State University

http://stm1.chem.psu.edu/~psw/Research.html

Exploring, probing, and manipulating interactions and dynamics at surfaces and interfaces

Princeton University

www.ee.princeton.edu/~chouweb

Nanofabrication
Nanoelectronics
Nanooptoelectronics
Nanomagnetics
Applications of nanostructures in other fields

Rice University

http://cnst.rice.edu

Educational consortium of university departments

Rutgers University

http://nanotech.rutgers.edu/nanotech

General clearinghouse for publications and nanotech information

Seoul National University

http://csns.snu.ac.kr

Molecular and atomic manipulation
Charge trap memory
Nanomagnetic memory
Nanoscale sensors and drivers

Stanford University

www-snf.stanford.edu

Provides researchers with effective and efficient access to advanced
nanofabrication equipment and expertise

State University of New York

http://dol1.eng.sunysb.edu/tsl/nano

Nanomaterials
Nanomaterials deposition and spraying

Technische Universitat Berlin

http://sol.physik.tu-berlin.de/htm_grdm/pg3mission.htm

Fabrication, characterization, and theoretical modeling of quantum
wires and quantum dots

Tufts University

http://ase.tufts.edu/chemistry/walt

Inorganic/polymer and metal/polymer composites
Self-assembly

Université Catholique de Louvain

www.cermin.ucl.ac.be

Chemical force microscopy
Diamonds
Mesoscopic semiconductor nanostructures
Microelectromechanical systems
Microwave magnetic nanostructures
Nanolithography
Nanomechanics

Nanoporous membranes
Nanotubes
Novel circuit architectures
Polymer nanostructures

University of Arizona

www.physics.arizona.edu/~stafford

Nanomechanics
Mesoscopic physics

University of Birmingham

http://nprl.bham.ac.uk/CNSD/index.html

Machining needed to develop novel scientific instruments for nanoscale research

University of California at Berkeley

http://argon.eecs.berkeley.edu:8080

Microelectromechanical systems

University of Cambridge

www.phy.cam.ac.uk/research/research

Quantum devices
Organic nanostructures
Monolayers
Nanomaterials

University of Chicago

http://mrsec.uchicago.edu/MRSEC/research.html

Mesoscopic self-assembly
Tunable quantum materials

University of Cincinnati

www.nanolab.uc.edu

Molecular-beam epitaxy and fabrication of rare earth–doped GaN electroluminescent devices

SiC chemical vapor deposition for advanced MEMS and high-power electronic applications
Focused ion-beam fabrication
Optical memory

University of Delaware
www.ece.udel.edu/cns

Nanomachined synthetic-quartz surfaces for use in photomasks

University of Glasgow
www.elec.gla.ac.uk/groups/nano

Dry etching (alternatives to lithography)
Lithography
Modeling
Semiconductor research
Quantum computing

University of Greenwich
http://cms1.gre.ac.uk/research/cnmpa/ns

Computational methods for nanostructures

University of Hamburg
www.uni-hamburg.de/&wlg_table=-3

Quantum materials

University of Illinois at Chicago
http://mclab.me.uic.edu/activities/projects.htm

Insitu investigation of fluid processes in a carbon nanotube
Hydrothermal formation of novel carbon structures: learning from nature and going beyond it
Hydrothermal behavior of carbon synthesis of sp^2- and sp^3-bonded carbon coatings
Synthesis and characterization of carbon coatings on the surface of carbides produced by etching in halogens

University of Illinois at Urbana-Champaign

www.beckman.uiuc.edu/research/menhome.html

Molecular and electronic nanostructures

University of Lausanne

www.unil.ch/ipmc/docs/wds/activities.html

Quantum confinement of electrons in nanostructures
Light emission from nanostructures
Manipulation of individual atoms, molecules, and clusters with the tip of a scanning tunneling microscope (STM)
Two-dimensional self-assembly phenomena
Chemical reactivity of size-selected metal particles on oxide surfaces: model catalysts

University of Leeds

www.amsta.leeds.ac.uk/cndm
www.chem.leeds.ac.uk/SOMS/home.html

Computational modeling of nanostructure electronics
Nanoscale molecular science

University of Michigan

http://nano.med.umich.edu/homepage.html

Nanoemulsions as agents for the disinfection and decontamination of surfaces
Smart nanodevices as anticancer therapeutics

University of Muenster

www.uni-muenster.de/Physik/PI/Fuchs/researchactivities/index.html

Surface-sensitive probes
Scanning-probe microscopy (atomic force microscope [AFM], scanning tunneling microscope [STM], scanning near-field acoustic microscope [SNAM], scanning near-field optical microscope [SNOM], scanning ion-conductance microscope [SICM])
Second-harmonic sum-frequency microscopy (nonlinear optics [NLO], second-harmonic microscope/sum-frequency microscope [SHM/SFM])

Standard surface-sensitive techniques (ultrahigh vacuum [UHV] and X-ray photoelectronic spectroscopy (XPS), ultraviolet photoelectronic spectroscopy [UPS], low-energy electron diffraction [LEED])

Computer simulations on organic/inorganic interfaces and molecular modeling

Self-assembly technique

Organic molecular-beam deposition

Nanostructuring by scanning-probe techniques

Self-organization methods

University of Nebraska

www.engr.unl.edu/ee/faculty/supriyo_bandyopadhyay/qdl1.html

Self-assembly of ordered quantum wire and dot arrays

Nonlinear magnetooptical properties of quantum wires

Hot electron transport in quantum wires

Collective computation and quantum computing with arrays of quantum dots

Quantum computing and spintronics

Fundamental issues in quantum mechanics

University of Newcastle

http://nanocentre.ncl.ac.uk

Ion-channel-based sensors

Microfabricated multianalyte amperometric sensors

Synthesis and tethering of biomolecules and biomembranes

Microsystems components and fabrication

Nano- and microelectronic devices

Fabrication of nanoscale structures

Thin films for smart technologies

Instrumentation for fabrication and characterization

Materials: structural and mechanical characterization, failure

University of North Carolina at Chapel Hill

www.physics.unc.edu/~zhou/muri
www.cs.unc.edu/Research/nano

New materials synthesis and fabrication

Mechanical properties

Electrical, magnetic, and optical properties

NanoManipulator system, an improved, natural interface to scanned-probe microscopes

University of Notre Dame

www.nd.edu/~ndnano

Molecular-based nanostructures
Semiconductor-based nanostructures
Device concepts and modeling
Nanofabrication characterization
Image and information processing
Functional systems design

University of Oxford

www.materials.ox.ac.uk/research/index.htm

Nanocrystaline materials
Nanofilms, -dots, and -wires
Nanocomposites
Polyrotaxanes
Carbon-nanotube emission displays
Microscopy
Self-assembly

University of Paris 13—CNRS

www-lplgb.univ-paris13.fr/Gb/Presentation/Presenta.htm

Quantum interferometry and optics
Nanophotochemistry

University of Pennsylvania

www.nanotech.upenn.edu
www.lrsm.upenn.edu/~fischer
www.seas.upenn.edu:8080/~bonnell

Electroactive Polymers
Buckminsterfullerene
Nanotubes
Lithium-carbon compounds
Electronic properties of conducting polymer nanofibers
Proximity effects in nanoelectronics
Charge-mediated assembly of nanoelectronics
New probes of local properties
Nanobiophysical engineering and synthetic mimicry
Nanoparticles in clinical applications

Theory and simulation of networked nanostructures
Nanofabrication

University of Southern California
http://lipari.usc.edu/~lmr/html/research.html

Automation of nanoparticle pattern construction
Layered fabrication of three-dimensional nanostructures
Deposition of material on nanoparticle patterns that serve as templates
Nanowires
Single-electron transistors
Chemical sensors
Manipulation and editing of DNA

University of Tennessee
Oak Ridge National Laboratory
www.ornl.gov/ment

Isolated biomolecules
Nanofabricated electrodes
Single-wall carbon nanotubes
Genetically engineered whole cells as microelectronic components
Vacuum nanoelectronics

University of Texas at Austin
www.botany.utexas.edu/facstaff/facpages/mbrown/nanopage

Single-wall carbon nanotubes
Linear acetylenic carbon
Enzyme complexes
Protein complexes
Polymers

University of Toronto
www.utoronto.ca/~ecan/projects.html

Transport and optical properties of low-dimensional quantum structures
Modeling SPM tip interactions with semiconductor surfaces
Virtual reality system for scanning-probe microscope (SPM) fabrication
    of multitip SPM arrays

Nanolithographic fabrication of novel quantum devices and their testing on a nanoscale
Studies of hybrid nanodevices and circuits

University of Wisconsin
http://mrsec.wisc.edu/irgsee.html

Nanostructured materials as interfaces to biology
Application of microelectromechanical systems to resonant ultrasound spectroscopy
Nanostructured shape-memory alloys

Washington University in St. Louis
http://bucky5.wustl.edu

Nanometer-sized metal particles and metal particle arrays
Growth and characterization of carbon fibers and nanotubes
Molecular-beam epitaxy with fullerenes
Biology and nanotechnology
Nanostressing stages, mechanochemistry, nanomanipulation, and measurement
Designer particles

Yale University
www.eng.yale.edu/uelm

Quantum devices
Advanced semiconductor devices
Nanoprobes
Nanofabrication

Organizations and Companies Affiliated with the Semiconductor Research Corporation

Advanced Micro Devices
Cadence Design Systems
Compaq Computer
CVC, Inc.
Defense Advanced Research Projects Agency (DARPA)
Eastman Kodak
Eaton Corporation
Etec Systems, Inc.
Flipchip Technologies, L.L.C.
Hewlett-Packard
IBM
Intel
Intersil
LSI Logic
Lucent Technologies
Mentor Graphics Corporation
Microbar
Microcosm Technologies
Mission Research Corporation
Mitre Corporation
Motorola
National Institute of Standards and Technology
National Science Foundation
National Semiconductor
Neo Linear, Inc.
Northrop Grumman

Novellus Systems, Inc.
Numerical Technologies, Inc.
Omniview, Inc.
PDF Solutions, Inc.
Physical Electronics
SAL Corporation
Sematech
Semiconductor Industry Association
Shipley Company
Silvaco Data Systems
Synopsys
Tessera, Inc.
Testchip Technologies
Texas Instruments
Ultratech Stepper
UMC
U.S. Army Research Office
Verity Instruments

Universities Affiliated with the Semiconductor Research Corporation

Interconnect Architecture

Carnegie Mellon University
Georgia Institute of Technology
Michigan State University
Oregon State University
City College of the City University of New York
State University of New York at Buffalo
University of Illinois, Urbana-Champaign
University of California, San Diego
University of Florida
University of South Florida
Yale University

Digital Implementation

Carnegie Mellon University
North Carolina State University
North Dakota State University
University of California, Los Angeles
University of Illinois, Urbana-Champaign
University of Massachusetts, Amherst
University of Southern California
University of Utah

Mixed-Signal Implementation

Duke University
Purdue University

University of Colorado
Virginia Polytechnic Institute and State University

Technology and Components

Boston University
Carnegie Mellon University
Illinois Institute of Technology
North Carolina State University
Oregon State University
Rensselaer Polytechnic Institute
University of Minnesota
University of Virginia

Wireless and Radio Frequency

Arizona State University
Carnegie Mellon University
George Washington University
Kansas State University
Ohio State University
Rice University
City College of the City University of New York
University of Washington
Washington State University

Companies Working with Nanotechnology

PRODUCT SORT

Information in the listings is current as of June 16, 2001. The listings exclude more than 750 microscopy companies and 120 semiconductor companies; some companies may have been inadvertently omitted. The author offers his apologies to those companies.

Many of the listed companies focus on other products and industries. Only the nanotechnology- or microelectromechanical systems (MEMS)-related products are listed here. Not all listed products are commercially available.

Acronyms used in the listings: AFM = atomic force microscope; EFM = electrostatic force microscope; ESEM = environmental scanning electron microscope; LEEM = low-energy electron microscope; LFM = lateral force microscope; MFM = magnetic force microscope; PAMAM = polyamidoamine (dendrimers); RF = radio frequency; SEM = scanning electron microscope; SNOM = scanning near-field optical microscope; SPM = scanning-probe microscope; STM = scanning tunneling microscope; TEM = tunneling electron microscope.

Nanotech/MEMS products	Company	Web Site
Biochemicals	Intergen	www.intergenco.com
	Promega	www.promega.com
Amino acids	Catalytica	www.catalytica-inc.com
Bio- and organic chemical synthesis	Sigma-Aldrich	www.sigma-aldrich.com
Biochips	Hewlett-Packard	www.hp.com
	Motorola	www.motorola.com
	Stratagene Cloning Systems	www.stratagene.com
DNA/RNA assays	Nanogen	www.nanogen.com

Nanotech/MEMS products	Company	Web Site
Gene chips	Pharmacia Biotech	www.jp.apbiotech.com/ie_index.asp
Scanners	Axon Instruments	www.axon.com
Bioinformatics	Merck	www.merck.com
Biotechnology	Kobe Steel	www.kobelco.co.jp/indexe.htm
Catalysts	Engelhard Corporation	www.engelhard.com
	NexTech Materials, Ltd.	www.nextechmaterials.com
Coatings	Aremco Products	www.aremco.com
	Materials and Electrochemical Research Corporation	www.mercorp.com/mercorp
	Materials Modification, Inc.	www.matmod.com
	Robert Bosch, GmbH	www.bosch.de/start/de/start/index.htm
Aligned nanotube arrays	NanoLab	www.nano-lab.com
Electrodeposited nanocrystalline materials	Integran	www.integran.com
Medical	Spire Corporation	www.spirecorp.com
Monomers and powders	Rohm and Haas	www.rohmhaas.com
Nanolayer	Technology Assessment & Transfer, Inc.	www.techassess.com
Combinatorial libraries for high-throughput screening	Nanoscale Combinatorial Synthesis, Inc.	www.nanosyn.com/company.html
Composites	Asulab	www.asulab.ch
	Materials and Electrochemical Research Corporation	www.mercorp.com/mercorp
Nanoclays	Nanocor, Inc.	www.nanocor.com
Powders	Materials Modification, Inc.	www.matmod.com
Design, Custom biosensors and nanotechnology applications	Keweenaw Nanoscience Center	www.portup.com/~funderdown
Designer drugs	Merck	www.merck.com

Nanotech/MEMS products	Company	Web Site
Designer molecules	Celanese	www.celanese.com
	Proctor & Gamble	www.pg.com
PAMAM dendrimers	Dendritech	www.mmi.org/mmi/ dendritech
Diamond coatings	Crystallume	www.crystallume.com
	Kobe Steel	www.kobelco.co.jp/ indexe.htm
Diamond coatings and diamondlike carbon products and coatings	Diamonex International, Ltd.	www.diamonex.com
Displays		
Large area displays using carbon nanofilms	SI Diamond Technology	www.carbontech.net
Nanotube-based field-emission displays	Dow Chemical	www.dow.com
Nanotube emitter displays	Noritake Company	www.noritake-elec.com
DNA genomics	Abbot Laboratories	http://abbott.com/news/ discovering_the _future.html
DNA sequencing	Beckman	www.beckman.com
DNA synthesis	Promega	www.promega.com
Fabrication technologies	Ennex Fabrication Technologies	www.ennex.com
High-temperature superconductors	Conductus, Inc.	www.conductus.com
Imaging		
Acquisition for microscopy	4Pi	www.4pi.com
Chemical	Bruker	www.bruker.com
Chemical phase	Advanced Surface Microscopy, Inc.	www.a1.com/asm
Interconnect devices	AMP, Inc.	www.amp.com
	Cinch	www.cinch.com
	IBM	www.ibm.com
Interconnection systems for microelectronics	Nanopierce	www.nanopierce.com
Lithography		
All aspects of semi- conductor litho- graphy including nanolithography	Leica	www.leica.com

Nanotech/MEMS products	Company	Web Site
Electron beam	Hitachi	www.hitachi.com
	Jeol USA, Inc.	www.jeol.com
Semiconductor	FEI	www.feicompany.com/ eng/index.html
Materials		
Advanced electronics materials	Dow Chemical	www.dow.com
Advanced semi-conductor materials	Hitachi	www.hitachi.com
	IBM	www.ibm.com
	Cabot Performance Materials	www.cabot-corp.com
Memory devices, nanoscale	IBM	www.ibm.com
MEMS	Analog Devices, Inc.	www.analog.com
	Asulab	www.asulab.ch
	Berkeley Sensor and Actuator Center	www.bsac.eecs.berkeley .edu
	Honeywell Microswitch Division	www.honeywell.com
	IBM	www.ibm.com
	Motorola	www.motorola.com
	Seiko	www.seiko.com
	Surface Technology Systems	www.stsystems.com
Accelerometers and optical reflectors	Tanner Research, Inc.	www.tanner.com
Biohazard detectors	System Planning Corporation	www.sysplan.com
Fabrication equipment	Plasma-Therm, Inc.	www.plasmatherm.com
Flow sensors	Perkin Elmer	http://fluidsciences .perkinelmer.com/ index.asp#
Fluidics	Alberta Microelectronics Center	www.amc.ab.ca
Mass storage	Nanochip	www.nanochip.com
Microrelays, optical attenuators, photonic switches	Cronos	www.memsrus.com
Microspectrometers, microfluidics	Microparts	www.microparts.de/ english/index.html
Microfluidics	Redwood Microsystems	www.redwoodmicro .com

Nanotech/MEMS products	Company	Web Site
Optical	Texas Instruments	www.ti.com
	Zygo Corporation	www.zygo.com
Optical switches, biomonitors, microfluidics	Intellisense Corporation	www.intellisense.com
Optical, RF, sequencing, assays, fluidics, sensors	Coventer	www.memcad.com
Oxygen and pressure sensors	Fujikura America, Inc.	www.faisensors.com
Piezo-based sensors	Kistler	www.kistler.ch
Plastic components	Jenoptik Mikrotechnik	www.jo-mikrotechnik.com/english/index.html
Pressure sensors	Lucas NovaSensor	www.novasensor.com
	Silicon Microstructures	www.si-micro.com
	Standard Mems	www.standardmems.com
Sensors	Delphi Delco Electronics Systems	www.delphiauto.com
	Druck, Inc.	www.druck.com
	Du Pont Electronics	www.dupont.com/automotive/applications/electronic
	Endevco	www.endevco.com
	Kulite	www.kulite.com
	Murata Electronics	www.iijnet.or.jp/murata
	SRI International	www.sri.com
3-D integrated circuits	Access/Valtronic	www.valtronic.ch
3-D optical	Integrated Micromachines	www.micromachines.com
Metrology	Archaeomation	www.edmondson.org/ArchaeoMation
	CVC Products	www.cvc.com
	Etalon, Inc.	www.etaloninc.com
	FEI	www.feicompany.com/eng/index.html
	Molecular Imaging	www.molec.com
	Nanometrics, Inc.	www.nanometrics.com
Microchannel plates, microdynode arrays	NanoSciences Corporation	www.nanosciences.com
Micromachining	Alberta Microelectronics Center	www.amc.ab.ca

Nanotech/MEMS products	Company	Web Site
Microplate readers	Molecular Devices	www.moleculardevices .com
Micropipettes	BioMetric Systems	www.biometricsystems .com
Micropositioners	Axon Instruments	www.axon.com
Microscopy	Archaeomation	www.edmondson.org/ ArchaeoMation
	SPI Supplies/Structure Probe, Inc.	www.2spi.com
AFMs	CVC Products	www.cvc.com
	Hewlett-Packard	www.hp.com
AFMs and related microscopy accessories	Technical Instruments	www.techinst.com
AFMs and SPMs	Topometrix	www.topometrix.com
AFM probes and tips	BioForce Labs	www.bioforcelab.com
AFMs, EFMs, LFMs, MFMs, STMs	Advanced Surface Microscopy, Inc.	www.al.com/asm
AFMs, STMs, SNOMs and other micros- copy products	DME	www.dme-spm.dk
Electron microscopy	Energy Beam Sciences	www.ebsciences.com
Electron microscopy instrumentation	Gatan	www.gatan.com
High-resolution magnetic scanners	Physical Sciences, Inc.	www.psicorp.com
LEEM	IBM	www.ibm.com
Nanoscopes	CVC Products	www.cvc.com
Probes and microimaging	Bruker	www.bruker.com
Sample preparation and imaging	Fischione Instruments	www.fischione.com
Scanning-probe position encoders	NanoWave, Inc.	www.nanowave.com
SEMs	Hitachi	www.hitachi.com
SEMs, TEMs, and accessories	Leo Electron Microscopy	www.leo.de
SEMs, TEMs, focused ion beam, ESEM	FEI	www.feicompany.com/ eng/index.html
SEMs, TEMs, STMs, other microscopy devices and components, wafer inspection	Jeol USA, Inc.	www.jeol.com

Nanotech/MEMS products	Company	Web Site
SNOMs, AFMs, and accessories	Park Scientific Instruments	www.park.com
SNOMs, SNOM probes, microscopy accessories	NT-MDT	www.ntmdt.ru
SPM calibration	Advanced Surface Microscopy, Inc.	www.al.com/asm
Microscopy, SPMs, AFMs, and other microscopy products	Digital Instruments	www.di.com
SPMs, metrology, accessories	Molecular Imaging	www.molec.com
STMs, positioning devices	McAllister Tech Associates	www.mcallister.com
Molecular analysis		
Systems and software	Nonius BV	www.nonius.com
Sensitive reagents for detecting biological molecules	Nanoprobes	www.nanoprobes.com
Molecular biology	Abbot Laboratories	abbott.com/news/ discovering_the _future.html
	Akzo Nobel	www.akzonobel.com
	Intergen	www.intergenco.com
Substances and tools	Calbiochem	www.calbiochem.com
Molecular electronics	Hewlett-Packard	www.hp.com
	Motorola	www.motorola.com
Molecular engineering	Aldrich Chemical Company	www.sigma-aldrich.com/ saws.nsf/Home ?OpenFrameset
	IBM	www.ibm.com
	Merck	www.merck.com
	SRI International	www.sri.com
Molecular medicine	Stratagene Cloning Systems	www.stratagene.com
Molecular modeling	American Chemical Society	www.acs.org
	Software	
	Kobe Steel	www.kobelco.co.jp/ indexe.htm
	Proctor & Gamble	www.pg.com
Nanoarrays	BioForce Labs	www.bioforcelab.com

Nanotech/MEMS products	Company	Web Site
Nanocomputing architectures	Hewlett-Packard	www.hp.com
Nanodevices	Hewlett-Packard	www.hp.com
	Hitachi	www.hitachi.com
Nanoelectronics	Bell Labs (Lucent)	www.lucent.com
	Hewlett-Packard	www.hp.com
	IBM	www.ibm.com
	Lucent	www.lucent.com
Nanoindentation	Advanced Surface Microscopy, Inc.	www.al.com/asm
Nanomanipulators	3rd Tech	www.3rdtech.com
Nanomaterials	Advanced Refractory Technologies	www.art-inc.com
	Akzo Nobel	www.akzonobel.com
	Engelhard Corporation	www.engelhard.com
	NanoMaterials Research Corporation	www.nrcorp.com
Carbon nanotube powders	NanoLab	www.nano-lab.com
Fuel cell materials	NexTech Materials, Ltd.	www.nextechmaterials .com
Fullerenes	Materials and Electrochemical Research Corporation	www.mercorp.com/ mercorp
	Strem Chemicals, Inc.	www.strem.com
Microspheres	Bangs Laboratories	www.bangslabs.com
Nano- and microparticles and spheres	Duke Scientific Company	www.dukesci.com
Nanocomposites	Hyperion Catalysis	www.fibrils.com
	Kobe Steel	www.kobelco.co.jp/ indexe.htm
Nanocrystalline materials	Altair International, Inc.	www.altairint.com
Nanocrystalline materials, nanotechnology consulting	Nanomat, Inc.	www.nanomat.com
Nanofibers and nanowebs	Espin	www.nanospin.com
Nanoparticles	Altair International, Inc.	www.altairint.com
Nanophase materials	Nanophase Technologies Corporation	www.nanophase.com

Nanotech/MEMS products	Company	Web Site
Nano–silica gels	Aldrich Chemical Company	www.sigma-aldrich .com/saws.nsf/Home ?OpenFrameset
Nanotubes	Materials and Electrochemical Research Corporation	www.mercorp.com/ mercorp
	Hyperion Catalysis	www.fibrils.com
	IBM	www.ibm.com
Carbon buckytubes, nanotubes, and manufacturing equipment	SES Research Corporation	www.sesres.com
Powders	Anhui Ultra-Fine Powders Developing Co., Ltd.	
	Kobe Steel	www.kobelco.co.jp/ indexe.htm
	NanoMaterials Research Corporation	www.nrcorp.com
Nanopowders, especially metals	Argonide	www.argonide.com
	Nanopowders Industries	www.nanopowders.com
Nanopowders, metallic (aluminum)	Technanogy	www.technanogy.net/ index.html
Single-wall carbon nanotubes	Carbolex	www.carbolex.com
	Carbon Nanotechnologies, Inc.	www.cnanotech.com
Nanopositioners	Polytech PI	www.polytecpi.com
Nanopositioning	Burleigh Instruments	www.burleigh.com
	JDS Uniphase	www.nanopositioning .com
Nanosensors	JDS Uniphase	www.nanopositioning .com
Nanotechnology product presentations	Nanologic, Inc.	www.nanologicinc.com
Nanowires	IBM	www.ibm.com
Organic vapor sensors	California Molecular Electronics Corporation	www.calmec.com
Particle characterization	Beckman	www.beckman.com
Photovoltaic manufacturing equipment	Spire Corporation	www.spirecorp.com

Nanotech/MEMS products	Company	Web Site
Piezo devices	Etalon, Inc.	www.etaloninc.com
	JDS Uniphase	www.nanopositioning .com
	Murata Electronics	www.iijnet.or.jp/murata
	System Planning Corporation	www.sysplan.com
Piezoelectric transducers	Kulite	www.kulite.com
Polymers, electroactive	SRI International	www.sri.com
Precious metal extraction using nanotechnology	Xenolix	www.xenolix.com
Precision photonic devices	Nanovation Technologies, Inc.	www.nanovation.com
Proteomics	Bruker	www.bruker.com
Quantum computing	IBM	www.ibm.com
Self-assembly devices	IBM	www.ibm.com
Semiconductor components and systems, advanced	Intel	www.intel.com
Semiconductor fabrication and test equipment	Newport Corporation	www.newport.com
Components, microscopy	SPI Supplies/Structure Probe, Inc.	www.2spi.com
Equipment	Galileo	www.galileo-tech.com
	Norton Company	www.nortonabrasive .com/electronics
	Plasma-Therm, Inc.	www.plasmatherm.com
	Seiko	www.seiko.com
	Structured Materials Industries	www.structured materials.com
	Surface Technology Systems	www.stsystems.com
	Varian	www.varian.com/ index2.html
	Veeco	www.veeco.com
	Zygo Corporation	www.zygo.com
Tools	Ceracon Corporation	www.ceracon.com
Semiconductor packaging	PSI Technologies	www.psitechnologies .com
Semiconductor packaging materials	Nissei Sangyo Company	www.nissei.com
Semiconductor processing components	Rohm and Haas	www.rohmhaas.com

Nanotech/MEMS products	Company	Web Site
Semiconductors	CVC Products	www.cvc.com
	Texas Instruments	www.ti.com
Semiconductors and equipment	Hewlett-Packard	www.hp.com
	Hitachi	www.hitachi.com
Semiconductor wafers	Virginia Semiconductor	www.virginiasemi.com
Software		
Bioinformatics, designer drugs	MDL Information Systems, Inc.	www.mdli.com
Chemical and chemistry modeling	Daylight Chemical Information Systems	www.daylight.com
Chemical and genetic analysis and modeling	Cherwell Scientific	www.cherwell.com
Chemical structure analysis and visualization	Cambridge Soft	www.camsoft.com
Chemistry	accelrys	www.accelrys.com
Image analysis for SEMs	Media Cybernetics	www.mediacy.com
Material characterization, microbiology	Jandel Scientific	www.jandel.com
Materials	accelrys	www.accelrys.com
MEMS and nanodevice design	Autodesk	www.autodesk.com
Microscopy visualization	Vaytek, Inc.	www.vaytek.com
Molecular modeling	Celanese	www.celanese.com
	Hypercube, Inc.	www.hyper.com
	Polyhedron Software	www.polyhedron.com
	Wavefunction, Inc.	wavefun.com
Molecular modeling and analysis	Cambridge Crystallographic Data Center	www.ccdc.cam.ac.uk
Molecular modeling and simulation	Gaussian, Inc.	www.gaussian.com
Molecular synthesis	Tripos, Inc.	www.tripos.com
Nanovision	American Chemical Society Software	www.acs.org
Sequencing	accelrys	www.accelrys.com
Visualization and imaging	Autometric	www.autometric.com
Visualization and various others	IBM	www.ibm.com

Nanotech/MEMS products	Company	Web Site
Technology transfer, microsystems technology transfer	VDI/VDE	www.vdivde-it.de
Thin films	Kobe Steel	www.kobelco.co.jp/ indexe.htm
Coatings	BeamAlloy Corporation	
	Bernex, Inc.	www.ionbond.com
	CVC Products	www.cvc.com
Diamond materials	Advanced Refractory Technologies	www.art-inc.com
Dielectric and ceramic materials	MRA Laboratories	www.ceramics.com/mra
Film and overlay	Nanometrics, Inc.	www.nanometrics.com
Oxides	Structured Materials Industries	www.structured materials.com
Ultramicrotomes	Energy Beam Sciences	www.ebsciences.com
Ultraprecision machining systems	Nanotechnology Systems	www.nanotechsys.com

COMPANY SORT

Information in the listings is current as of June 16, 2001. The listings exclude more than 750 microscopy companies and 120 semiconductor companies; some companies may have been inadvertently omitted. The author offers his apologies to those companies.

Many of the listed companies focus on other products and industries. Only the nanotechnology- or microelectromechanical systems (MEMS)-related products are listed here. Not all listed products are commercially available.

Acronyms used in the listings: AFM = atomic force microscope; EFM = electrostatic force microscope; ESEM = environmental scanning electron microscope; LEEM = low-energy electron microscope; LFM = lateral force microscope; MFM = magnetic force microscope; PAMAM = polyamidoamine (dendrimers); RF = radio frequency; SEM = scanning electron microscope; SNOM = scanning near-field optical microscope; SPM = scanning-probe microscope; STM = scanning tunneling microscope; TEM = tunneling electron microscope.

Company	Web Site	Nanotech/MEMS products
3rd Tech	www.3rdtech.com	Nanomanipulators
4Pi	www.4pi.com	Imaging acquisition for microscopy
Abbot Laboratories	abbott.com/news/ discovering_the _future.html	DNA genomics Molecular biology
accelrys	www.accelrys.com	Chemistry, materials, and sequencing software
Access/Valtronic	www.valtronic.ch	MEMS, 3-D integrated circuits
Advanced Refractory Technologies	www.art-inc.com	Nanomaterials Thin-film diamond materials
Advanced Surface Microscopy, Inc.	www.al.com/asm	Chemical phase imaging Microscopy: AFM, EFM, LFM, MFM, SPM Calibration, STM Nanoindentation
Akzo Nobel	www.akzonobel.com	Molecular biology Nanomaterials
Alberta Microelectronics Center	www.amc.ab.ca	MEMS, fluidics Micromachining
Aldrich Chemical Company	www.sigma-aldrich.com/ saws.nsf/Home ?OpenFrameset	Molecular engineering Silica gel nanomaterials
Altair International Inc.	www.altairint.com	Nanocrystalline nanomaterials Nanoparticles
American Chemical Society Software	www.acs.org	Molecular modeling Nanovision
AMP, Inc.	www.amp.com	Interconnect devices
Analog Devices, Inc.	www.analog.com	MEMS
Anhui Ultra-Fine Powders Developing Co., Ltd.		Nanomaterial powders
Archaeomation	www.edmondson.org/ ArchaeoMation/	Metrology Microscopy
Aremco Products	www.aremco.com	Coatings
Argonide	www.argonide.com	Nanomaterial powders, especially nanometals

Company	Web Site	Nanotech/MEMS products
Asulab	www.asulab.ch	Composites MEMS
Autodesk	www.autodesk.com	MEMS and nanodevice design software
Autometric	www.autometric.com	Visualization and imaging software
Axon Instruments	www.axon.com	Biochip scanners Micropositioners
Bangs Laboratories	www.bangslabs.com	Microspheres
BeamAlloy Corporation		Thin-film coatings
Beckman	www.beckman.com	DNA sequencing Particle characterization
Bell Labs (Lucent)	www.lucent.com	Nanoelectronics
Berkeley Sensor and Actuator Center	www-bsac.eecs.berkeley.edu	MEMS
Bernex, Inc.	www.ionbond.com	Thin-film coatings
BioForce Labs	www.bioforcelab.com	AFM probes and tips Nanoarrays
BioMetric Systems	www.biometricsystems.com	Micropipettes
Bruker	www.bruker.com	Chemical imaging Microscopy probes and microimaging Proteomics
Burleigh Instruments	www.burleigh.com	Nanopositioning
Cabot Performance Materials	www.cabot-corp.com	Semiconductor materials
Calbiochem	www.calbiochem.com	Molecular biology substances and tools
California Molecular Electronics Corporation	www.calmec.com	Organic vapor sensors
Cambridge Crystallographic Data Center	www.ccdc.cam.ac.uk	Molecular-modeling and analysis software
Cambridge Soft	www.camsoft.com	Chemical structure, analysis, and visualization software
Carbolex	www.carbolex.com	Single-wall carbon nanotubes
Carbon Nanotechnologies, Inc.	www.cnanotech.com	Single-wall carbon nanotubes
Catalytica	www.catalytica-inc.com	Biochemicals, amino acids

Company	Web Site	Nanotech/MEMS products
Celanese	www.celanese.com	Designer molecules Molecular-modeling software
Ceracon Corporation	www.ceracon.com	Semiconductor fabrication tools
Cherwell Scientific	www.cherwell.com	Chemical and genetic analysis and model-ing software
Cinch	www.cinch.com	Interconnect devices
Conductus, Inc.	www.conductus.com	High-temperature superconductors
Coventer	www.memcad.com	Optical, RF, sequencing, assay, fluidics, and sensor MEMS
Cronos	www.memsrus.com	Microrelays, optical attenuators, photonic switches
Crystallume	www.crystallume.com	Diamond coatings
CVC Products	www.cvc.com	AFMs Metrology Nanoscopes Semiconductors Thin-film coatings
Daylight Chemical Information Systems	www.daylight.com	Chemical and chemistry modeling software
Delphi Delco Electronics Systems	www.delphiauto.com	MEMS sensors
Dendritech	www.mmi.org/mmi/ dendritech	PAMAM dendrimer designer molecules
Diamonex International, Ltd.	www.diamonex.com/	Diamond coatings and diamondlike carbon products and coatings
Digital Instruments	www.di.com	SPMs, AFMs, and other microscopy products
DME	www.dme-spm.dk	AFMs, STMs, SNOMs, and other microscopy products
Dow Chemical	www.dow.com	Nanotube-based field-emission displays Advanced electronics materials
Druck, Inc.	www.druck.com	MEMS sensors
Duke Scientific Company	www.dukesci.com	Nanomaterials, Nano- and micropar-ticles and spheres

Company	Web Site	Nanotech/MEMS products
Du Pont Electronics	www.dupont.com/ automotive/ applications/electronic	MEMS sensors
Endevco	www.endevco.com	MEMS sensors
Energy Beam Sciences	www.ebsciences.com	Electron microscopy Ultramicrotomes
Engelhard Corporation	www.engelhard.com	Catalysts Nanomaterials
Ennex Fabrication Technologies	www.ennex.com	Fabrication technologies
Espin	www.nanospin.com	Nanofibers and nanowebs
Etalon, Inc.	www.etaloninc.com	Metrology Piezo devices
FEI	www.feicompany.com/ eng/index.html	Semiconductor lithography Metrology Microscopy: SEMs, TEMs, focused ion beam, ESEM
Fischione Instruments	www.fischione.com	Microscopy sample preparation and imaging
Fujikura America, Inc.	www.faisensors.com	MEMS oxygen and pressure sensors
Galileo	www.galileo-tech.com	Semiconductor fabrication equipment
Gatan	www.gatan.com	Electron microscopy instrumentation
Gaussian, Inc.	www.gaussian.com	Molecular-modeling and simulation software
Hewlett-Packard	www.hp.com	AFMs Biochips Molecular electronics Nanocomputing architectures Nanodevices Nanoelectronics Semiconductors and equipment

Company	Web Site	Nanotech/MEMS products
Hitachi	www.hitachi.com	Advanced semi-conductor materials Electron beam lithography Nanodevices Semiconductors and equipment SEMs
Honeywell Microswitch Division	www.honeywell.com	MEMS
Hypercube, Inc.	www.hyper.com	Molecular-modeling software
Hyperion Catalysis	www.fibrils.com	Carbon nanotubes Nanocomposites
IBM	www.ibm.com	Advanced semi-conductor materials Carbon nanotubes Interconnect devices Memory devices, nanoscale MEMS Microscopy, LEEM Molecular engineering Nanoelectronics Nanowires Quantum computing Self-assembly devices Visualization and various other software
Integran	www.integran.com	Electrodeposited nanocrystalline material coatings
Integrated Micromachines	www.micromachines.com	3-D optical MEMS
Intel	www.intel.com	Advanced semi-conductor components and systems
Intellisense Corporation	www.intellisense.com	MEMS optical switches, biomonitors, microfluidics
Intergen	www.intergenco.com	Biochemicals Molecular biology

Company	Web Site	Nanotech/MEMS products
Jandel Scientific	www.jandel.com	Material characterization, microbiology software
JDS Uniphase	www.nanopositioning .com	Nanosensors Nanopositioning Piezo devices
Jenoptik Mikrotechnik	www.jo-mikrotechnik .com/english/index .html	Plastic MEMS components
Jeol USA, Inc.	www.jeol.com	Electron beam lithography Microscopy: SEMs, TEMs, STMs, other microscopy devices and components, wafer inspection
Keweenaw Nanoscience Center	www.portup.com/ ~funderdown/	Design of custom biosensors and nanotechnology applications
Kistler	www.kistler.ch	Piezo-based MEMS sensors
Kobe Steel	www.kobelco.co.jp/ indexe.htm	Biotechnology Diamond coatings Molecular modeling Nanocomposites Nanomaterial powders Thin films
Kulite	www.kulite.com	MEMS sensors Piezoelectric transducers
Leica	www.leica.com	All aspects of semi-conductor lithography including nanolithography
Leo Electron Microscopy	www.leo.de	SEMs, TEMs, and accessories
Lucas NovaSensor	www.novasensor.com	MEMS pressure sensors
Lucent	www.lucent.com	Nanoelectronics

Company	Web Site	Nanotech/MEMS products
Materials and Electrochemical Research Corporation	www.mercorp.com/ mercorp	Coatings Composites Fullerenes Nanotubes
Materials Modification, Inc.	www.matmod.com	Coatings Composite powders
McAllister Tech Associates	www.mcallister.com	STMs, microscopy positioning devices
MDL Information Systems, Inc.	www.mdli.com	Bioinformatics and designer-drug software
Media Cybernetics	www.mediacy.com	Image analysis software for SEMs
Merck	www.merck.com	Bioinformatics Designer drugs Molecular engineering
Microparts	www.microparts.de/ english/index.html	Microspectrometers, microfluidics
Molecular Devices	www.moleculardevices .com	Microplate readers
Molecular Imaging	www.molec.com	Metrology SPMs, metrology, and accessories
Motorola	www.motorola.com	Biochips MEMS Molecular electronics
MRA Laboratories	www.ceramics.com/mra	Thin-film dielectric and ceramic materials
Murata Electronics	www.iijnet.or.jp/murata	MEMS sensors Piezo devices
Nanochip	www.nanochip.com	MEMS mass storage
Nanocor, Inc.	www.nanocor.com	Composite nanoclays
Nanogen	www.nanogen.com	DNA/RNA biochip assays
NanoLab	www.nano-lab.com	Aligned nanotube array coatings Carbon nanotube powders
Nanologic, Inc.	www.nanologicinc.com	Nanotechnology product presentations
Nanomat, Inc	www.nanomat.com	Nanocrystalline materials, nanotechnology consulting

Company	Web Site	Nanotech/MEMS products
NanoMaterials Research Corporation	www.nrcorp.com	Nanomaterial powders
Nanometrics, Inc.	www.nanometrics.com	Metrology Thin film and overlay
Nanopierce	www.nanopierce.com	Interconnection systems for microelectronics
Nanophase Technologies Corporation	www.nanophase.com	Nanophase materials
Nanopowders Industries	www.nanopowders.com	Nanopowders, especially metals
Nanoprobes	www.nanoprobes.com	Sensitive molecular analysis reagents for detecting biological molecules
Nanoscale Combinatorial Synthesis, Inc.	www.nanosyn.com/ company.html	Combinatorial libraries for high-throughput screening
NanoSciences Corporation	www.nanosciences.com	Microchannel plates, microdynode arrays
Nanotechnology Systems	www.nanotechsys.com	Ultraprecision machining systems
Nanovation Technologies, Inc.	www.nanovation.com	Precision photonic devices
NanoWave, Inc.	www.nanowave.com	Scanning-probe position encoders
Newport Corporation	www.newport.com	Semiconductor fabrication and test equipment
NexTech Materials, Ltd.	www.nextechmaterials .com	Catalysts Fuel cell nanomaterials
Nissei Sangyo Company	www.nissei.com	Semiconductor packaging materials
Nonius BV	www.nonius.com	Molecular analysis systems and software
Noritake Company	www.noritake-elec.com	Nanotube emitter displays
Norton Company	www.nortonabrasive .com/electronics	Semiconductor fabrication equipment
NT-MDT	www.ntmdt.ru	SNOMs, SNOM probes, microscopy accessories
Park Scientific Instruments	www.park.com	SNOMs, AFMs, and accessories

Company	Web Site	Nanotech/MEMS products
Perkin Elmer	http://fluidsciences .perkinelmer.com/ index.asp#	MEMS flow sensors
Pharmacia Biotech	www.jp.apbiotech.com/ ie_index.asp	Gene biochips
Physical Sciences, Inc.	www.psicorp.com	High-resolution magnetic scanners
Plasma-Therm, Inc.	www.plasmatherm.com	MEMS fabrication equipment Semiconductor fabrication equipment
Polyhedron Software	www.polyhedron.com	Molecular-modeling software
Polytech PI	www.polytecpi.com	Nanopositioners
Proctor & Gamble	www.pg.com	Designer molecules Molecular modeling
Promega	www.promega.com	Biochemicals DNA synthesis
PSI Technologies	www.psitechnologies .com	Semiconductor packaging
Redwood Microsystems	www.redwoodmicro.com	MEMS microfluidics
Robert Bosch, GmbH	www.bosch.de/start/de/ start/index.htm	Coatings
Rohm and Haas	www.rohmhaas.com	Monomer and powder coatings Semiconductor processing components
Seiko	www.seiko.com	MEMS Semiconductor fabrication equipment
SES Research Corporation	www.sesres.com	Carbon buckytubes, nanotubes, and man-ufacturing equipment
SI Diamond Technology	www.carbontech.net	Large area displays using carbon nanofilms
Sigma-Aldrich	www.sigma-aldrich.com	Biochemical and organic chemical synthesis
Silicon Microstructures	www.si-micro.com	MEMS pressure sensors
SPI Supplies/Structure Probe, Inc.	www.2spi.com	Semiconductor fabrication compo-nents, microscopy

Company	Web Site	Nanotech/MEMS products
Spire Corporation	www.spirecorp.com	Medical coatings
		Photovoltaic manufacturing equipment
SRI International	www.sri.com	MEMS sensors
		Molecular engineering
		Electroactive polymers
Standard Mems	www.standardmems.com/	MEMS pressure transducers
Stratagene Cloning Systems	www.stratagene.com	Biochips
		Molecular engineering, molecular medicine
Strem Chemicals, Inc.	www.strem.com	Fullerenes
Structured Materials Industries	www.structuredmaterials .com	Semiconductor fabrication equipment
		Oxide thin films
Surface Technology Systems	www.stsystems.com	MEMS
		Semiconductor fabrication equipment
System Planning Corporation	www.sysplan.com	MEMS biohazard detectors
		Piezo devices
Tanner Research, Inc.	www.tanner.com	MEMS accelerometers and optical reflectors
Technanogy	www.technanogy.net/ index.html	Metallic (aluminum) nanopowders
Technical Instruments	www.techinst.com	AFMs and related microscopy accessories
Technology Assessment & Transfer, Inc.	www.techassess.com	Nanolayer coatings
Texas Instruments	www.ti.com	Optical MEMS
		Semiconductors
Topometrix	www.topometrix.com	AFMs and SPMs
Tripos, Inc.	www.tripos.com	Molecular synthesis software
Varian	www.varian.com/ index2.html	Semiconductor fabrication equipment
Vaytek, Inc.	www.vaytek.com	Microscopy visualization software
VDI/VDE	www.vdivde-it.de	Microsystems technology transfer

Company	Web Site	Nanotech/MEMS products
Veeco	www.veeco.com	Semiconductor fabrication equipment
Virginia Semiconductor	www.virginiasemi.com	Semiconductor wafers
Wavefunction, Inc.	wavefun.com	Molecular-modeling software
Xenolix	www.xenolix.com	Precious metal extraction using nanotechnology
Zygo Corporation	www.zygo.com	Optical MEMS Semiconductor fabrication equipment

European Innovation Relay Center Locations

Country and City	IRC Name
Austria	
Wien	Bureau for International Research and Technology Cooperation
Belgium	
Brussels	Technopol Brussel-Bruxelles asbl
Brussels	VIA—IWT Vlaams Instituut voor de bevordering van het Wetenschappelijk-Technologisch onderzoek in de industrie
Jambes (NAMUR)	Direction Générale des Technologies, de la Recherche et de l'Energie—Ministère de la Région Wallonne (DGTRE-CRIW)
Bulgaria	
Sofia	Applied Research and Communications Fund (ARC Fund)
Cyprus	
Lefkosia	Cyprus Institute of Technology (CIT)
Czech Republic	
Prague 6	Technology Centre AS CR
Denmark	
Copenhagen V	EuroCenter—Danish Agency for Trade and Industry
Estonia	
Tartu	Archimedes Foundation
Finland	
Länsi-Pasila, Helsinki	Tekes—the National Technology Agency
France	
Dijon	Chambre Régionale de Commerce et d'Industrie de Bourgogne

Country and City	IRC Name
France *(Continued)*	
Limoges	Agence Nationale de Valorisation de la Recherche—Limousin
Lyon Cedex 03	Chambre Régionale de Commerce et d'Industrie de Rhône-Alpes
Marseille	Méditerranée Technologies
Nancy	Chambre Régionale de Commerce et d'Industrie de Lorraine
Paris Cedex 01	Chambre de Commerce et d'Industrie de Paris
Rennes	Bretagne Innovation
Germany	
Hannover	NATI Technologieagentur Niedersachsen GmbH
Leipzig	Agentur für Innovationsförderung & Technologietransfer GmbH Leipzig
Mülheim	ZENIT—Zentrum für Innovation & Technik in Nordrhein-Westfalen GmbH
Nürnberg	Bayern Innovativ Gesellschaft für Innovations- und Wissenstransfer mbH
Stuttgart	Steinbeis-Europa-Zentrum der Steinbeis Stiftung für Wirtschaftsförderung
Teltow/Berlin	VDI/VDE Technologiezentrum Informationstechnik GmbH
Wiesbaden	TechnologieStiftung Hessen GmbH
Greece	
Athens	Foundation for Research and Technology—Hellas (HELP-FORWARD)
Athens	National Documentation Centre/Hellenic Research Foundation
Hungary	
Budapest	National Technical Information Centre and Library (OMIKK)
Ireland	
Dublin	Enterprise Ireland
Israel	
Tel-Aviv	MATIMOP, the Israeli Industry Center for R&D
Italy	
Bologna BO	Ente per le Nuove Tecnologie, l'Energia e l'Ambiente ENEA—IRC IRENE
Catania	Consorzio Catania Ricerche
Milano	Consorzio per la Costituzione del Milano Ricerche Centro per l'Innovazione in Città Studi

Country and City	IRC Name
Pisa	Consorzio Pisa Ricerche
Roma	Consiglio Nazionale delle Ricerche
Torino	Camera di Commercio Industria Artigianato e Agricoltura di Torino
Valenzano (BA)	Tecnopolis Csata Novus Ortus s.c.r.l.
Latvia	
Riga	Latvian Technological Center
Lithuania	
Vilnius	Lithuanian Innovation Centre
Luxembourg	
Luxembourg/Kirchberg	Luxinnovation GIE, Agence nationale pour la promotion de l'innovation et de la recherche
Netherlands	
Den Haag	Senter
Norway	
Trondheim	SINTEF Industrial Management
Poland	
Kraków	Cracow University of Technology
Warsaw	OPI—Information Processing Centre
Wroclaw	Wroclaw Centre for Technology Transfer
Portugal	
Oeiras	Instituto de Soldadura e Qualidade
Porto	Agência de Inovaçao S.A.
Romania	
Bucharest	The Foundation Romanian Center for Small and Medium Sized Enterprise
Slovakia	
Bratislava	BIC Bratislava
Slovenia	
Ljubljana	Josef Stefan Institute
Spain	
Alicante	Universidad de Alicante—OTRI
Barcelona	Centre d'Informació i Desenvolupament Empresarial
Bilbao	Sociedad para la Promoción y Reconversión Industrial, S.A.—SPRI
Madrid	Dirección General de Investigación Consejería de Educación Comunidad de Madrid
Oviedo	Fundación para el Fomento en Asturias de la Investigación Científica Aplicada y la Tecnología

Country and City	IRC Name
Spain *(Continued)*	
Sevilla	Instituto de Fomento de Andalucía
Zaragoza	Instituto Tecnológico de Aragón
Sweden	
Mölndal (Göteborg)	The Swedish Institute of Production Engineering Research
Umeå	Uminova Center AB
Uppsala	Uppsala University
Switzerland	
Lausanne	Centre d'appui scientifique et technologique—Cast EPFL
United Kingdom	
Belfast	Local Enterprise Development Agency
Bristol	South West of England Regional Development Agency
Cambridge	St. John's Innovation Centre Ltd.
Canterbury—Kent	Kent Technology Transfer Centre Ltd.
Cardiff	Welsh Development Agency
Coventry	Coventry University Enterprises Ltd.
Glasgow	Targeting Technology Ltd.
Sunderland	RTC North Ltd.

German Companies Involved in Nanotechnology

Aixtron AG
AMO GmbH
Angewandte Werkstoff-Forschung GmbH
ATOS GmbH
Atotech
Audi AG
BASF AG
BASF LYNX
Bioscience AG
Bayer AG
Beiersdorf AG
BioTul GmbH
BMW AG
Boehringer
Brain GmbH
Bruker-AXS
Carl Zeiss
Daimler Chrysler
Dornier GmbH
Focus GmbH
Freiberger Compound Materials GmbH
FRT GmbH
Henkel KGaA
Hoechst AG
IBM Deutschland
ICT GmbH
Intop
Ion-Tof GmbH
Jenoptik L.O.S. GmbH
Kleindiek Nanotechnik

Klocke Nanotechnik
Kugler GmbH
Lambda Physik
Laser- und Medizintechnologie
Leica Lithographie Systeme
Leica Mikroskopie und Systeme GmbH
Mediport
Merck KGaA
Mineralien-Werke
Nanofilm Technologie GmbH
NanoPhotonics AG
Nanosol Gesellschaft
Nanoview GmbH
Omicron Vakuumphysik GmbH
Opal Jena GmbH
Plasma Consult GmbH
Porsche AG
Qiagen GmbH
Raith GmbH
Robert Bosch GmbH
Rollei Fototechnik
Siemens AG
Surface Imaging Systems
H. C. Starck GmbH & Co. KG
Team Nanotec GmbH
Technics Plasma GmbH
Telekom AG
Triple-O Microscopy GmbH
Volkswagen AG
WITec

Countries Covered by the Institute of Nanotechnology

Austria
Czech Republic
Denmark
Finland
Flanders
France
Germany
Ireland
Italy
Lithuania
The Netherlands
Norway
Romania
Spain
Sweden
Switzerland

Japanese Companies Involved in Nanotechnology

Advantest Corporation
Canon, Inc.
Daiichi Pharmaceutical Co., Ltd.
Dainippon Screen Mfg. Co., Ltd.
Disco Corporation
Fuji Electronics Co., Ltd.
Fuji Photo Film Co., Ltd.
Fujitsu, Ltd.
Hitachi, Ltd.
Hoden Seimitsu Kako Kenkyusho Co., Ltd.
INAX Corporation
Japan Aviation Electronics Industry, Ltd.
JEOL
Kao Corporation
Matsushita Electric Industrial Co., Ltd.
Matsushita Electric Works, Ltd.
Mitsubishi Chemical Corporation
Mitsubishi Electric Corporation
Mitsui High-tec, Inc.
NEC Corporation
Nikon Corporation
Nippon Telegraph and Telephone Corporation
Noritake Co., Ltd.
Olympus Optical Co., Ltd.
Osaka Gas Co., Ltd.
Sapporo Breweries, Ltd.
Sekisui Chemical Co., Ltd.
Sharp Corporation
Shimadzu Scientific Instruments.
Showadenko, K.K.

Sony Corporation
Takeda Chemical Industries, Ltd.
Tokyo Electron, Ltd.
Tokyo Seimistu Co., Ltd.
Topcon Corporation
Toray Industries, Inc.
Toshiba Corporation
Toyota Motor Corporation

Chinese Universities and Institutions Involved in Nanotechnology

Beijing Industrial University
Nanometer Crystal Laboratory

Beijing University
Chemistry and Molecular Project Institute
Nanotechnology and Technical Research Center

Chinese Mining Industry University
Ultrafine Material Research Institute

Huadong Technical University
Ministry of Education National Laboratory
Superfine Material Program

Nanjing Technical University
Advanced Scientific Technical Research Institute
Ultrafine Dust Materials Project Center

National Chemical Industry Powder Body Engineering Design
    Technology Center

Qingdao Chemical Industry Institute
Nanotechnology Research Institute

Qinghua University
Powder Body Project Laboratory

Shandong Building Materials Industrial Institute
Particle Test Research Institute

Shanghai Huaming High-Tech Group Company
National Superfine Powder Engineering Research Center

Shanghai Silicate Research Institute
High-Performance Ceramics and Ultrastructure National Laboratory

Shanghai Technical University
Particle Technology Laboratory

Sichuan Union University
Chemical Industry Institute
Powder Material Research Institute

Sichuan University (West Campus)
Ultrafine Powder Body Material Research Institute

Wuhan Industrial University, Material Institute
Material Compound New Technology National Laboratory

Xi'an Architectural Scientific and Technical University
Powder Material Engineering Research Institute

Zhongshan University Physics Department
Superfine Material Research Center

Chinese Companies Involved in Nanotechnology

Taiwan Nanometer Components Laboratory
Chineses Academy of Sciences Institute of Chemistry, Primitive Micro-instrument Center
Shanghai Bena Science and Technology Development, Ltd. Co.
Shanghai Aijian Manometer Science and Technology Development, Ltd. Co.
Shandong Zheng Yuan Nanometer Material Engineering, Ltd. Co.
Jiangsu WuLing ChangTai Nanometer Material, Ltd. Co.
Zhejiang Lishui Jindiyia Manometer Material, Ltd. Co.
Taixing Nanometer Material Factory
Shandong Ultramicro Particle Research Institute
Shanghai Ultramicro Material Science and Technology, Ltd. Co.
Suchuan Electronic Powder Factory

Contact Information

CHAPTER 1

National Nanotechnology Initiative

NSTC's Subcommittee on Nanoscale Science, Engineering and
Technology (NSET)
c/o National Science Foundation
4201 Wilson Blvd., Suite 525
Arlington, VA 22230
Web site: www.nano.gov

CHAPTER 3

Department of Commerce

National Institute of Standards and Technology (NIST)
100 Bureau Drive, Stop 3460
Gaithersburg, MD 20899-3460
Phone: (301) 975-NIST (6478)
Web site: http://patapsco.nist.gov/ts_sbir/awards.htm

Department of Defense

Web site: www.dodsbir.net/awardlist/awardlist.htm

Department of Energy

Web sites:
http://sbir.er.doe.gov/sbir/Awards_Abstracts/award_Abstract_main.htm
http://sbir.er.doe.gov/sbir/Awards_Abstracts/sttr/sttr_a&a_main.htm

Department of Transportation

Web site: www.volpe.dot.gov/sbir/previous.html

National Aeronautics and Space Administration
Web site: http://sbir.gsfc.nasa.gov/SBIR/awdarch.htm

National Institutes of Health
Web site: http://grants.nih.gov/grants/funding/sbir.htm#data

National Science Foundation
Web site: www.fastlane.nsf.gov/a6/A6AwardSearch.htm

National Technology Transfer Center
316 Washington Avenue
Wheeling, WV 26003
Phone: (800) 678-6882
Fax: (304) 243-4388
Web site: www.nttc.edu

Small Business Administration
Web site: www.sba.gov/INV

CHAPTER 4

Association of University Technology Managers
60 Revere Drive, Suite 500
Northbrook, IL 60062
Phone: (847) 559-0846
Fax: (847) 480-9282
Web site: www.autm.net

Nature
Web site: www.nature.com/nature

Science
Web site: www.sciencemag.org

CHAPTER 5

Atomasoft
Web site: www.atomasoft.com

MEMX

5600 Wyoming Blvd. NE, Suite 160
Albuquerque, NM 87109
Web site: www.memx.org

Nanotechnology Holding Corporation

Web site: www.nanotechnologyholdingcorp.com

Semiconductor Research Corporation

P.O. Box 12053
Research Triangle Park, NC 27709-2053
Phone: (919) 941-9400
Web site: www.src.org

Zyvex

1321 N. Plano Road
Richardson, TX 75081
Phone: (972) 235 7881
Web Site: www.zyvex.com

CHAPTER 6

Community Research and Development Information Service (CORDIS)

Web site: www.cordis.lu/nanotechnology

EO, P.L.C.

Web sites: www.eo.net
www.epo.com

EUREKA

EUREKA Secretariat
107 rue Neerveld
B-1200 Brussels
Phone: 32 2 777 09 50
Fax: 32 2 770 74 98
Web site: www.eureka.be

EXIST

Bundesministerium für Bildung und Forschung
EXIST

Referat 326
53170 Bonn
E-mail: exist@bmbf.bund.de

Institute of Nanotechnology
Web site: www.nano.org.uk

KITC Co., Ltd.
Web site: www.hantotams.com

Korea Trade-Investment Promotion Agency, KISC program
Web site: www.kisc.com

Korean Trade-Investment Promotion Agency
300-9 Yorngok-dong
Seocho-ku
Seocho P.O. Box 101
Seoul, Korea
Phone: 82 2 3460 7114
Fax: 82 2 3460 777-8

Tokyo IPO Corporation
Web site: www.ipotokyo.com

CHAPTER 12

RHK Technology, Inc.
1050 East Maple Road
Troy, MI 48083
Phone: (248) 577-5426

ThermoMicroscopes
1171 Borregas Avenue
Sunnyvale, CA 94089-1304
Phone: (408) 747-1600

Glossary

501(c)(3)   The tax code referring to a nonprofit corporation.

accelerometer   A device that measures changes in motion.

accredited investor   An investor that meets specific requirements of the SEC and is permitted to participate in private placements.

ADP   Adenosine diphosphate: The reduced component of ATP after energy production.

AFM   Atomic force microscope: A device that creates an image of individual atoms based on the electron charge of the atoms.

AIST   National Institute of Advanced Industrial Science and Technology (Japan).

algorithm   An ordered set of instruction steps intended to produce a specific outcome.

angstrom   A unit of length equivalent to one ten-billionth of a meter.

apoptosis   The process of programmed cell death in the normal development of a multicellular organism.

assembler   A device that creates objects by placing atoms into the object one atom at a time.

atom   The fundamental unit of matter.

ATP   Adenosine triphosphate: The organic molecule responsible for most of the energy production systems in the living cell.

AUTM   Association of University Technology Managers

bioengineered   Referring to characteristics of plants or animals that are added or deleted for a commercial purpose.

biomimetic   Replicating functions of parts of living creatures with fabricated devices.

bit   The primal unit of computation in a conventional computer.

brownian motion   The mechanical motion caused by the thermal interaction of small objects and their medium.

CAD   Computer-assisted design.

capacitor   A device that stores and releases electrons.

carbon nanotube   A cylindrical object constructed of atoms of carbon at the nanometer scale.

CMOS   Complimentary metal oxide semiconductor: A fabrication technique for integrated circuits.

combustion   A chemical reaction that principally releases heat.

conductor   A material that unconditionally permits the flow of electrons.

DARPA   Defense Advanced Research Projects Agency.

diamonoid   A nanoscale tool fabricated out of diamond.

DNA   Deoxyribonucleic acid: The molecule that encodes the functions and replication process of a living organism.

DNA sequencing   Determining the order of the four molecular coding components of DNA.

DoD   Department of Defense.

DOE   Department of Energy.

dot-com company   Any of the companies focused on generating revenues through functionality provided by Internet services.

DVD   Digital versatile (video) disk.

electron   The fundamental unit of charge.

electrostatic force   The force of attraction or repulsion between electrons and protons.

Fast Track   Either an STTR or SBIR program that includes direct investment by private investors.

FDA   Food and Drug Administration.

fluidics   The engineering practice dealing with managing the flow of low-speed fluids or gases.

fullerene   Materials with a regular atomic structure similar in appearance to the dome structures developed by Buckminster Fuller.

GDP   Gross domestic product: A measure of the value of the annual productivity of a country.

genome   The map depicting the genetic content of a single species derived from DNA sequencing.

gigahertz   1 billion repetitions per second

hydrodynamics   The study of fluid and gas flow and the interactions with objects in the path of the flow.

IMI   Intelligent Micromachine Initiative: A program managed by Sandia National Laboratory.

industrial sector   A collection of industries or stocks of companies that produce and sell products to a common customer base.

integrated circuit   A collection of discrete electronic devices, fabricated at the same time, typically through selective deposition and etching of layers of semiconductor and conductor materials.

IPO   Initial public offering: The time when a company's stock is first offered for sale to the public

IRC   Innovation Relay Center (Europe).

JVC   Japan Victor Corporation.

ligand   An ion that binds together other atoms or molecules.

magnetosensor   A device that measures the ambient magnetic field.

MARCO   Microelectronics Advanced Research Corporation: A subsidiary of the SRC.

mask   The optical pattern that exposes a photoresist.

MAV   Micro air vehicle.

megahertz   1 million repetitions per second.

MEMS   Microelectromechanical systems: Devices fabricated using semiconductor techniques that include a moving part.

mesoscopic   Systems composed of many discrete atoms or molecules.

METI   Ministry of Economy, Trade, and Industry (Japan)

micro   Referring to an object smaller than the unaided human eye can see.

microbe   A single-celled living organism, typically living autonomously.

microbial   Coming from a microbe.

microelectronics   Devices fabricated from microscopic electronic components.

micromachine   A device, the smallest component of which is fabricated at the micrometer scale.

micromechanics   The study of motion and interactions at the micrometer scale.

micrometer   A unit of length equivalent to one-millionth of a meter.

microscopy   The collection of devices and techniques used to create pictures of objects as small as an atom, or larger.

millikelvin   A unit of temperature equivalent to one-thousandth of a degree Kelvin; 0 K is equal to absolute zero.

MIT   Massachusetts Institute of Technology.

mitochondria   Organelles within a cell responsible for providing energy resources to the cell. These organelles have their own DNA and are possibly organisms captured by larger cells eons ago.

molecular biology   The study of organic processes at the molecular level.

molecule   A collection of tightly coupled atoms with unique chemical properties.

molecular electronics   Electronic circuits in which the individual components are single molecules.

monolayer   A layer of a material one atom or molecule in thickness.

Moore's law   The observation that the density of electronic components doubles every 18 months.

MOSFET   Metal oxide semiconductor field-effect transistor: A highly sensitive electronic device.

MWNT   Multiwalled nanotube.

nanotube   A cylindrical object consisting of atoms at the nanometer scale.

nanocomposites   Materials fabricated out of materials including nanomaterials.

nanodot   A device that contains a single unit of charge.

nanoelectronics   Electronic devices fabricated at the atomic or molecular scale.

nanofabrication   The production of parts by addition or deletion of material at the nanometer scale.

nanolithography   A process that creates structures at the nanometer scale.

nanomachine   A device, the smallest component of which is fabricated at the nanometer scale.

nanomagnetics   Magnetic fields at the atomic scale.

nanomanipulator   A device capable of positioning individual atoms or molecules.

nanomaterial   Any material, the smallest components of which are materials fabricated at the nanometer scale.

nanomechanics   The study of motion and interactions at the atomic scale.

nanometer   A unit of length equivalent to one-billionth of a meter.

nanophase   Changes in chemical or other properties that occur at the nanometer scale.

nanoporous   Having the attribute of permitting diffusion of materials or gases measured in nanometers.

nanoscale   Referring to objects the smallest of which are measured in nanometers.

nanostructure   Objects measured in nanometers.

nanowire   A linear structure, usually conductive, at the nanoscale.

NASA   National Aeronautics and Space Administration.

NIH   National Institutes of Health.

NNI   National Nanotechnology Initiative: U.S. Government funding program supporting national policies for nanotechnology development.

NORAD   North American Air Defense Command.

NSF   National Science Foundation.

NSTC   National Science and Technology Council.

NTTA   National Technology Transfer Act.

NTTC   National Technology Transfer Center.

OEM   Original equipment manufacturer: A manufacturer that sells to other manufacturers rather than end users.

optical   Referring to the use of light.

paradigm   The dominant logical system of scientific enterprise.

pathogen   In biology, typically a process or organism that destroys the functioning of a larger organism from within.

photoelectric   The process of converting light into electricity.

photolithography   The process of etching a surface into its final form by use of light-sensitive chemistries.

photoresist   A thin chemical layer that provides protection to the underlying surface when exposed to light.

photovoltaics   Devices that generate electricity when exposed to light.

piezoelectric   A material that translates current into motion, motion into current, or both.

pixel   Picture element: The smallest discrete element of a digital picture.

plasma   A high-energy state of matter, usually consisting of highly energized atoms used for abrasion processes.

polymer   A material composed of repeating patterns, usually a plastic.

pre-IPO   A company that is intending to, but has not yet executed an IPO.

private company   A company that has never sold stock to the public.

private placement   The sale of stock by a company to accredited investors or institutions.

public company   A company that has sold stock to the public to acquire capital, and whose stock is listed on a stock exchange.

quantum   Usually refers to the physics of quantum mechanics or quantum physics.

quantum computer   A device predicated on the ability to perform computational operations using quantum mechanics.

quantum mechanics   The models used in physics to describe the interactions of matter at the atomic and subatomic scales.

quantum physics   The physics which describes the interactions of matter at the atomic and subatomic scales.

qubit   The fundamental unit of computation in a quantum computer.

R&D   Research and development.

replication   The ability of something to make a copy of something.

replicator   A device that makes copies of something.

resistance   A measurement of the efficiency of flow of electrons through a material.

RITTS   Regional Innovation and Technology Transfer Strategy program (Europe).

ROI   Return on investment.

S&P 500   Standard & Poor's 500 Stock Index: An index of stocks, usually associated with traditional manufacturing sector companies.

S.E.C.   Security and Exchange Commission: The federal agency responsible for the regulation of public companies and the trade of stock.

SETI   Search for Extraterrestrial Intelligence: A privately funded program searching for radio broadcasts from other civilizations.

SBA   Small Business Administration.

SBIR   Small Business Incentive Research program.

self-assembly   The process by which objects create structures by the nature of their physical interrelationships.

self-organization   Processes by which objects arrange themselves without external manipulation.

self-replication   The ability of something to make a copy of itself.

SEM   Scanning electron microscope: A microscope using electron beams to image objects with submicrometer resolution.

semiconductor   A material that permits the flow of electrons through the material conditional on the proximity of other electric fields.

sensor   A device that measures the presence or absence of something.

SIA   Semiconductor Industry Association.

silicon   The material on which electronics are fabricated.

SNOM   Scanning near-field optical microscope.

SRC   Semiconductor Research Corporation.

STM   Scanning tunneling microscope: A variation on the electron microscope.

STTR   Small Business Technology Transfer program

subatomic   Smaller than an atom

superconductor   A material that permits the flow of electrons with zero resistance.

swarm   A large collection of devices intended to collectively operate toward some common objective.

SWCNT   Single-walled carbon nanotube.

SWNT   Single-walled nanotube.

terahertz   1 trillion repetitions per second

thin film   A layer of material a few atoms in thickness.

transistor   The basic device in electronics that provides either switching or amplification.

tribology   The science of interactions of surfaces at the nanometer scale including friction, lubricity, and other near-surface phenomenon.

ultrasonic   Frequencies of sound higher than the range of normal human hearing.

van der Waals force   The electrostatic fields surrounding atoms or molecules.

VHS   Video Home System: A video recording format.

VLSI   Very large scale integration or very large scale integrated circuits.

wafer   A flat circular plate of silicon on which integrated circuits are fabricated.

Index